ISBN 978-1-331-98888-5
PIBN 10205499

1 MONTH OF
FREE
READING

at

www.ForgottenBooks.com

By purchasing this book you are eligible for one month membership to ForgottenBooks.com, giving you unlimited access to our entire collection of over 700,000 titles via our web site and mobile apps.

To claim your free month visit:

www.forgottenbooks.com/free205499

Similar Books Are Available from
www.forgottenbooks.com

HIS LIFE, LETTERS AND FRIENDS

BY A. M. BROADLEY

JOINT-AUTHOR OF "NAPOLEON AND THE INVASION OF ENGLAND" AND
"DUMOURIEZ AND THE DEFENCE OF ENGLAND AGAINST NAPOLEON," ETC.

AND R. G. BARTELOT, M.A.

AUTHOR OF "A HISTORY OF CREWKERNE SCHOOL"
VICAR OF ST GEORGE'S, FORDINGTON, DORCHESTER

LONDON
JOHN MURRAY, ALBEMARLE STREET
1909

TO

THOMAS HARDY

PRESIDENT OF THE SOCIETY OF DORSET MEN IN LONDON

WHOSE HISTORICAL NOVEL THE "TRUMPET MAJOR" AND EPIC
POEM "THE DYNASTS" HAVE DONE SO MUCH TO AWAKEN
PUBLIC INTEREST IN THE STIRRING TIMES DURING
WHICH HIS GALLANT DORSET NAMESAKE
FOUGHT FOR HIS COUNTRY UNDER
NELSON

THIS VOLUME IS WITH HIS PERMISSION
DEDICATED

BY THE AUTHORS

GEORGE III., PITT AND HARDY AT WEYMOUTH

SCENE FROM "THE DYNASTS," VOL. I., ACT IV., SCENE I.

[Reprinted by permission of Mr Thomas Hardy.]

KING.   And now he has left Boulogne with all his host?
Was it his object to invade at all,
Or was his vast assemblage a mere blind?

PITT.   Undoubtedly he meant invasion, Sir,
Had fortune favoured.   He may try it yet.
And, as I said, could we but close with Fox——

KING.   But, but ;—I ask, what is his object now?
Lord Nelson's Captain—Hardy—whose old home
Stands in a peaceful vale hard by us here—
Who came two weeks ago to see his friends,
I talked to in this room a lengthy while.[1]
He says our navy still is in the dark
As to the aims by sea of Bonaparte
Now the Boulogne attempt has fizzled out,
And what he schemes afloat with Spain combined.
The *Victory* lay that fortnight at Spithead,
And Nelson since has gone aboard and sailed ;
Yes, sailed again.   The *Royal Sovereign* follows,
And others her.   Nelson was hailed and cheered
To huskiness while leaving Southsea shore,
Gentle and simple, wildly thronging round.

[1] See pp. 134-135.

PREFACE

OF all the subordinate characters in the tragedy of Trafalgar, the personality of Thomas Masterman Hardy is unquestionably by far the most interesting, striking, and attractive. The "Kiss me, Hardy" of the dying Nelson has perhaps taken a firmer hold on the popular imagination than either the "Remember" of Charles Stuart, or the real or supposed "My country, oh my country" of William Pitt.

Another of the "greatest sailor's" utterances during the brief interview which preceded Hardy's return to his duties on deck, within about half an hour of "his Lord's" death, is scarcely less distinctly graven on men's minds. It was, as we are told by the able author of *Nelson and his Captains*, the timely quotation of the words, "Anchor, Hardy, anchor," more than forty years later, by which Sir Herbert Edwardes steadied in a moment of supreme difficulty the iron nerve of the worn-out and over-wrought Sir John Lawrence.[1]

Twenty-eight years have passed away since another Thomas Hardy (scarcely less famous in his generation than his great naval namesake) gave to the world that delightful novel *The Trumpet Major*, the scenes of which are laid in Dorset during the later days of the "Great Terror" (1796-1805). Its author had talked to many men and women who vividly remembered the events of that momentous period of our history when George III. reviewed his troops

[1] *Nelson and his Captains*, W. H. Fitchett, p. 63.

—Regulars and Volunteers—on the heights above Weymouth, and the arrival of the "dreaded Corsican" on our shores was hourly expected.[1] Mrs Charteris, the daughter of Sir T. M. Hardy, was then alive, and it was from her description of her father that Thomas Hardy wrote the vivid pen-picture to be found in Chapter XXXIII. of his book, in which love-sick Bob Loveday of the mercantile marine is made to visit the captain of the *Victory* at Portisham with a view to volunteer for service on board Nelson's flag-ship. The author of *The Trumpet Major* had many long talks with Mrs Charteris, who, amongst other things, informed him that during the last illness of her revered father she had burned, by his directions, the whole of his correspondence. It is evident that she spoke only of communications addressed to Hardy, for Hardy's own letters are constantly turning up, very often throwing fresh light on the events in which he played a more or less important part, and always adding to one's appreciation of his amiable and unselfish character. A good many letters of Hardy have come to light since the first issue of the biography in *The Three Dorset Captains at Trafalgar*. The most important of these will be found in the last chapter of this volume.[2] "The Captain," writes his namesake, "at this time was thirty-five, rather short in build, with light eyes, bushy eyebrows, a square, broad face, plenty of chin, and a mouth whose corners played between humour and grimness."

In the result, Loveday, who had successfully resisted the snares of the press-gang, fought at Trafalgar on board the *Victory*, although for obvious reasons he does not appear under that name in the muster-roll. By permission of the author, further reference will be made in our text to

[1] Full particulars of the various schemes projected for the defence of Dorset and other interesting details will be found in *Napoleon and the Invasion of England*, by H. F. B. Wheeler and A. M. Broadley (1907), and *Dumouriez and the Defence of England against Napoleon*, by Dr J. Holland Rose and A. M. Broadley (1908).

[2] See *post*, p. 245.

the allusions to "Nelson's Hardy," both in the *Dynasts* and
The Trumpet Major.   Thomas Hardy's graphic account of
the meeting between the captain of the *Victory* and his
Sovereign has already been printed after the dedication.

No sooner did the belated news of the battle of
Trafalgar reach England than the whole kingdom was
flooded with popular mementoes of the great event which
had saved her from the long-feared foreign invasion, while
depriving her of her foremost sailor.   In all these
souvenirs—songs, broadsides, glass-pictures, engravings,
or pottery—the favourite theme was that of the most
familiar death scene in naval history—Nelson expiring
in the arms of Hardy.   Two-and-twenty years after
Trafalgar, the late Admiral Sir W. William Phipps Hornby
was serving with Hardy, then Commander-in-Chief of the
Experimental Squadron at Portsmouth.   Shortly before
his death, Sir William Hornby communicated to Mr Henry
Newbolt an old Trafalgar song, "The Quarter-gunner's
Yarn,"[1] containing the following verses:—

> "Our captain was Hardy, the pride of us all,
> I'll ask for none better when danger shall call,
> He was hardy by nature and Hardy by name,
> And soon by his conduct to honour he came.
>
> The *Victory* led, to her flag it was due,
> Though the *Téméraires* thought themselves admirals too,
> But Lord Nelson he hailed them with masterful grace,
> 'Cap'n Harvey I'll thank you to keep in your place.'
>
> To our battering next the *Redoubtable* struck,
> But her sharpshooters gave us the worst of the luck,
> Lord Nelson was wounded, most cruel to tell,
> 'They've done for me, Hardy,' he cried as he fell.
>
> When the captain reported a victory won,
> 'Thank God,' he kept saying, 'my duty I've done';
> At last came the moment to kiss him good-bye,
> And the captain for once had the salt in his eye.

---

[1] *The Year of Trafalgar*, by Henry Newbolt, pp. 232-3-4. London:
John Murray, 1905.

'Now anchor, dear Hardy,' the admiral cried,
But before we could make it he fainted and died ;
All night in the trough of the sea we were tossed,
And for want of ground tackle good prizes were lost.

Then we hauled down the flag, at the fore it was red,
And blue at the mizzen was hoisted instead
By Nelson's famed captain, the pride of each tar
Who fought in the *Victory* off Cape Trafalgar."

In the times immediately following Trafalgar the "Mummers Play" was still enacted every succeeding Christmastide in the mansions and farmhouses of the West, and specially in the county of Hardy's birth. "St George," "Captain Bluster," "Room," and the "Egyptian King," may claim direct descent from the Middle Ages, but an interlude was added dealing with the absorbing topic of the hour, and in which the sole *dramatis personæ* were Nelson and Hardy. For the nonce the floor of the room in which the rustic actors performed was supposed to be the deck of the *Victory*. The following dialogue, for half a century at least, never failed to provoke the utmost enthusiasm :—

NELSON. "Hardy, I be wownded."
HARDY. "Not mortually I hopes, my lord."
NELSON. "Mortually I be afeared. Kiss me, Hardy, thank God I've done my duty."

The friendship which existed between Nelson and Hardy for over ten years was of the closest description. Nothing could ever interrupt it. Nelson regarded Hardy not merely as a "right-hand man" like the resourceful Berry, or an able and courageous seaman like Ball, Troubridge, Keats, and others. Hardy possessed all their good qualities, but he had other attributes which led Nelson to feel he might safely make him the recipient of his most intimate confidences. Possibly the strong union of sympathy which linked them together was intensified by their strange diversity of both temperament and physique. It is difficult to imagine a more striking contrast than that presented by the pale-faced, stunted, and attenuated admiral—"that cripple-gaited, one-eyed, one-armed little naval critter," as Sam Slick has been made to describe him—and the captain—tall, broad-shouldered, muscular, robust, rubicund of countenance and hearty in manner, like his stalwart Dorset forebears. Nelson was habitually moody, sensitive, and fretful; at times he was despondent, but Hardy could always cheer him with a ringing laugh, an unruffled temper, and a constant disposition to look on the bright side of things. The intense personal regard for one another of these two comrades imparts a peculiar interest to the letters of Hardy which will now be read for the first time.

At Nelson's funeral it was Thomas Masterman Hardy who bore the "banner of emblems." It must not be forgotten that Hardy took part in all Nelson's principal naval engagements—St Vincent, the Nile and Copenhagen, as well as Trafalgar—but so important was the *rôle* played by Hardy at Trafalgar that it overshadows many notable occurrences in his career both before and after the most memorable 21st October of history. From December 1796, when Nelson hoisted his broad pendant on board the *La Minerve*, of which ship Hardy had been appointed lieutenant on the preceding 20th August, they became inseparable friends. The victor of the Nile very soon realised the merits of the future captain of the *Victory*. "I never knew Hardy wrong upon any professional subject," said Nelson; "he seems imbued with an intuitive right judgment." It was not, therefore, surprising that Nelson trusted Hardy implicitly, and the same confidence was placed in him by Lady Nelson and other members of their family. To all of them he was "dear Hardy," and their affection was repaid by the most sterling loyalty. Hardy was ever jealous of the fair fame of the great admiral, who regarded him as one of his best friends and ablest officers almost from the day he saved him from capture by the Spaniards in February 1797. That Hardy often told Nelson home truths is abundantly evident from the voluminous correspondence which now sees the light.

When Hardy returned to England after Trafalgar he was in his thirty-seventh year. He survived Nelson for four-and-thirty years, dying in harness as Governor of Greenwich Hospital on the 20th September 1839, having served the State under no less than four sovereigns, including her late Majesty, Queen Victoria. Between 1806 and 1827 (when he finally struck his flag), on the 22nd anniversary of Trafalgar, Hardy rendered invaluable services to his country both on the North and South America Stations. It has even been said that his tact and prudence alone saved England from a third war with the United States.

From a comparatively early stage in his career Hardy enjoyed the intimate friendship of at least two of the Royal Dukes. In the autumn of 1812 he thus wrote to the Duke of Clarence, afterwards William IV.:—

Sept. 16th, 1812.

SIR,

I have the honour to acknowledge the receipt of your Royal Highness's letter of the 14th of last month, which I only received yesterday from Lieut. Hay, who is now in the *Barfleur.* I am appointed to the *Ramillies,* and if I possibly can I will take young Hay with me should either of the lieuts. not join that are now named to her. I have great pleasure in stating to your Royal Highness that during the time Mr Hay was under my command he has at all times conducted himself most fully to my satisfaction, and I have no hesitation in saying that he will turn out a most excellent officer. I feel quite grateful to your Royal Highness for your kind remembrance of me, and I beg to subscribe myself your Royal Highness's

Dutiful humble servant,

T. M. HARDY.

In 1830, when Lord Grey formed his first Cabinet, William IV. only accepted the nomination of Sir James Graham (whose name he declared he had never heard of) to the post of First Lord of the Admiralty on the understanding that Sir T. M. Hardy, whom he knew well, and of whose ability and prudence he entertained the highest opinion, should be First Sea Lord. Hardy moved to Whitehall, where for four years he threw all his constitutional energy into the discharge of his official duties. In the traditions of the Admiralty he is remembered as one of the best and most far-sighted men who ever held that responsible post. A portion of the Hardy correspondence deals with that all-important epoch of his career, as well as with the closing days of his life, which he spent in company with many other Trafalgar survivors at Greenwich Hospital, of which he became Governor, and where he more than once welcomed his brother sailor, the "jolly young tarry breeks" of 1782, now known as "Good King William."

It is somewhat surprising that the life of Thomas Masterman Hardy has never been written, and that until less than three years ago, the places of his birth and baptism were matters of historic doubt. In July 1905, however, a Nelson and Trafalgar Exhibition was held at Dorchester, the capital of Hardy's county, under the auspices of the Rev. S. E. V. Filleul, Rector of All Saints' Church in that town, assisted by a local committee. The result of the activity of Mr Filleul and his associates was to bring together, in one room, a number of rare, and in many cases unique, relics connected not only with Lord Nelson himself, but with the life and exploits of Thomas Hardy, captain of the *Victory*, and other famous Dorset sailors from Elizabethan times downwards. The portion of the Dorchester Exhibition devoted to Hardy was of quite exceptional interest, for it contained relics of every description, ranging from medals and miniatures to the watch he wore while he held the dying Nelson in his arms, the pencil-case he used to note the signals during the battle of Trafalgar, with the marks of his teeth still clearly visible upon it, and the silver shoe-buckle, shattered by a splinter only a few minutes before the British Commander-in-Chief received his death wound.

Mr Filleul was fortunate enough to obtain the active co-operation of Hardy's direct descendants and representatives, including Sir Malcolm MacGregor, Lady Helen MacGregor, Mrs John Thynne, and Mr Atholl Macgregor, while Mrs Manfield and her son, Mr William Hardy Manfield, the present possessors of Sir T. M. Hardy's old home at Portisham, contributed other objects of great historic value. The loan was also obtained of several autograph letters written by Hardy to his brother-in-law, Mr John Callard Manfield, a former Mayor of Dorchester, who, in the days of Trafalgar, and for some years previously, carried on the solicitor's business which has now, after various changes, passed into the hands of Mr H. A. Huxtable, like his predecessor, an ex-Mayor of Dorchester, and who now holds the post of Town Clerk of Weymouth. The presence of these autographs in the exhibition eventually led to the discovery of several other bundles of Hardy's letters, beginning 26th May 1798, and ending 29th April 1839, less than five months before his death. Mr Manfield died 21st June 1808, and the latter portions of the Hardy correspondence are addressed to Joseph Hardy, the admiral's elder brother, who survived him.

In addition to this unlooked-for discovery of hitherto unknown Hardy letters, the writers have been enabled to use other important MSS., including a letter written by Hardy to his brother Joseph at the age of thirteen, now in the possession of Mrs John Thynne, and other communications addressed by him to Mr Edmund Noble, Sir Benjamin Hallowell-Carew, K.C.B., and others.

The captain of the *Victory* had no pretence to scholarship in the modern sense of the word. He often wrote in a hurry, and under circumstances of considerable excitement. Sometimes he is racked with anxiety for the reputation of his "dear Lord"; other letters are jotted down in the intervals of travel by land or sea. Occasionally he writes with the din of battle still ringing in his ears, to give the Dorset folk the earliest news of great victories and stirring events, *quorum pars magna ífuit*, for Thomas Masterman Hardy was ever in the thickest of the fight. From first to last, Hardy wrote from the heart, and it has been deemed expedient to publish the letters just as he penned them, with the errors uncorrected.

Hardy's letters may not throw an important light on the larger questions of naval history, but they certainly very materially help us to a closer acquaintance with the personality of Nelson, as well as that of all those who played a prominent part in the great naval drama, of which he was the central figure. They are remarkable also for the spirit of affectionate regard to his own people which they breathe throughout, and the deep love he entertained for his native county. With him, charity always commenced at home. Digby might want him to give a berth to the son of some meritorious clergyman, but Hardy preferred the recommendations which came from Dorchester or "Possum." In very many of these letters we have ample evidence of his constant care for the boys from Dorset—the Balstons, the Robertses, and the Manfields—as well as of that singular sweetness of disposition and temper which endeared him to "old Nelson" (as Hardy affectionately called him), who, just after Copenhagen, wrote to Alexander Ball at Malta : "All in the fleet are so truly kind to me that I should be a wretch not to cheer up. Foley has put me under a regimen of milk at four in the morning; Murray has given me lozenges—*Hardy is as good as ever.*" The picturesque side of life in the Navy during the Great War, as graphically depicted in Commander C. N. Robinson's deservedly popular *British Fleet*, is reflected throughout the earlier portions of the Hardy correspondence.

b

Without the information there given, it would have been difficult to understand many of the matters to which Hardy frequently alludes.

The Appendix contains a complete pedigree, not only showing Hardy's lineal connection with Clement le Hardi, Bailly and Lieutenant-Governor of Jersey in 1483 and 1488, but giving the names of the whole of his descendants alive at the centenary of Trafalgar. It is certainly an auspicious coincidence that Hardy's grandson, Sir Evan MacGregor, K.C.B., was Permanent Secretary of the Admiralty up till 1907. The room he so long occupied was in close proximity to the apartments tenanted sixty-three years since by Sir Thomas and Lady Hardy, the latter of whom lived till 1877, and is vividly remembered by Sir Evan. "Little," writes Sir John Briggs,[1] "could Lord Nelson's favourite captain have anticipated that his own grandson would, at the end of the nineteenth century, assist in carrying out the views he entertained, and the opinions he expressed as First Sea Lord of Sir James Graham's Board of 1830, and as his representative witness all those great and important changes which he then predicted science and steam would render inevitably necessary throughout every branch of the Naval Service."

From two roughly-bound folio volumes of stamped receipts in the possession of Messrs Maggs, of 109 Strand, the writers have been enabled to compile a complete and accurate muster-roll of the *Victory* on the 21st October 1805. The earlier of these records, dated August 1806, deals with the division *pro rata* of the £300,000 voted by Parliament for the whole of the Trafalgar Fleet, while the latter, begun in April 1807, shows in the minutest detail the distribution of the sum total of the Trafalgar Prize Money and Bounty Bills. The first Page of the *Victory* section of both these valuable registers (which should certainly find a home either at Whitehall or in the British

---

[1] *Naval Administrators*, 1827-1892. London, 1897, p. 44.

Museum) have been reproduced (by Messrs Maggs' permission) amongst our illustrations.

In order to explain as far as possible the true import of Hardy's letters, and to give something like an adequate idea of the invaluable services rendered to his "king and country" by the captain of the *Victory* during a career extending over nearly sixty years, the writers have had recourse to the works of standard authors dealing with our naval annals between the years 1780 and 1840. They desire to express the deep obligations they are under to Captain Mahan,[1] Mr Henry Newbolt,[2] Commander Charles N. Robinson,[3] Mr W. H. Fitchett, B.A., LL.D.,[4] Professor John Knox Laughton,[5] Secretary of the Navy Records Society (probably the greatest living authority on Nelson bibliography), Mr David Hannay,[6] and last but not least, the able correspondent of *The Times*,[7] whose masterly elucidation of the tactics of Trafalgar in a series of articles recently published, has been the admiration of all those interested in the achievements of Lord Nelson and his captains.

While the sheets of the first issue of this work were going through the press, another very interesting discovery was made, viz., the "remark-book" of Richard Francis Roberts, one of Hardy's midshipmen on board the *Victory* at the battle of Trafalgar. It was used with the sanction of its owner, Miss Roberts of the Grove, Burton Bradstock, in the chapter relating to that momentous event in Hardy's career. Miss Roberts has since then come across a series

---

[1] *The Life of Nelson*, Captain A. T. Mahan.   London : Sampson, Low, Marston & Co., 1897.

[2] *The Year of Trafalgar.*   London : John Murray, 1905.

[3] *The British Fleet*, Commander C. N. Robinson.   London : George Bell, 1896.

[4] *Nelson and his Captains.*   London : Smith, Elder & Co., 1904.

[5] *The Nelson Memorial*, by John Knox Laughton.   London : George Allen, 1896.   *Biography of Nelson in D.N.B.*, etc., etc.

[6] Introduction to reissue of Southey's *Life of Nelson.*

[7] *The Times*, September 16, 19, 26, 30, and October 19, 1905.

of interesting letters from her ancestral kinsman, giving a minute account of the action of October 21, 1805, and the events which immediately followed it. The interest of these letters, written at the time of the momentous occurrences they deal with, is very great, and Chapter XXIII. of the present volume is devoted to their publication.

For many years a *Dorset* or *Dorsetshire* figured in the list of British ships-of-war. The first *Dorsetshire*, a third-rate of 80 guns, was built at Southampton in 1694. She was a vessel of 1176 tons, and carried a crew of 476 men. She was rebuilt at Portsmouth in 1712, and finally taken to pieces in 1749. Then came the *Dorset*, a large yacht with swivel guns only, constructed at Deptford, November 1752 —August 1753. She survived the Great War, and in the spring of Waterloo year fetched £330. The second *Dorsetshire* was a third-rate of 80 guns, built at Portsmouth in 1757. She was broken up in 1775. Two men-of-war have been named after Lord Hood—like Hardy, a native of Dorset—viz., the *Hood* (late *Edgar*), a second-rate of 80 guns, launched in 1856, and sold in 1888 for £5000. The existing *Hood*, a battleship of 14,150 tons, was completed for sea at Chatham in 1893, and is now in commission in reserve at Devonport. The disappearance of *Dorsetshire* and *Dorset* as ship names is unaccountable, and for a time the county of Hardy and the Hoods has had to console herself with the reflection that the ancient regiment of foot, bearing her name, can still boast of the proud device, "Primus in Indis," as well as that of "Mortis Insignia Calpe." If, in years to come, the name of the *Dorset*, the *Dorsetshire*, or possibly the *Hardy*, be bestowed on one of the armour-clad, of which the First Sea Lord of 1830-4 foretold the existence and realised at least some of the possibilities, the life-story of "Nelson's Hardy" will not have been told in vain.

A. M. B.

Jany. 1, 1909.

CONTENTS

APPENDICES

LIST OF ILLUSTRATIONS

xxiii

THE THREE DORSET CAPTAINS AT TRAFALGAR

CHAPTER I

DORSET AND HER FAMOUS SAILORS

ALTHOUGH Dorset is one of the smallest of the maritime counties of England, she has played an important part in our naval annals ever since the far-off days of the ninth century, when the Wessex fishermen and peasantry looked down with dismay from the cliffs of Golden Cap and Thorncombe Beacon on the destruction of the fleet of King Ethelwulf by their Danish adversaries. The disaster of A.D. 843 was evidently taken to heart by the vanquished Saxons, for thirty-four years later it was signally avenged by the brilliant victory won by the marine forces of King Alfred in Swanage Bay, when no less than 120 Danish ships were sunk and the few vessels which contrived to evade pursuit were dashed to pieces on the Peverel Rocks. The Dorset littoral from Liliput Hill and Canford Cliffs on the east to Lyme Regis and Charmouth on the west, measures about 70 miles. In the centre the peninsula of Portland, assuming the shape of a booted foot, apparently kicking contemptuously at any possible invader of England's shores, helps to form West Bay on one side of the Chesil Beach and Weymouth Bay on the other. The latter terminates in the chapel-crowned headland of St Aldhelm (commonly known as St Alban), while further eastwards, towards the

A

Hampshire borders, lie the smaller bays of Swanage and Studland, and the land-locked harbour of Poole, once securely guarded by the castle of Brownsee or Branksea Island. Lines of lofty cliffs, bare of verdure, inaccessible and often well-nigh perpendicular, broken here and there by verdant valleys and stretches of golden sand, are the characteristic features of the Dorset sea-board, the scene of some of the most terrible shipwrecks of history and the home of many generations of sturdy sailors. The Dorset smuggler was in his day quite as adventurous as his Cornish *confrère*, and in the beautiful and picturesque hinterland hidden behind the yellow cliffs, all sorts of cleverly-contrived hiding-places and over-spacious cellars still keep the memory of their prowess green. In the print-room of the British Museum may be seen a set of maps portraying the coast of Dorset as it was in Henry VIII.'s time. They are embellished with rude drawings of towns, castles, churches, ships, and beacons, to say nothing of sundry stately swans and stags with enormous antlers. The greater part of the names (notwithstanding the primitive spelling) are easily recognisable, and the "Cobbe" at Lyme Regis looks very much like what it is now and what it must have been two hundred and twenty years ago, when the luckless Monmouth stumbled and fell as he set his foot upon it on his way to Sedgemoor and Tower Hill. These charts demonstrate sufficiently the importance of Dorset as a naval centre in the middle of the sixteenth century, which was to close with the complete discomfiture of the Armada called "Invincible," off Portland Bill.

We must not forget, however, that long before that "crowning victory" was achieved, Weymouth, Poole, Lyme Regis, and Wareham had all made notable con-tributions of men and ships to the force which crossed the Channel to win the battle of Creçy and cover the English arms with glory. In this expedition, at least 31 Dorset ships and 479 Dorset mariners took part. As far back as King John's reign the best cordage came from Bridport, which, as "Byrportte," figures conspicuously in the suggestive sketches of the Tudor hydrographer. In 1322 Sir Nicholas Cheney, Sheriff of Dorset, sought in vain to recover from the king his out-of-pocket expenses—70 shillings and some odd pence—incurred by the dispatch of six "ropers" from Bridport to Newcastle-upon-Tyne. About the time of the elaboration of these early maps of the Dorset littoral, an Act of Parliament made short work of unauthorised "ropers" on the ground that "Time-out-of-mind Bridport ('Byrportte') had made all the great cables, ropes, hawsers, and other tackling for the Royal Navy and the most part of other ships within this realm." The ingenious Leland came to Bridport and was evidently taken in by the ancient joke arising out of the varied uses to which good rope was put, for he asserts gravely that "at Bridportt be made good daggers." The old saw about being "stabbed by a Bridport dagger" (*i.e.*, hanged), was evidently in vogue in the days when Sir Richard Bingham [1528-1598-99], the first of Dorset's famous sea-dogs, was giving proof of his skill as a sailor, soldier, and statesman. The captain of the *Swiftsure* eventually became Marshal of Ireland, but died before he could assume the reins of office. As Governor of Connaught, ten years before, he had mercilessly butchered the Spanish sailors who had survived the engagement off Portland Bill, only to meet with a still more terrible fate on the rock-bound shores of Ireland. Bingham's native county had placed 8 ships and 340 men at the disposal of the Lord High Admiral, who commenced the destruction off the Dorset coast, on which various relics of the Armada have been cast up by the waves ever since.

Sir George Summers or Somers [1554-1610], the ship-mate of Raleigh and the discoverer of the Bermudas, was born at "Lyme of the King." Summers was one of the boldest and most successful of the early sixteenth-century "adventurers." Having taken many prizes, including a particularly rich "carrack" off Lisbon, he came home to be knighted by James I., and sit in Parliament for Lyme Regis. Having escaped the perils of the Gunpowder Plot, he once more crossed the Atlantic to colonise Virginia and discover the Bermudas, where he unfortunately died " of the surfeit of eating of a pig." His nephew and heir, Matthew Summers, brought his embalmed body back to Berne Manor, the mansion on the banks of the Char which he had purchased with the proceeds of his " prize-taking." The house still exists, but American travellers look in vain for his grave or any memorial of him in the beautiful church of St Candida and Holy Cross, where he was laid to rest. Forty-three years after the death of Summers, the Portland waters were again the scene of another memorable engagement. For three entire days (February 18-20), Robert Blake maintained a death-struggle with Van Tromp, upon whom he finally inflicted a complete defeat, capturing 11 men of war and 30 merchantmen.

Within easy walking distance of Summers' home at Whitchurch is the modernised farmhouse of Little Windsor, where, in Charles II.'s reign lived Alexander Hood, from whom the six seamen bearing that name are descended. Lieutenant Arthur Hood, R.N., lost on the *Pomona*, Captain Alexander Hood, who fell in the naval duel between the *Mars* and the *Hercule* on the 21st April 1798, and Admiral Sir Samuel Hood, were his great-grandchildren, through his eldest son and namesake ; while from the youngest, the Rev. Samuel Hood, Vicar of Thorncombe and Master of the Beaminster Grammar School, sprang the much more celebrated Admiral Samuel Hood, Viscount Hood, and Admiral Alexander Hood, Viscount Bridport. From the cliffs of West Bay (the modern name for what was only twenty years ago generally known as Bridport Harbour), one can see Thorncombe Beacon to the west, as well as the heights of Lewesdon and Pillsdon (the " Cow " and " Calf " of the sailors of Nelson's time), which rise above the aboriginal home of the Hoods at Little Windsor and the old-fashioned town of Beaminster where Samuel

Hood, the schoolmaster, espoused Mary Hoskins the mother of two naval peers—Lord Hood and Lord Bridport. The Bullens, from whom came Admiral Sir Charles Bullen, who commanded the *Britannia* at Trafalgar, have long been associated with Charmouth, which immediately adjoins both Lyme Regis and Whitchurch — the birthplace and burial-place of Summers.

Close to Thorncombe, Charmouth, and Whitchurch is Hawkchurch, whence came Admiral Sir William Domett [1752-1828], another hero of the Great War, who distinguished himself as flag-captain to Lord Bridport, assisted Thomas Hardy to promotion in the earlier days of his career, and eventually represented the united boroughs of Weymouth and Melcombe Regis in the House of Commons. Sir William Domett sleeps in his native village, in one of the most romantic of Dorset God's acres, where a lengthy inscription on a tablet inside the church sets forth all his professional achievements.

Admiral Robert Digby [1752-1815], the first instructor of William IV. in his "jolly young tarry breeks" days, and Admiral Henry Digby [1770-1842], who commanded the *Africa* at Trafalgar, are both associated with Minterne in central Dorset, but turning eastwards on the rising ground above West Bay, a massive column some seven miles away at once arrests the view. It stands out boldly on the grassy summit of Blagdon on Blackdown Hill, where, as at Thorncombe, Norchard, Lewesdon, Cerne Abbas, Badbury, Bubb Down, Blackdown (in Hawkchurch), Bulbarrow, Frampton, Lytchett, Ridgeway, Woodbury, and Penbury Hills, the Dorset yeomen in 1805, and the years which preceded it, guarded and watched the beacons which were to announce the always-expected arrival of the "Corsican ogre" on these shores. The obelisk in question commemorates the valour and virtues of Dorset's favourite naval hero, Thomas Masterman Hardy, captain of the *Victory*, at once the most intimate and the most trusted of all Nelson's companions in arms, and to whom the dying

admiral murmured his last words on the afternoon of the
21st October 1805, while the shadows of night were falling
fast on distant Dorset, and Joseph Hardy, the captain's
elder brother, unconscious of what was taking place off the
coast of Spain, was climbing up the steep sides of Blackdown Hill to tend the beacon, the lighting of which was no
longer necessary.

The Hardy Monument (as it has been called for
nearly three-quarters of a century) possesses no artistic
or architectural merits, but its position is singularly appro-
priate. It dominates the greater part of that Dorset
littoral and its hinterland which has given England so
many brave sailors in the past and from which the crews of
His Majesty's fleet are still largely recruited. It is in
immediate proximity to Kingston Russell, where Hardy
was born in the same eventful year as Napoleon and
Wellington, while his parents lived in the old home of
the Dukes of Bedford, as well as to Portisham, the
" Possum " of his correspondence, where Hardy spent the
greater part of his boyhood, and which, almost unchanged
and untouched since Hardy left it, still shelters many of
the most characteristic and interesting relics and mementos
of Thomas Masterman Hardy. The object of the following pages is to tell as briefly as may be, and as much as
possible in his own words, the hitherto unrevealed story of
the life of the captain of the *Victory*—Nelson's "dear
Hardy," on many ships and in many lands.

CHAPTER II

THE DORSET HARDYS AND THEIR JERSEY FOREBEARS

THOMAS MASTERMAN HARDY was the last of four distinguished admirals who could one and all claim descent from Clement le Hardy or Hardi, Bailly of Jersey in 1483, and five years later Lieutenant-Governor of that island, where the Le Hardis had flourished exceedingly during the Middle Ages, and from whence the younger son of Bailly John Hardy emigrated to England *vers l'ouest, i.e.*, to Dorsetshire.[1] The first of the four admirals Hardy, was, like the last, named Thomas. He was the son of John Hardy, Solicitor-General of Jersey. Born in the year of the great fire of London, he won a knighthood at the hands of Queen Anne for the share he took in the complete destruction of the combined fleets of France and Spain in Vigo Bay. Having represented Weymouth in Parliament for some years, Sir Thomas Hardy died in 1732 and was buried in Westminster Abbey, where his tomb is still to be seen. The first Sir Charles Hardy was born in 1680, his father Philip Hardy, son of John Hardy, the Jersey Solicitor-General, holding the office of commissioner of garrisons in

---

[1] A pedigree of French Hardys of Vicques and Beaulieu in France is in possession of Mrs J. C. Thynne. Although the Christian names are often identical, it establishes no connection with the Hardis of Jersey.

7

Guernsey.   Having commanded with distinction the *Weymouth* and the *Guernsey*, he earned a knighthood in consideration of long service in the royal yacht, the *Carolina*, and died in 1744 a Lord Commissioner of the Admiralty.   His son, afterwards Sir Charles Hardy the younger, was born amidst the excitement occasioned by the Old Pretender's bootless invasion of England in 1715. He won his first laurels as captain of the *Jersey* in a severe action fought off the Portuguese coast with the French ship *Saint Esprit*.   Ten years later (1755) he was appointed Governor of New York, and before leaving England was knighted by George II.   In 1759 he was second in command when Sir Edward Hawke won his memorable victory in Quiberon Bay.   Sir Charles Hardy (who sat for a time in the House of Commons as M.P. for Portsmouth) was for nine years Governor of Greenwich Hospital, where his portrait by Romney still hangs in the Painted Hall.

The relations between the Channel Islands, and the Dorset littoral which directly faces them, have always been of a very intimate character ever since the days of William the Norman.   For a time they both formed part of the same ecclesiastical diocese, and Weymouth has always been the port through which the produce of the fertile Channel Islands reached the English markets. This traditional intimacy accounts for the presence on the Dorset coast of such names as the Poole Havillands, Jolliffes, and Filliters ; the Swanage Chinchins ; the Parmiters of Corfe Castle ; the Loups and Lerousses of Wareham ; the Russells and Keynells of Weymouth and Kingston Russell; the Halletts, Traverses, Denziloes, Gerrards, and Jeffords of Bridport ; and the Perrotts, Limbrys, and Dollings of Lyme Regis and Charmouth.   Another well-known descendant of the Jersey Hardys was Sir Thomas Duffus Hardy [1804-1878], Deputy-Keeper of the Public Records, whose pedigree in some detail figures in the *Armorial of Jersey*, edited by Mr J. Bertrand Payne.

There are few places on the Dorset sea-board which have not at some time or other been the homes of the Hardys. In the sixteenth and seventeenth centuries they possessed land at Toller Whelme, Wolcombe Matravers, Sydling, Frampton, Frome St Quintin, Melcombe Regis, Compton Abbas, Askerswell, Abbotsbury, and Portisham. In the "Herald's Visitations of 1565" the right of the Hardys of Toller Whelme and Wolcombe Hall to bear the same arms as the Le Hardis or Hardys of Jersey was recorded and subsequently confirmed by Sir William Dethick, the Garter King at Arms (see Pedigree). The Grammar School at Dorchester was founded by Thomas Hardy, of Melcombe Regis Priory, in 1569, and after the lapse of three centuries his crest—a wyvern's head —is still worn on the cricket caps of the Dorchester *alumni*. It is from a nephew of this Thomas Hardy that the Portisham branch of the family, to which Sir T. M. Hardy's immediate ancestors belonged, traces its descent.

Portisham, a typical Dorset village of the more prosperous kind, nestles amongst the hills within two miles of the coast, in the hinterland of Abbotsbury and the Chesil Beach. It will be further alluded to in the chapter dealing with the upbringing and the boyhood of the future captain of the *Victory*. Here, in the principal house of the parish, the foundations of which were laid in Tudor times, lived generation after generation of Hardys, who farmed their own estate, brewed their own beer, and pressed their own cyder. While the Frampton Hardys sided with the Parliamentarians, Joseph Hardy, of Portisham (Sir T. M. Hardy's great-great-great uncle) and his loyal brother-in-law, William Weare, of the same village, declared boldly for church and king,[1] suffering thereby a sequestration of their property and enduring much persecution. The Hardys and Weares sleep side by side in vaults both below and

[1] See Mayo's *Dorset Committee*, p. 452, and Hutchin's *History of Dorset*, 3rd ed., vol. ii., p. 765.

around the beautiful old church of Portisham, of which they were often wardens and eventually became patrons. In the exterior of the southern wall may still be seen the time-worn and lichen-stained monument of William Weare, on which the following curious inscription is still decipherable :—

> " William Weare lies Heere in dust,
> As thou and I and all men must,
> Once plundred by Sabaean force
> Some cald it war but others worse
> With confidence he pleads his cause,
> And Kings to be above those laws.
> September's eyghth day died hee
> When neare the date of 63
>   Anno Domini 1670."

William Weare married Joane, daughter of Anthony Hardy, of Portisham, on the 3rd May 1646, and mentions his brother-in-law, Mr Joseph Hardy, in his will, dated 1670. The "Sabaean" force alluded to in the inscription, refers to the sequestration of stock, valued at £140, in 1644 by order of the Roundhead Committee. In the reigns of William III., Queen Anne, and George I., II., and III., Joseph Hardy, Thomas Masterman Hardy's grandfather, lived at Portisham House, where he died on 16th January 1778, when in his eighty-ninth year. He had married his cousin, the grand-daughter of that ardent royalist, William Weare, thus still further cementing the alliance between the two families. Thomas Masterman Hardy must have known his venerable grandfather, who lived till he was nine years old. Nearly thirty years later, when the Heralds College was busily engaged over the record of his pedigree, in accordance with the stipulations of the patent of baronetcy won at Trafalgar, he wrote thus to his brother-in-law at Dorchester :—

" Mr Nayler[1] wants to know who was the Father of my Grandmother Hardy. Of course my Aunt can tell and

[1] Sir George Nayler, York Herald, Garter King-of-Arms, 1822.

then I believe the Pedigree will be finally settled ; at least I hope so."

Doubtless the information thus asked for was immediately forthcoming, but the pedigree which appears in the Appendix is the only one which can claim anything like completeness, for, as has already been mentioned, the actual place of Hardy's birth was unknown until the summer of 1905. Sir T. M. Hardy neither sought for nor adopted the Trafalgar augmentations of arms so freely granted by Sir Isaac Heard[1] to the fortunate winners of so much prize money. He continued to use the old Jersey coat and crest of the Le Hardis, notwithstanding the slight changes introduced into his armorial bearings previous to the issue of the baronetcy grant. Nor, as far as it can be ascertained, does it appear that he ever adopted the naval crown and dragon's heads allotted him, or the motto " Anchor, Hardy, Anchor," suggested by the sailor prince, under whom, when the latter became King of England, he was destined to serve as First Sea Lord of the Admiralty.

[1] Garter King-of-Arms, 1784-1822.

CHAPTER III

THE BIRTH, BIRTHPLACE, AND BOYHOOD OF THOMAS MASTERMAN HARDY

THE future captain of the *Victory* was born at Kingston Russell House, in the heart of the beautiful valley of the Bride, on the 5th April 1769—the eventful year which gave the world so many of the principal actors in the drama of the Great War, including Napoleon Bonaparte, Arthur Wellesley and Nicholas John de Dieu Soult. Hardy was the junior by four weeks of the Duke of Wellington, and by four months the senior of the great master of statecraft, whose ambitious schemes of invasion and conquest he helped so materially to combat.

He was the second son of Joseph Hardy, of Portisham [1733-1785], and Nanny, his wife [1737-1799], daughter and co-heiress of Thomas Masterman, gentleman, of Kingston Russell and Winterbourne St Martin. For at least seven years prior to Thomas Hardy's birth, his parents had resided at Kingston Russell House, which had previously been tenanted by Nanny Hardy's parents, Thomas and Mary Masterman, who died there in 1763 and 1757 respectively. Like the Hardys, the Mastermans were honoured in the parish registers with the title of " Esquire," and may be presumed, therefore, to have been at least small landowners farming their own estate. Like the Hardys and the Weares, the Mastermans were originally natives of Portisham, where, as far back as 1690, they held the farm of Friar Waddon, and where a Masterman Charity still keeps them in remembrance. Kingston

LONG BREDY CHURCH, DORSET

Where Sir T. M. Hardy was christened in 1769.

To face page 2.

Russell House was a mansion of more than ordinary importance. Although the façade of Portland stone is in the severest form of that classical architecture which delighted the soul of Christopher Wren, the back still retains high mullioned Tudor windows, from which the brittle bluish glass of Elizabethan times has not wholly disappeared. It was, in some shape or other, the aboriginal home of the wealthy and powerful Russells (once probably Rousselles), from which John Russell,[1] afterwards the first Earl of Bedford, is supposed to have started on the journey across the hills to Wolfeton or Wolveton House (now the property of Mr Albert Bankes), where by his linguistic skill he won the favour of the shipwrecked Archduke Philip of Austria, son-in-law of King Ferdinand of Spain, and laid the foundations of the fortunes of his family.

Opposite the entrance of Portisham House, to which Thomas Masterman Hardy's father and mother removed in 1778, on the death of Joseph Hardy, the elder, stands a weather-worn sun-dial, which they must have brought with them from Kingston Russell. It bears the following inscription : " Joseph Hardy, Esq., Kingston Russell, 1767. Lat. 50. Fugio fuge." In accordance with the custom of the times, in the case of the upper classes, Thomas Masterman Hardy was christened privately two days after his birth. Four weeks later he was taken in due course to Long Bredy Church, where his father and mother had been married from Kingston Russell House on the 31st March 1755, and there publicly received " into the Congregation." The entry in the Long Bredy register runs as follows :—
" Baptized, Anno Dom[ni] 1769, Thomas Masterman, son of Joseph Hardy, and Nanny his wife, was baptized April 7th, and rec[d] into the Church, May 4th."

The early years of Hardy's life were indeed cast in pleasant places, for there is nothing more picturesque to be found in the whole of Wessex than the verdant valley through which the limpid Bride winds, now swiftly and now

[1] John Russell, Earl of Bedford [1485-1555].

slowly, from its source in the Bridehead hills, past Kingston Russell, the two Bredys, Litton Cheney and Barwick, until it joins the sea some 6 miles to the west at Burton Bradstock, formerly known as Briditon or the town of the Bride, just as Bridport is the town of the Brit, the sister river which rises in the neighbourhood of Beaminster and joins the Channel at a short distance from the mouth of the Bride.   Little is known of this the most peaceful portion of Hardy's life.   He probably saw the sea for the first time when carried over a spur of the hill, now crowned by the Hardy Monument, to see his octogenarian grandfather at Portisham House.   He may also have visited his Hardy cousins, who lived at the Hyde, near Bridport, obtaining from the road beyond Burton a glimpse of the glories of West Bay and the cliffs of Thorncombe Beacon, and Golden Cap.   It is possible he was also taken to Shapwick, near Blandford, where lived a number of somewhat distant Masterman kinsmen.

A series of gates, not too easy to open, has as yet saved the road from Burton to Kingston Russell from the invasion of the motor-car, and even the cyclist finds his progress a matter of difficulty.   It would, however, be well-nigh impossible to discover a more delightful afternoon's walk than that which Thomas Masterman Hardy, his brothers Joseph and John, and his sisters Elizabeth, Ann, Mary, Catherine, Martha, and Augusta must often have taken.   The oldest of them all was Elizabeth, who was twelve years of age when her afterwards celebrated brother was born.   His brother John was only two years his junior, and the baby of the youthful party at Kingston Russell was his sister Augusta, born only twelve months before the *lares et penates* of the Hardys were finally transferred to the family house at Portisham.   The scene has changed very little during the century and a quarter which have rolled by since then. It is true that the early Victorian restorer has wrought sad havoc in the quaint churches of the Bride Valley, from which many memorials of the past have vanished for ever,

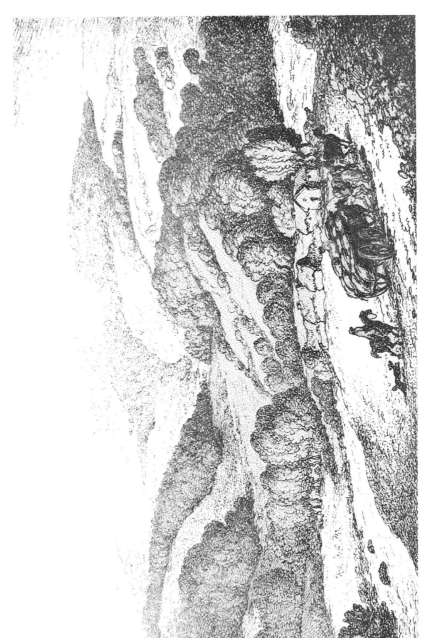

THE BRIDE VALLEY

As sketched in Wa er-colour by Thomas Row andson in 1 99.

To face page 1

but the banks of the Bride are not a whit less lovely now than they were then, and the hedgerows which border the narrow road are still a delightful tangle of maple and hazel, alder and "snag," wild hops and "withy wind," "old man's beard" (clematis) and honeysuckle.   Sleek cattle graze knee-deep in rich meadows by the water side, in the shade of giant elms and venerable oak trees, beneath which Thomas Hardy and his brothers and sisters may have played, while in search of the primroses, bluebells, "ragged Robin," "Stars of Bethlehem," "cherry pie" (soap wort), and the lilac "butter burr," which grow in profusion between Kingston Russell and Burton.   On one side of the vale, far above the stretches of purple heather and bracken fern, are perched the villages of Puncknowle and Swyre, the homes of many a Dorset sailor who fought with "Cap'n Hardy on the deck of the *Victory*"; on the other rises the keel-shaped hill of Shipton Beacon (a favourite haunt of the smuggler), towering far above the tiny church of Chilcombe, which still shelters a rude-carved altar-piece of cedar wood, saved as tradition asserts from the oratory of one of the Armada wrecks.   Next comes Litton Cheney, erstwhile the residence of those doughty warriors, the Cheneys, kinsmen of the stalwart and valiant Sir John Cheney, whose exploits at Creçy were chronicled by Froissart, where palms and other sub-tropical plants grow luxuriantly amongst a series of fish-ponds formed in the grounds of the rectory by one of the tributaries of the Bride rushing down the hill slopes.   In the same parish stands Baglake Farm, once the abode of the Dorset Napiers, and the scene of a well-known Civil War ghost-story.

Leaving Long Bredy Church behind you, you traverse the broad meadows over which Thomas Masterman Hardy must have been carried to his christening. A wire fence now surrounds the historic and once stately home of the Russells, the Mastermans, and the Hardys, which the Dukes of Bedford are allowing to become a ruin, although the massive roof still remains intact. The arms of the Russells have been cut bodily out of the centre of the heavy pediment which surmounts the façade. Doors and windows have been removed, and the empty spaces thus created are now filled up with brickwork. In the interior all is fast falling into decay. The oak wainscoting has gone to Woburn; the main staircase will soon be altogether inaccessible; but the spacious corridor, which should be lighted by the half closed-up Tudor windows, retains something of its pristine charm, and traces are still discernible of old glass, neglected pictures, dilapidated hangings, and elaborate decoration. Above the intruding brickwork, which has replaced the ponderous front door, is a stone slab on which the astonished pilgrim in the footsteps of Hardy reads the words :—"John Lothrop Motley, Minister of the United States, Historian of the Dutch Republic, died at Kingston Manor House, May 20th, 1877." The swallows have made their nests in the spaces once covered by the dethroned panelling, but the broad flight of eight steps leading up to the entrance hall defies alike the ravages of time and weather. As far as Kingston Russell is concerned, the presence of the Hardys is clean forgotten, although the public memorial to the great sailor born there is plainly seen on the bleak summit of Blagdon or Blackdown Hill. You contrive to creep over a heap of rubbish into the death-chamber of Motley; possibly it was also the birth-room of Hardy. In any case, your guide remembers the time before the desertion of the old house was decreed, when "Duke William" and "Duke Hastings" came down to Kingston Russell to walk the boundaries. Surely the preservation of the home of the Dorset Russells, the birthplace of Thomas Masterman Hardy, and the scene of the death of John Lothrop Motley, would be worthy of the present bearer of the motto, " Che sara sara " —the owner of the green meadows and fertile fields of the beautiful valley of the Bride?

KINGSTON RUSSELL HOUSE, DORSET.

An Ancient Seat of the Duke o Bedford. where T. M. Hardy was born and J. L. Mo ley died.

To face page. 6.

CHAPTER IV

HARDY'S SCHOOLDAYS AT CREWKERNE AND MILTON
ABBAS. HIS EARLY EXPERIENCES IN THE NAVY
AND MERCHANT SERVICE [1778-1790]

THE spring of 1778 witnessed the removal of the whole
of the Hardy family from Kingston Russell to
"Possum." The eldest of Joseph Hardy's children,
Elizabeth, was just of age and about to marry John
Thresher, who belonged to another ancient Portisham
family, established there some years before the defeat of the
Spanish Armada by Lord Howard of Effingham off Portland Bill might have been clearly seen from the high land
above the village, the leading inhabitant of which, one John
Studley, had contributed £25 to the national defence fund.
Her next sister, then a girl of twenty, remained all her life
unmarried, but the third and fourth daughters of Joseph
and Nanny Hardy—Mary and Catherine—in 1778, aged
eighteen and sixteen respectively, in the course of the next
few years became the wives of James Balston and John
Callard Manfield, the latter of whom was destined to
become Thomas Hardy's legal adviser and the recipient of
his confidential correspondence. Their two youngest
sisters, Martha and Augusta (the latter in 1778 a baby),
never married. Of Thomas Hardy's two brothers, Joseph,
the elder (aged fourteen in 1778) was five years his senior.
In after life he married Miss White of Cerne and resided
at Charminster, where he died some years after the demise
of the captain of the *Victory*. John, the youngest of

Joseph Hardy's sons (a child of seven when his parents went to live at Portisham) never married, and after he reached manhood farmed the Hardy lands in and near their native village until he died, on the 25th April 1822. If the childhood of Thomas Hardy and his brothers and sisters at Kingston Russell is clean forgotten as far as the dwellers in the Bride Valley are concerned, their life at "Possum" is still the subject of local legend. Joseph Hardy offered his sons ponies to scour the bridle-paths of the Dorset downs, but the proffered favour was declined by the embryo sailor, who replied that "Joe and Jack might have horses, but that he wanted a wooden one," thereby meaning that he intended to go to sea.

In the latter half of the eighteenth century, country squires like Joseph Hardy were in the habit of sending their sons to school at an age which would now be regarded as abnormally early. As far as grammar schools are concerned, Dorset could boast of something approaching an *embarras de richesses*. Within easy reach of Portisham and the Valley of the Bride were the flourishing educational establishments of Wimborne (founded in 1496 by the Countess Margaret, only daughter of John Beaufort, Duke of Somerset); Milton Abbas, established a quarter of a century later by William Middleton, Abbot of Milton; Sherborne (chartered on the 13th May 1550 by Edward VI. of pious memory), and Dorchester (built and endowed in 1569 by Thomas Hardy of Melcombe Priory, an ancestral kinsman of the Portisham Hardys), to say nothing of minor seminaries at Beaminster, Gillingham, and Cranborne. Thomas Hardy, however, was at first sent to none of these. Just across the Somerset border, and not more than 18 miles from Portisham, prospered exceedingly the ancient grammar school of Crewkerne, which had originated at the end of the fifteenth century in the munificent benefactions of John de Combe, Precentor of Exeter and formerly Rector of the picturesque little town then called

Photo by

Evans, Dorcheste

HARDY's HOME AT PORT SHAM.

Crokehorn.[1]   Between 1762 and 1787 the fortunes of John de Combe's foundation were entrusted to two worthy pedagogues, who enjoyed something more than merely local fame.   The first of these was the Rev. Robert Burnett Patch, B.A., Fellow of Exeter College, Oxford, who in 1780 was succeeded by the still better known Rev. Robert Hoadly Ashe, D.D., a connection of the celebrated Bishop Hoadly, of Salisbury and Winchester, who had at one time no less than eighty boarders.   It was to this school that Thomas Masterman Hardy went soon after the settling-down of his parents at Portisham House.

The old building in which Hardy, and in all probability his two brothers, acquired the rudiments and doubtless received correction at the hands of the worthy Mr Patch and the eminent Dr Ashe, both stern and uncompromising believers in the theory and practice of King Solomon's precept on the subject of the rod, still exists close to Combe's old church of St Bartholomew.   The ancient brass over the entrance, with its curious inscription ending in the lines, "Venite filii obedite mihi timorem domini ego vos docebo," was about a quarter of a century ago transferred to a new and more ornate school-house.   Although the whole of the registers prior to 1828 have disappeared, there is no lack of information as to the state of the school about the time Hardy must have arrived there, probably after a long ride over Blagdon Hill, and through the two valleys of the Bride and the Brit.   The following were the modest requirements of a Crewkerne boarder in the matter of wardrobe :—

> "Ten shirts
> Eight 'necks'
> Six pair of stockings
> Four handkerchiefs
> One worsthred nightcap
> One white waistcoat."

[1] See *History of Crewkerne School*, by the Rev. R. Grosvenor Bartelot, M.A. ; Crewkerne, James Wheatley, 1899.

The diversions at Crewkerne were by no means confined to such orthodox games as cricket and football.
Onè learns from the MS. common-place book of John
Banger Russell, of Beaminster, himself an old Crewkernian,
that on every Shrove Tuesday the boys were accustomed
to indulge in cock-fighting in the school-room and under
the superintendence of the masters.   After the contests
the victor was expected to write a copy of verses on his
triumph.   If success fell to a youth of tender years he
was required to procure a poetic effusion from one of
his seniors.   Mr Russell observes that the contending
cocks at Crewkerne were armed with steel spurs, and
adds naïvely that "such indulgences were calculated to
give boys a fondness for that cruel and unmanly diversion."
Amongst Hardy's Crewkerne contemporaries was one
at least who won name and fame in after life, viz., William
Draper Best, a day boy, who eventually held the office
of Chief Justice of the Common Pleas, and was subsequently created Baron Wynford.   In 1816, as Serjeant
Best[1] he represented Sir T. M. Hardy in a delicate and
important lawsuit, in which he won a verdict for his client.

Hardy's lesson-books were soon closed, for a time at
least, for in the late autumn of 1781 he returned to Portisham to prepare for joining H.M.'s brig *Helena*, then
commanded by Captain Francis Roberts of Burton Bradstock, a relative of the Churchills of West Compton or
Compton Abbas and the Browns of Mappercombe, all
of them neighbours of the Hardys in the Kingston
Russell days.[2]   On the 30th November of this year

---

[1] See *post*, p. 168.

[2] Francis Roberts (born 1749, died 1794). As first lieutenant, he was
the only surviving officer of the *Quebec* frigate after the famous engagement with the *Surveillante*.   In the same year that Hardy joined the
Helena, Roberts had acquired fresh distinction by carrying despatches
in her to Gibraltar, through the thick of the fire of the enemy's flotilla.
He died on board the *Success*, of yellow fever, off Jamaica, 1st September
1794, aged 45, after thirty-six years' service in the navy.   His nephew,
R. F. Roberts, served with Hardy as midshipman on the *Victory* at

From a Pen-and-Ink Drawing by   F. J. Broadley.

CREWKERNE SCHOOL.   To face page 0.

begins Hardy's naval record. He was rated as "Captain's servant," in conformity with the then existing custom by which commanders of ships were permitted, under this designation, to initiate promising youths into the mysteries of seamanship. It was with the same qualification that Dorset's famous Admirals, Lord Hood and Lord Bridport, first went to sea.[1] Three months passed away, and a letter addressed to his brother Joseph (now aged eighteen) arrives at Winterbourne St Martin (Martinstown), on the other side of Blagdon Hill, whither he had gone to learn something of practical farming. It runs as follows :—

"HELENA," DOWNS,
March 6th, 1782.

DEAR BROTHER,

I received your letter on the 18th of last month and was glad to hear Father, Mother, Sisters and Brother and all our relations were well. We anchored here yesterday from Ostend where we went with a convoy and to bring one back. I was going to wright to Father when we were at Portsmouth but our sailing from there so soon prevented me, and my having so much to say. We put in there from chesing of another Privateer which got away again after they had struck owing to very bad weather so bad that we could not hoist our boat out and it being very dark. The bow (boy?) and Bounce[2] are

Trafalgar. Another nephew, Francis, was an officer with Hardy on board the *Triumph* and *Barfleur*. The Grove, the home of the Robertses at Burton Bradstock, sheltered by a gigantic mulberry tree, has changed very little since 1781. It belongs now to Staff Commander Roberts, R.N., and is tenanted by Miss M. M. Roberts, who possesses many interesting relics of her nautical ancestors, including a fine portrait of Francis Roberts and several letters from Hardy to members of the Roberts family.

[1] See D. N. B. under Hood (Samuel) and Hood (Alexander). For much interesting information as to qualification of "Captain's servant," see *The British Fleet*, by Commander C. N. Robinson, p. 316.

[2] Hardy's favourite dog at Greenwich Hospital, fifty-five years later, also bore the old name of "Bounce."

safe on board. I was very angry with Bounce, he would not know me till I had put on my old coat. Captn. Roberts likes him very much and everybody. He has promised when an opportunity offers to send me home to go to school for some time to learn navigation and everything that is proper for a sailor, therefore should be glad if you would ask Father to look out for a good school for me as I am resolved to learn everything as fast as I can. The close Mr Bagter sent are to large but they do prety well. Please to direct to me in the Downs as this is the place we always come to after our cruise is out. Capt. Roberts desiers his best compts. to you and all our family. Remember my duty to Father and Mother and Aunt Hardy and Love Sisters and Brother John and am Dear Brother

Yours affectionately

THOS. MASTERMAN HARDY.[1]

JOSEPH HARDY
Martinstown, Dorchester.

The receipt of this letter must have given much satisfaction both at Portisham and Martinstown, for it bears the following endorsement in the handwriting of Captain Francis Roberts :—

DEAR SIR,

I am happy to hear, by ·your letter to Thomas, that all your family are well. I thank you for your information of my friends; I have by the same post received letters from them. Am glad to inform you that Thomas is a very good boy, and I think will make a com plete seaman one day or other. He is now very desirous of learning; and please to make my compliments to your

---

[1] This letter was printed in the *United Service Journal*, November 1839, with the spelling corrected. It is now reproduced as Hardy wrote it, by permission of its present owner, Mrs John C. Thynne, Sir T. M. Hardy's granddaughter.

CAPTAIN FRANCIS ROBERTS
of Burton Bradstock, Dorset, with whom Hardy first went to sea on board
the *Helena* Brig.

[*To face page* 22.

father, and tell him I think in two or three months, if he approves of it, and can procure him a good school, to send him home for an education ; as it is impossible for him to learn everything that is proper for him on board ship. We were glad to find the dog safe ; I think him a very fine one. My best compliments to yourself and family, and am,

Dear Sir,

Your obedient humble servant,

FRANCIS ROBERTS.

So far, at any rate, Hardy had justified his choice of the "wooden horse." On the 9th April 1782, his name disappeared from the books of the *Helena*, and three weeks later was entered under the same rating in those of the *Seaford*, to which Captain Roberts was promoted, and where he remained for exactly twelve months. For nine months, *i.e.*, from 26th April 1783 to 24th January 1784, he seems to have remained on shore, and if current tradition on the subject may be trusted, went, for the purposes set forth in his own letter, to the Grammar School at Milton Abbas, then presided over by John Warton, a near relative of Thomas Warton, the poet laureate, and Joseph Warton, the author of the once famous critical " Essay on the Genius and Writings of Pope." The Rev. Herbert Pentin, Vicar of Milton Abbas, and secretary of the Dorset Field Club, writes as follows : " That Hardy was educated at Milton there is no doubt. The father of the old parish clerk in Mr Roberts's time (Roberts was appointed vicar in 1842) knew the boy Hardy well at school, and the anecdote related of him in Vol. XXV. of the *Proceedings of the Field Club* was found amongst Mr Roberts's papers." The story here alluded to by Mr Pentin is as follows :—

" When Hardy (afterwards Admiral Sir Thomas Masterman Hardy—Nelson's friend) was at the (Milton Abbas) School, it is recorded that he mounted the abbey tower one day with another boy, and they let down the headmaster's son (James Wood) over the tower to take a nest from the head of the stack pipe. Hardy then threatened to cut the rope unless Wood promised to give him two out of the four eggs."

The absolute authenticity of this legend must certainly remain a matter of doubt. In the first place, the Rev. James Wood resigned his post as Headmaster of Milton School in 1780, when Hardy was only eleven and scarcely likely to indulge in so perilous an adventure. Moreover, in an official record published in 1808, Crewkerne School is clearly stated to have been the place of his early education and upbringing. If Hardy ever went to Milton Abbas at all, it was at the epoch of his career above indicated, when Mr Wood was no longer headmaster, although it is just possible his son may have remained at the school. The story itself little accords with the generous and open character of Hardy, whose constant aim through life was to take a paternal care of the youths under his command. At Milton Abbey still hangs a fine portrait said to be that of Hardy. It has been ascribed to Gainsborough, as well as to Beach (the latter a native of Milton). It represents a naval officer, in a captain's uniform, of the period of 1780-81. It bears no resemblance whatever to the authentic miniature of Hardy which prefaces this volume, or either of the other acknowledged portraits of the captain of the *Victory*. By the kind permission of Mr Everard Hambro, the alleged Hardy portrait has been photographed, but competent critics have pronounced decidedly against its relation to Thomas Masterman Hardy, quite apart from the incompatibility of naval costume it discloses. Another painting, professing to portray the features of Hardy, is in the collection of the Baroness Burdett-Coutts, but its authenticity is denied by Hardy's descendants.

The month of January 1784 once more sees the name of Thomas Masterman Hardy appearing on the muster-roll of the *Carnatic* guardship as "Captain's servant." He continued to be thus rated until the 16th October 1785, but it has been alleged that he really remained at school during the whole of this time. Be this as it may, from this date until the 5th February 1790, no further mention of him occurs in the archives of the Navy Office. His father died on the 24th April 1785, at the comparatively early age of fifty-two. This is recorded on a memorial ring, which once belonged to Sir T. M. Hardy, and is now in possession of the Manfields of Portisham. Nanny Hardy was thus left a widow, with the care of a large family, of which several were still minors. It seems probable that from motives of economy, and possibly from an unselfish wish to assist his mother in her difficulties, Hardy at this juncture resolved, for a time at least, to leave the navy and join the merchant service.[1] As far as can be ascertained, no correspondence or records exist which can throw any light on Hardy's life and adventures in the mercantile marine. He doubtless acquired much valuable experience, which stood him in good stead throughout the whole of the brilliant career, which began on the 5th February 1790, when, just a month before his twenty-first birthday, he joined the *Hebe* as midshipman, under that brave Dorset sailor, Captain Alexander Hood, who, like his younger brother, Sir Samuel, was born at Kingsland Farm, Netherbury, at the head of the Valley of the Brit.

[1] The biographer of Hardy, in the *United Service Journal* of 1839, Part 3, pp. 383-4, accounts for Hardy's temporarily joining the merchant service by the commission of some "youthful transgression," adding that he "shipped on board a West Indiaman in London in some inferior capacity and served for some time before his friends knew what had become of him." The present writers have failed to find any grounds for such an insinuation, and it must not be forgotten that the same biographer located Hardy's birth erroneously at Martinstown, which he actually described as "a small town near Dorchester." It was in Hardy's time, and is still, only a village of less than 400 inhabitants.

CHAPTER V

HARDY AS MIDSHIPMAN AND LIEUTENANT [1790-1797]

THROUGHOUT the whole of the latter half of the eighteenth century, the Hoods were the naval heroes *par excellence* of the Dorset littoral. Their exploits formed the constant subject of conversation in the chimney-corners of cottage, tavern, and farm, and afforded congenial material for many a stirring song and rudely-printed broadside. While Hardy was at Crewkerne School, he was within an easy walk of the homes of the Hoods at Mosterton, Little Windsor, and Kingsland, and we are indebted to the personal influence of Alexander Hood for the return of Hardy to his first love—the king's navy. His wish to do so was doubtless facilitated by his coming of age and inheriting his share of the paternal estate.

After joining the *Hebe* frigate as midshipman, he went for several cruises in the Channel, and before the year was out (December 8, 1790) was promoted to be master's mate on board the same ship. This position he filled until the 5th March 1792, when the crew was paid off. On the next day his name appears as " A.B." on the *Tisiphone* sloop of twelve guns, Captain Anthony Hunt. He was again rated as midshipman in the same vessel in the month of October following, and when Captain Hunt assumed the command of the *Amphitrite* frigate of twenty guns, in May 1793, he took Hardy with him (once more as midshipman), and they joined Lord Hood's fleet in the Mediterranean. The French Revolution had now broken out, and the story of Lord Hood's operations before

26

Marseilles and Toulon, and the embarrassments caused by the dual command (for joint powers were exercised by Hood, then on board the *Victory*, and the Spanish admiral, Don Juan de Langara) has been often told. The golden opportunity which presented itself of entirely wiping out the fleet of the French Convention was lost, but Hardy must have distinguished himself, for on the 10th November he was promoted to the rank of lieutenant on board the *Meleager* frigate, Captain (afterwards Sir Charles) Tyler.[1] It was now that Hardy first came in contact with Captain Nelson, for the *Meleager* was attached to Nelson's squadron off Genoa. In June 1794, Captain Cockburn (thirty-four years later, Hardy's immediate predecessor as First Sea Lord of the Admiralty) succeeded Captain Tyler in the command of the *Meleager*. Between midsummer 1794, and August 1796, Hardy remained on board this vessel, which served as a repeating ship in Hotham's two actions off Toulon (March 14 and July 13, 1795). During the last twelvemonth of that period, *i.e.*, from July 1795 to August 1796, the *Meleager* was employed in the Gulf of Genoa, under the immediate orders of Captain Nelson, to whom Cockburn (and it may be presumed Hardy) gave unqualified satisfaction. On the 20th August 1796, Hardy (still only a lieutenant) moved with his captain into the *Minerve*,[2] a large frigate lately captured from the French, and in which, in the following month of December, Nelson (who had become a commodore of the second class on the previous 4th April) was to hoist his broad pendant.

On the 15th December 1796, the *Minerve* and the

[1] Wounded while commanding the *Tonnant* at Trafalgar. Died an admiral in 1835.

[2] On the 3rd July 1803, the *Minerve*, which played so important a part in the careers of both Nelson and Hardy, struck on a cone in Cherbourg harbour and was compelled to surrender to the French. Her officers and crew were conveyed to Verdun, where such of them as could not escape were detained for many years. The MS. journal of William Sweeting, of Huntingdon, one of the prisoners, rated as first-class boy in the ship's books, has lately been acquired by Mr Broadley.

Blanche sailed from Gibraltar, and five days later, off Carthagena, fell in with two Spanish frigates, the *Sabina* and the *Ceres*. The *Minerve* attacked the former, which was commanded by Don Jacobo Stuart, a descendant of the Duke of Berwick. After a prolonged resistance the *Sabina* surrendered, and Lieutenants Culverhouse and Hardy commanded the prize crew which took possession of the ship. Meanwhile the *Ceres* had struck her colours to the *Blanche*, but before a prize crew could be sent on board, a Spanish squadron of two ships of the line, accompanied by two frigates, hove in sight. The *Blanche* at once made sail, and, being some distance to leeward, escaped, but the *Minerve* was only saved by the courage and adroitness of Hardy. He ran up the English ensign in the *Sabina*, with the humiliated Spanish flag floating beneath it, an indignity which so irritated the commander of the largest Spanish ship, that he stopped his pursuit of the *Minerve*, and made for the *Sabina*, which he soon recaptured after her masts had gone over the side, and thus Culverhouse and Hardy became prisoners of war.[1] They were conveyed to Carthagena, where they were promptly exchanged for the unlucky scion of the House of the Stuart, who had surrendered his sword on board the *Minerve*, on the taking of his ship by the English. Hardy again joined the *Minerve* at Gibraltar, after her return from Elba, on 9th February 1797, so that his enforced absence from his ship was little more than six weeks.

On the following day, an incident occurred which not only demonstrated Nelson's regard and esteem for Hardy, but won for him the undying gratitude of his Dorset *protégé*. The *Minerve*, with the Spanish in chase, was passing through the Straits of Gibraltar in order to join the admiral, Sir John Jervis, when a man fell overboard, and Hardy, without the slightest hesitation, jumped into the jolly-boat and put off with

---

[1] Nelson's unqualified praise of this evidence of Hardy's courage and alertness will be found in Sir H. Nicolas's *Collection of Nelson's Despatches and Letters*, ii. 315.

her crew to save the drowning sailor. The boat and Hardy in it were being fast borne by the current towards the leading enemy's ship. It seemed as though he must be taken prisoner once more; but Nelson, who knew the value of a brave man, said: "By G—, I'll not lose Hardy; back the mizen topsail." It was instantly done; the effect was electrical. The Spanish saw the *Minerve* slowing down, and at once themselves started shortening sail, and this allowed Hardy to be picked up by the *Minerve*, which three days later joined the English Fleet just in time to take a frigate's part in the brilliant victory off Cape St Vincent (14th February 1797), in which Nelson won the star of a K.B., which he is supposed to have preferred to a baronetcy.

With the news of Jervis' glorious success ringing throughout the length and breadth of the land, begins most appropriately the newly discovered Hardy corre-spondence, to which the present chapter and those which preceded it, serve only as an introduction. The letter which Hardy addressed, after this momentous affair, to his brother-in-law, the Dorchester attorney, John Callard Man-field, has been lost, but one obtains a good notion of its contents from the communication which Manfield subse-quently addressed to Captain, afterwards Sir William Domett, another of the Dorset naval heroes of the Great War. Mr Manfield's epistle ran thus:—

DORCHESTER, 18*th April* 1797.

SIR,

I ought to apologize for not answering your letter of 25 Febry long before now but very soon after I received it I read in the papers your having sailed on a cruise—since which for these last six weeks I have been very ill indeed and not able to attend to business of any kind. I observe what you say respecting the Estates at Westhay[1] in your brother's occupation and agree with you that a lease ought to have been granted before this time

---

[1] Westhay, in Hawkchurch, Captain Domett's paternal home.

but the reason why it was delayed was owing to the
Tenements falling into hand from time to time as the
Lives droppd.—But now I have prepared a Draft of the
intended Lease of the whole in your brother's occupation
which only waits for his Lordship,[1] coming into the
Country when I will take care to get the lease executed.
If anything should fall into Hand convenient to be
occupied with what your Mother & Brothers have at
present you might depend on my giving them the preference.   I have a Brother-in-Law (T. M. H.) in the Navy.
He is now serving on Board the *Minerve* Frigate of which
he is First Lieutt. and was with Admiral Nelson when he
engaged and took the Spanish Frigate which was afterwards retaken by the Fleet and Mr Hardy (who was then
2nd) with Mr Culverhouse the first Lieutt. was carried into
Carthagena prisoners of war.   However they got their
liberty and joined the *Minerve* again two days previous
to the late Glorious Action off St Vincent.   If at any
time it should lye in your power to serve him I shall
consider it an obligation conferred upon me—and I trust
on enquiry into his conduct he will be found deserving
of it.

I am, etc.,

JOHN CALLARD MANFIELD.

Captn. DOMETT.

The covering letter written by Captain Domett to
his legal representative at Dorchester is missing, but its
enclosure, *i.e.*, a letter addressed to Domett by Sir Robert
Calder, who had been knighted some ten weeks previously,
on bringing home the first intelligence of Jervis's victory,
speaks for itself.   It runs as follows :—

[1] The Earl of Dorchester who purchased the Hawkchurch estate
from the Henley family.

"VILLE DE PARIS,'
AT ANCHOR OFF CADIZ,
28*th May* 1797.

DEAR DOMETT,

Many thanks for your kind congratulations, and for all your good wishes; rest assured you have mine in return and I hope that we shall soon meet at Southwick to talk over all our adventures since we parted over a good Bottle of the best.

Lieutenant Hardy of *La Minerve* is very highly spoken of by all who know him and I shall have great pleasure whenever in my power to give him a helping hand not only as one in whom you are interested but from his general good character. I have the pleasure to tell you *La Minerve* is now gone on a very good cruize with the *Lively* and I am in great hopes they will have it in their power to do something to get both money and promotion to the first Lieuts.

The Dons promise to come out when ready with a very large force, some say 33 sail of the line and 12 Frigates etc., etc. They also count upon having down from Toulon and Carthagena from 10 to 12 ships of the line and Frigates, possibly we may put a little salt upon their tails in their way to Cadiz should they attempt a junction. We have now here with us at anchor 22 sail of the line, one 50 gun ship, and 5 or 6 Frigates cruizing about us. We are all tolerably healthy and in very high spirits, so far so good, this goes a great way.

I beg my respects to Lord Bridport and best regards to Rear Admiral Pole,

I am, Dear Domett,

Ever yours truly,

ROBERT CALDER.

To Captn. WILLIAM DOMETT
H.M. Ship *Royal George*, Spithead.
[Re-directed to Torbay, Postage 1s. 9d.]

The high hopes which Sir Robert Calder had imparted to Captain Domett were speedily realised. On the very next day after he had penned his encouraging epistle, the *Minerve* and the *Lively* discovered the presence of a French brig of war, the *Mutine*, a beautiful vessel of 16 guns, in the Bay of Santa Cruz. Lieutenant Hardy was placed in command of the boats sent to cut her out. He performed the duty allotted to him in so dashing and skilful a manner that complete success rewarded his efforts. Although the taking of the *Mutine* was effected in broad daylight, not a single man was lost, but Hardy received a wound in the head, from the effects of which he afterwards suffered at intervals. The *Mutine* was captured (29th May 1797), and Hardy not only gained his promotion to the rank of commander, at the hands of Lord St Vincent, but was appointed to the prize, in the securing of which he had played so important a part. No one was more delighted at Hardy's success than Nelson, who hastened to express his warm approval of the appointment made, in the following words:—" My dear Admiral the Capture of the *Mutine* was so desperate an enterprise that I should certainly have promoted Lieut. Hardy so that neither you, Hallowell, nor Cockburn have any debtor account to me on this occasion. He has got it by his own bat and I hope will prosper." Thomas Masterman Hardy was only twenty-eight, and now commanded a ship of his own. He had got his " wooden horse " at last, and the gossips at Dorchester and " Possum " prophesied that his fortune was as good as made. From that time forth his relatives at home evidently thought it worth while to preserve the bulk of his correspondence. History will assuredly be no loser by the decision which they arrived at.

CHAPTER VI

HARDY AS COMMANDER OF THE "MUTINE" [JUNE 16, 1797—AUGUST 3, 1798]

FOR the remaining months of 1797 and those of the following year which preceded the never-to-be forgotten naval engagement at the mouth of the Nile, Hardy was busily engaged in executing, with admirable promptitude, the orders of Lord St Vincent and Sir Horatio Nelson. The *Mutine*, a fast-sailing brig and the only single-decked vessel in the squadron,[1] was in constant requisition during the momentous events which culminated in the battle of 1st August 1798. In the intervals of keeping up communication between St Vincent and Nelson, Hardy was lucky enough to capture a few prizes, which not only helped to swell his balance with his agents, but materially increased his popularity with his crew. Few men ever had a more ardent love of glory or keener sense of duty to king and country, but Hardy after all was human, and his letters, especially the earlier ones, disclose a pardonable weakness both for prize-money and promotion. In April 1798, the successes of Bonaparte in Italy impelled the British ministers to impress strongly on Lord St Vincent the absolute necessity of striking a decisive blow in the Mediterranean, with the view of thwarting once and for all the projects of the Toulon fleet. "Either our Government," wrote the victorious French generalissimo at this

[1] *Gentleman's Magazine*, vol. xii., new series, p. 650.

time, "must destroy the English monarchy, or must expect itself to be destroyed by the corruption and intrigue of those active islanders."[1]   The reply to this was Earl Spencer's despatch to Lord St Vincent informing him that reinforcements were to be sent out at once, and suggesting that Nelson might achieve such a triumph as would "bring about a new system of affairs in Europe which shall save us all from being overrun by the exorbitant power of France."   This despatch reached the Commander-in-Chief on the 10th May, and was followed a week later by more urgent messages of the same nature.   On the 19th May, Hardy was ordered to notify Nelson that a squadron of 10 ships of the line and the *Leander* of 50 guns, under the orders of Captain (afterwards Sir Thomas) Troubridge, were about to join him from Cadiz, in order to facilitate his operations against the enemy.   A week later, Hardy, on his way to join Nelson, put in at Gibraltar, whence he wrote as follows to his brother, now occupying the family house at Portisham :—

"LA MUTINE," GIBRALTAR,
May 26th, 1798.

DR BROTHER,

We are bound to Naples under the Command of Sir Horatio Nelson & you may expect to hear of something handsom being done very soon by his Squadron which at present is small but I believe will consist of eighteen sail of the Line.

I hope Sir Horatio will have it in his power to do something for me before our Cruise is out.   I find by Sir Robert Calder[2] my Friend Captain Domett has written to him in my behalf & Sir Robert appears very much inclined to assist me.   Should Manfield write to Cap^n Domett I hope he will not forget to add my thanks to him for his attention to me.   I have sent my Journals To Mr Hartwell for the *Meleager* & *La Minerve*.   Should you or Manfield

[1] Mahan's *Life of Nelson*, vol. i., p. 318.
[2] See Letter of Sir Robert Calder, Chapter V., p. 31.

go to London I'll thank you to call on him & inquire if he has recd them & add I am very anxious to hear from him. Should you find he *rides the High Horse* act as you think proper & if he has not received my Prize Money for the Spanish Squadron do tell him it has been payable some Months by Cook & Halford, Strand. Should he be careless I think they had better be appointed, & I can easily send a Power of Attorney for that Purpose. We have been fortunate enough to have two Newtral Vessels condemned it is supposed ten Thousand Pound however if half I shall be satisfied as Appeals are dangerous. I shall not think of meddling with the Cash until twelve Months are expired after that period all will be safe. *La Mutine* was alone at their Capture.

If you write to me within these two [months] from this Date I wish you to direct to me at Naples to the Care of Sir Wm Hamilton his Majesty's Consul. I'll thank you to tell Tulledge's Friends that he is well & I assure you he behaves remarkably well. Jas Dine is on board the *Hector* he has applied to me to get him with me but as yet I have not been able he is well & desires to be remembered to his Mother.

I thank you to give my duty, Love, &c., to all friends and remain,

Yours Affectionately,

T. M. HARDY.

Tell Ann I have written her a long letter but fear the conveyance was not good however shall write again from the first Port we put in not in the Mediterranean.

JOSEPH HARDY, Esq.,
    Portisham, near Dorchester,
        Dorset.

The *Mutine* joined Nelson somewhere near Elba on the 5th June, and Hardy found the Rear-Admiral was much depressed by an untoward series of accidents. The French transports had successfully evaded his pursuit; a storm had dismasted his flag-ship, the *Vanguard*, and other mishaps had plunged Nelson in one of his gloomy and desponding moods. No messenger was ever the bearer of more welcome intelligence than his loyal and loving friend, Thomas Hardy. Sir Horatio Nelson now realised the fact that at last a supreme chance was to be vouchsafed him. The promised reinforcements arrived, although three frigates, upon which he greatly relied, still tarried at Gibraltar, and the ever-useful *Mutine* was all he had to replace them. On the 5th June the chase began. A fortnight later the *Mutine* conveyed Troubridge to Naples with letters from Nelson for Acton, the Neapolitan Premier, and Sir William Hamilton, the British Minister. On Troubridge rejoining the squadron, 10 miles off the Italian coast, Nelson sailed for Aboukir Bay.

For the story of the Battle of the Nile the reader is referred to the pages of Captain Mahan and other standard authorities. Suffice it to say, the *Mutine* did excellent service. When Troubridge's ship, the *Culloden*, grounded, Hardy went to his assistance, and the continued absence of the missing frigates must have appreciably enhanced the value of the good work done by the only brig in Nelson's fleet. Once more, in the hour of victory, the wounded Admiral remembered his friend Hardy. Edward Berry, Nelson's flag-captain on the *Vanguard*, and often described as his "right-hand man," was sent home with despatches in the *Leander*, while the *Mutine* followed her with the duplicates. Hardy, however, was no longer her commander. On the 4th August 1798, one of Hardy's cherished dreams of promotion was realised. Two days before Berry sailed for England, Hardy replaced him as Nelson's flag-captain on board the *Vanguard*. At this time he was still on the sunny side of thirty.

CHAPTER VII

HARDY AS FLAG-CAPTAIN OF THE "VANGUARD" AND
"FOUDROYANT." WITH NELSON IN NAPLES AND
SICILY [4TH AUGUST 1798—12TH OCTOBER 1799]

THE gratitude of England to Nelson was unbounded. The thanks of Parliament and a pension of £2000 a year were voted him. He was also made a Peer of the Realm under the style of Baron Nelson of the Nile. His wound proved very troublesome, but it began to heal at last; and after the essential repairs of the damaged ships had been effected, and the most worthless of the prizes destroyed, the *Vanguard* set sail for Naples, where she arrived on the 22nd of September towed in by a frigate, her foremast having gone by the board in a squall which she encountered a week previously. The arrival of her "two crippled consorts," on the 16th of the same month, enabled the King and Queen of Naples, as well as Sir William and Lady Hamilton, to prepare a series of those public rejoicings so dear to the hearts of the Neapolitans. Hardy is silent on the subject of the meeting of Nelson and Lady Hamilton and other incidents about which so much has lately been written. The succeeding four months must have been busy ones for Hardy. They were crowded with events as momentous to the future of Nelson as to the history of the kingdoms of Sicily and Naples. On the 15th October, Hardy sailed in the *Vanguard* with Nelson for Malta, the blockade of which island had been resolved upon. Three other ships accompanied them. By the 5th November they were back in Naples, and on the 22nd of that month the *Vanguard* and the rest of the squadron, with 5000 troops on board, set out for Leghorn. A week later the *Vanguard*, with Nelson and Hardy, returned to Naples. Then came the total rout of the Neapolitan rabble army, 40,000 of the soldiers bolting at the sight of barely 10,000 French. Nelson waxed furious. With grim humour he writes: "The Neapolitan officers have not lost much honour, for God knows they have but little to lose, but they lost all they had. Cannons, tents, baggage, and military chest—all were left behind." The invaders marched on Naples. The royal family, the English minister and his wife, the British residents, the most prominent sympathisers with King Ferdinand (irreverently called *il vecchio Nasone*—"old Nosey"), and the tactless Queen Caroline, went on board the flag-ship and three British transports which happened to be in the harbour. The King and Queen of Naples, as well as Sir William and Lady Hamilton, were the guests of Lord Nelson on board the *Vanguard*, freighted also with treasure in jewels and specie of enormous value. On the evening of 23rd December she sailed for Palermo, where she arrived three days later, after a most tempestuous passage. Never did Nelson or Hardy spend a more uncomfortable Christmas Day. Before the Sicilian coast was sighted, the youngest of the sons of King Ferdinand died of convulsions, in the arms of Lady Hamilton. Exactly one month later, Hardy addresses the following letter to his brother-in-law :—

"VANGUARD," PALERMO MOLE,
Jan. 26th, 1799.

DR MANFIELD,

I received your letter a few days ago and am much obliged to you for the trouble you have taken to settle between Mr Hartwell & me. I also very much approve of taking my business out of his hands. As he says I am indebted to him two hundred & fifty pounds & since that time I have drawn on him for at least one hundred pounds more It is necessary that should be settled. I have therefore enclosed my Power of Attorney to Messrs Cook & Halford & written to them on that head. The day I received your letter I got my Commissions for the *Meleager, Falcon* (I suppose *Mutine*) & *Alligator* all in a blank cover I suppose from Mr Hartwell tho' he has not even written me a word. The Commission given me by Lord Nelson was dated 2nd of August which was sent to Mr Hartwell, that from the Admiralty is dated the 2nd of October therefore I lose two months. If there are many Captains made between the 2nd of August & the 2nd of October I shall lose that rank unless some good friend at home represents it to the Admiralty, should no one be made between those two dates it will be of little or no consequence. That will be easily seen by looking at the last Steel's List. The French have not as yet possession of Naples but are within twelve miles of it and we have little doubt but they will soon garrison the City. Captain Troubridge is gone off Alexandria with three Bomb Vessels. I believe the intention is to make a dash which I hope and trust will succeed. The surrender of Malta is I believe near at hand. We have accounts today of our ships having possession but it wants confirmation.[1] There is little doubt but the *Vanguard* will soon go to England with the Admiral & Sir William Hamilton's family. If I can get a frigate in this Country I shall not refuse, if not I think you will see me in the course of three months. I am sorry to hear of my Brothers illness but hope Spring will recover my Mother & him. Give my love to Catherine[2] & all my little Nephews and Nieces. Wishing you health & happiness I remain

Dear Manfield,
Yours Affectionately,
T. M. HARDY.

JOHN CALL. MANFIELD, Esqr.
Dorchester, Dorset.

---

[1] Malta did not, however, surrender until 5th September 1800.
[2] Hardy's sister, the wife of John Callard Manfield.

Three weeks later he again writes :—

"VANGUARD," PALERMO MOLE,
Feby 17th, '99·

DR MANFIELD,

I received your letter of the 19th of Novr
three Weeks ago & answered it the next day but as letters
frequently miscarry & you wished to know if I approved
of the exchange of Agents I again repeat my approbation
& thanks to you for the trouble you have taken with that
Obstinate Gentleman Mr Hartwell. I this day have sent
my Power of Attorney &c. &c. to Messrs Cook & Halford
& have requested them to settle with Mr Hartwell & send
me his Account.[1] I suppose there wil be no difficulty in
settling with him provided my Pay &c. does not amount
to the sum which I am indebted to him as my Prize
money for the 1st of August will be greatly in my favour.
I find the Admiral is not so anxious to quit this Country
as when I wrote you last ; therefore my going to England
greatly depends on Captn Berry's coming to join the
Vanguard.

The Politicks of this Country appears to me to be
nearly in the same state as those of Naples were three
Months ago & if I judge right, which I very much fear I
do, the French will have possession of this Island in the
course of this Summer & what will become of the poor
Royal Family God knows but I suppose we shall have to
carry them to Trieste.

The French have full possession of the Kingdom of
Naples & have given it the name of Vesuvian Republick.
We expect to have orders from this Court in a few days
to make reprisals on all Neapolitans. The blocade of
Malta will I fear be much prolonged owing to a Frigate
having got in with a Quantity of Stores & Provisions,
however as the winter is almost over I hope & trust no
more will escape the indefatigable exertions of Captn

[1] See Appendix, p. 294.

Ball.[1]   I am very sorry to hear of my Mother[2] & Brothers indisposition but hope soon to hear of their perfect recovery.   Give my love to Catherine my little Nephews & Nieces & all friends.

I remain, yours Affectionately,

T. M. HARDY.

JOHN CALLD. MANFIELD, Esq.
Dorchester, Dorset.

For five months we have no more letters from Hardy. In the interval, Naples had been taken possession of by the French (January 1799), who shortly afterwards withdrew, leaving only the fortress of St Elmo and one or two other forts occupied by their troops.   A counter revolution now became possible, the project being doubtless diligently fomented by the fugitives at Palermo.   The appearance in Mediterranean waters of a naval force under Admiral Bruix aroused Nelson from the lethargy plainly hinted at by Hardy, and he lost no time in summoning his ships to a rendezvous off Maritimo, so as to be able to assist Lord St Vincent or strike another blow on his own account. The order was dispatched on the 12th May.   On the 23rd of that month, Nelson and 7 ships were waiting for reinforcements at Maritimo.   No sooner did they arrive than Bruix, seeing his plans were thwarted and presumably overawed by the demonstrations, precipitately retired through the Straits of Gibraltar.   On the 8th June, Nelson, once more at Palermo, transferred his flag to the *Foudroyant*, which had arrived there two days previously, taking Hardy with him.   On Midsummer Day—a fortnight later—with the whole of his squadron, he entered the Bay of Naples, and apparently acting as representative of the king, annulled the existing armistice and demanded the

---

[1] Ball had been sent on the previous 4th October (1798) in the *Alexander* to conduct the blockade of Malta, and eventually became British Governor of the Island and was knighted.

[2] Mrs Joseph Hardy died at Portisham in March 1799.

surrender of the rebels. On the 14th July, Hardy thus writes to his brother-in-law at Dorchester :—

"FOUDROYANT," NAPLES BAY,
July 14th, 1799.

DR MANFIELD,

I received your letter a few days ago & take the opportunity of sending this by Liut Parkinson who takes home the Admiral's dispatches with the accounts of the surrender of St Elmo which Castle commanded the whole City of Naples. Captain Troubridge & Hallowell had the Command of the Marines of the Squadron & after a close siege of ten days they got possession of it yesterday. The loss on our side has been very small that of the French about 20 killed and forty wounded. They set off to-morrow for Capua a garison town about sixteen miles from Naples. As the strength on our side will be very formidable we soon expect to place the King of Naples on his throne. He is now on board the *Foudroyant* waiting the event. The lower & middling class of People who have little or nothing to lose all appear to be loyal. The Nobles are almost all Republicans & the greater part of them are now in irons on board the Fleet. One only as yet has been hanged,[1] but the tryals come on to-morrow & we expect that at least a hundred more will share the same Fate & the lowest Rank will be that of a Bishop or a Knight. The Queen & Royal family are still at Palermo but we expect very soon to go for them. We have been in the *Foudroyant* about a month she is one of the finest two Deck Ships in the service but I do not think Lord Nelson will remain in her long as Lord St Vincent is gone

---

[1] Francesco Caracciolo, the Neapolitan leader, who had been captured in disguise and brought on board the *Foudroyant* on the 29th June 1799. After a trial, before a court-martial of Neapolitan officers, he was sentenced to death, and hanged at 5 P.M. from the fore yard-arm of the *Minerve*. This vessel belonged to the Neapolitan Navy, and must not be confused with Hardy's ship, *La Minerve*, originally a French prize.

FERDINAND IV., KING OF NAPLES.

From an original Water-colour once in possession of Sir T. M. Hardy.

[*To face page* 42.

home. I think it more than probable he will follow if not we shall I think go in to the *Ville de Paris*—however this is all conjecture—Lieut Parkinson came out in the *Vanguard* & has been 1st Lieut about 4 Month it gives me great pleasure at this opportunity as he is a very good young man & it will insure his promotion. I think it likely he will call on you & I am certain you will find him a very pleasant young man. I'll thank you to tell my brother that I wish my proportion of every description (left by my Father & Mother) to be equally divided between my three unmarried Sisters & I shall be much obliged if you will beg of them to accept it. I have not yet heard from Cook & Halford but hope they have recd my books of the *Mutine* &c. &c. Give my best love to Catherine and the little ones & to all Friends & remain

Dr Manfield

Yours affectionately

T. M. HARDY

JOHN CALLARD MANFIELD, Esq.,
Dorchester, Dorset.

Hardy's service as flag-captain to Nelson on board the *Foudroyant* was now drawing rapidly to a close. As he anticipated, Captain Berry (by this time Sir Edward) returned to the Mediterranean, and on the 12th October 1799, relieved him of the post which he had held for over fourteen months. Two days later, Nelson appointed him Captain of the *Princess Charlotte*. In less than a month he was on his way home, reaching London a week before Christmas, when he wrote the following brief letter to Dorchester, announcing his arrival :—

BEAUFORT BUILDINGS,
Decr. 18*th*, '99.

DR MANFIELD,

I arrived last night too late to save the Post ; therefore it is likely you will see my Name in the papers before you receive this.

I shall come in the Country as soon as I possibly can, I think the 24th will be the day,

I remain,

Dr Manfield, in great haste,

Yours most sincerely,

T. M. HARDY.

JOHN MANFIELD, Esq.,
   Dorchester, Dorset.

On Christmas Eve the Dorchester coach deposited Nelson's flag-captain at the door of the "King's Arms." After a short drive over execrable roads, Hardy and his brother-in-law, Manfield, were welcomed by Joseph and John Hardy, and their three unmarried sisters, to the old home at "Possum," where the villagers accorded him the welcome he merited after his prolonged absence.

The church bells rang out many a merry peal, and Thomas Hardy spent his Christmas in good old Dorset fashion in the shadow of the rugged hill now surmounted by the memorial of his valour and victories.

CHAPTER VIII

HARDY'S HOLIDAY IN ENGLAND. HE AWAITS THE RETURN OF NELSON

HARDY'S sojourn with his kinsfolk at "Possum" was not destined to be of long duration. A week after the dawn of 1800 (then erroneously considered to be the first year of a new century), the Dorchester coach brought him back to London. Society as well as dear Dorset had now its claims on Nelson's flag-captain, and a presentation at court was, of course, inevitable. On the 8th January he thus writes from 1 Cecil Street, Strand :—

DR MANFIELD,

I am this moment arrived from Court, there were so many presentations that the King had but little time to talk to any of us. Genl Stewart, Admirals Harvey[1] & Mitchell[2] were honored with the Order of the Bath. The Cermony was very short & simple.

Lord Spencer has been out of Town until this Morning. I shall wait on him to-morrow morning, & should he give me any promises, I will let you know. There will not be a Drawing Room till the Birth Day, & I am advised to go to it, & I think I shall leave Town on that day or the day following, for Portsmouth. To-morrow I shall call on

[1] Sir Henry Harvey [1737-1810].
[2] Sir Andrew Mitchell [1757-1806].

Mary Thresher,[1] Martha desired me to get her something, but I quite forget what it was, do inquire & let me know. With Love & Compliments, I remain,

Dr Manfield,

Yours most Sincerely,

T. M. HARDY.

Three months elapse, and one hears of Hardy dining with Lady Nelson, who had already interested herself in his welfare. In a hitherto unpublished letter to her husband, dated 10th December 1799 (a week before Hardy's arrival in England), she says: "I long to hear what you have done for Captain Hardy. His character is indeed excellent." Hardy's solicitude for the comfort of Nelson's father, the venerable rector of Burnham Thorpe, is indeed touching. His next letter to Mr Manfield runs thus:—

1 CECIL STREET, STRAND,
April 12th, 1800.

DEAR MANFIELD,

I Dined yesterday with Lady Nelson; Mr Nelson has been very ill but is getting better and can eat nothing but light food; he expressed a wish to her Ladyship whilst at dinner that some Sea Cale may be procured for him & I verily believe there is none to be got in London. As I know Mrs Manfield has plenty I am certain she will spare me some & I recommend it to be sent by the Balloon[2] as the Guard comes to London. If he is asked I doubt not he will deliver it himself in Cecil Street & the Carriage had better not be paid as I think my being in his debt will assist his memory.

Yesterday being Good Friday no business was done at the Admiralty, nor have I been able to see Lord Spencer as yet. When I do I will write again. Lady Nelson has

---

[1] Hardy's niece. Daughter of John and Elizabeth Thresher of Corfe Hill and Portisham.

[2] A well-known Dorchester coach.

FRANCES HERBERT, VISCOUNTESS NELSON

From a Miniature, taken in 1804, in the possession of Mrs Eccles, Sherwell House, Plymouth.
(Copyright).

[*To face page* 46.

not heard from Lord Nelson but thro' Mr Morris[1] Nelson
of the Navy Office, who I shall not see before Tuesday &
from whom I expect some hints concerning his Lordship's
movements. If Mrs Balston[2] should have some young
Chicken or Ducks a Couple will be very acceptable to
old Mr Nelson. Spinage would be a valuable article if
the Country produces it fit for use.

I am sorry I have no news for you, but hope Tuesday
will furnish me with some. With Love and Coms. to all
friends,

I remain, Dr Manfield,

Yours most sincerely,

T. M. HARDY.

The results of this appeal for Dorset table-delicacies
seemingly proved satisfactory. So much so that Lady
Nelson desired to cultivate the vegetable her father-in-law
longed for in her own garden. Three days later Hardy
again writes :—

April 15th, 1800.

DR MANFIELD

I'll thank you if you can Provide some Sea
Cale Seed & send it as directed on the other side.[3] If you
can also inquire of some of the Gardners at Dorchester
and inform Mr Fuller the manner in which it is sown Lady
Nelson will be obliged to you as it is for her Ladyship's
Garden.

Yours truly,

T. M. HARDY.

Mr MANFIELD,
Dorchester, Dorset.

Hardy now begins a dreary course of lobbying at
Whitehall, an experience to which Nelson himself in days

[1] Maurice Nelson, Lord Nelson's elder brother [1753-1801].
[2] One of Hardy's married sisters, then living in or near Dorchester.
[3] Mr Fuller, Cauldwell Hall, Near Ipswich, Suffolk.

gone by was not wholly a stranger.   He writes no longer of sea-cale or spinach, but of his own professional prospects.

CECIL STREET,
Apl. 19*th*, 1800.

DEAR MANFIELD,

I shall not be able to see Lord Spencer before Tuesday next & as I have determined with Mr John Browne[1] to leave London on Thursday (should nothing at the Ameralty prevent me) I will thank you to desire John to send my Horse to your house by Wednesday next & Mr Browne's Servant will call for it on Thursday.   There appears little doubt but Lord Bridport will strike his Flag very soon & it is equally clear in the Opinion of the folks in this part of the World that Lord St Vincent is to have the Command of the Channel Fleet.   I waited on His Lordship the day before yesterday He was extremely polite & advised me not even to refuse a *Troop Ship* should it be offered me.   Mr Browne received a very satisfactory letter from Jos yesterday.   I expect to hear from you on Monday with the Name of the Man of whom I am to get a Saddle for you.

Mr Bagster[2] has not got a Measure for Mrs Balston later than the year '96 therefore he is afraid to begin her habit until he hears from her again—

Give my Love to all the Family

I remain Dr Manfield

Yours most sincerely,

T. M. HARDY.

[1] Francis John Browne of Frampton Court, sometime M.P. for Dorset.   He held a commission as Captain in the regiment of Dorset Yeomanry raised to resist the threatened invasion of the Dorset littoral by Bonaparte.   In 1801 the defence of the seventh division was allotted to him.   It extended from the Fleet River (Weymouth) to the Bride or Bredy, and included Portisham, Abbotsbury, Kingston Russell, Shipton Gorge, and Burton Bradstock.   His portrait by Thomas Beach is to be seen at Came House, Dorchester.

[2] A lady's tailor of the period.

The ante-chambering at the Admiralty (where thirty years hence he was to reign as First Sea Lord) continues. July comes round and Hardy is still waiting for a ship. He now writes :—

No. 8 CECIL STREET,
July 25th, 1800.

DEAR MANFIELD,

Thank you for your letter & my friend Parker's[1] *long* Epistle which if I was obliged to answer *line* by *line* I think I should eat nothing for these three days to come, however as there is no Fleet (except the prison) in this great City his letter will be answered in one side & an half.

I am happy to hear that the Castle Yacht sails *uncommon* well & am sorry I had not the pleasure of being with you.

Mary[2] & I slept at Salisbury & came on next morning in the Coach we arrived at Prospect House about 9 o'clock on Monday evening & her Governess was very happy to see her tho' a fortnight before the Vacation was ended.   I have reduced the Impress to £331 : 7 : 6 & expect to pass my Accounts as soon as I hear from the Pursur of the *Vanguard* whom I wrote to yesterday.   I saw a letter from Leghorn, dated 23rd of June, saying that Lord Nelson had actually sail'd for Gibraltar in the *Culloden* on his way to England & he is hourly expected at the Admiralty; however as I can always be in London so shortly after his arrival I am determined to quit Town as soon as I possibly can for no man would remain here for pleasure that could exist on bread and water in the Country.

As I cannot determine on when I leave town I will

---

[1] Parker was one of the many young naval officers in whose career Hardy took a kindly interest.   He afterwards died at Deal, September 28, 1801, of wounds received in the unsuccessful attack on Boulogne; *vide* p. 71.

[2] His niece Mary, daughter of J. C. Manfield.

D

give you a line before I quit it.   Give my love to Catherine the Children & all friends

I remain Dear Manfield,

Yours sincerely,

T. M. HARDY.

P.S.—As I have no *female correspondence* I'll thank you to open all the letters that come for me.

Everybody goes out of town and further lobbying would be a bootless task.   Hardy resolves to give himself a holiday in Dorsetshire.

LONDON,
July 28th, 1800.

DEAR MANFIELD,

I leave London tomorrow evening in the Mail and will Dine with you on Wednesday

Yours truly,

T. M. HARDY.

Nelson's homeward journey has occupied nearly the whole of the summer, and in October Hardy returns to London to await his arrival.

NEW EXCHANGE COFFEE HOUSE,
STRAND, *Octr.* 15*th*, 1800.

DEAR MANFIELD,

I did not write to you before because I had nothing to say.   Lord Nelson's arrival has been hourly expected till yesterday when it was proved they knew nothing about it.

I saw Mr Sylvester (the Messenger) who tells me he saw his Lordship on the 4th inst two stages this side of Dresden with Sir Wm & Lady Hamilton and my good friend Miss Knight[1] &c.   The Roads are so extremely bad that they with great difficulty got on at

---

[1] A literary friend of Lady Hamilton at Naples.   Afterwards an authoress.

the rate of four Miles an hour with eight horses in each Carriage however he thinks we may expect them in about a week. Ned Balston[1] has been on board his Ship a week & is expected in town tomorrow. I wrote to John requesting him to send the stock of my single barrell gun which is not come, but suppose I have only to blame the tardyness of Russell's Waggon.

Give my love to Catharine the Children & all relations

I remain

Dr Manfield

Yours sincerely,

T. M. HARDY.

A fortnight passes and still no news of "his lordship" and his companions. Hardy has now secured lodgings in the West End near those of Lady Nelson. He writes as follows :—

No. 9 DUKE STREET,
ST JAMES'S SQUARE, *Octr.* 30*th*, 1800.

DEAR MANFIELD,

I suppose you have given me up for lost long ago ; however here I am within a half a Dozen Dores of Lady Nelson who arrived last Week to wait her Lord's arrival & I am just informed by Mr Wagstaff (the Messenger) that arrived this Morning from Vienna that his Lordship with Sir Wm & Lady Hamilton & Lord Whitworth had been waiting fifteen Days at Hamburgh for a fair Wind & he has no doubt but they sailed last Sunday the Wind being then fair & the Frigate waiting to take them on board so I think we may expect to hear of his arrival within a day or two. Do tell Mr Oakley that the Hamper which he sent Lady Nelson was so badly packed that eighteen Bottles were broken & the corks so *extremely* short and bad that several had flown. However

---

[1] Hardy's nephew, who by this time had entered the Navy under his auspices.

the Beer that remained was the best ever drank in Norfolk [1] therefore I think with the precautions above mentioned another hamper will not be amiss against his Lordship's arrival which you will have the goodness to order to be sent to me here as soon as possible. As Mr Bagster has not received the Beer ordered for him will you at the same time enquire if it is sent; if not if there is any chance of its being sent; the old Gentleman never sees me without asking me about it.

Give my Duty to my Aunt when you see her & say I am indebted to her twenty-two shillings and sixpence. I received a good Basket of Game two or three Days ago. I suppose I am to thank Mr Travers [2] for it but do not know as the Direction was torn off before I saw it. Ned Balston has told you how much I am tired of London therefore I need say nothing on that head. I think what with the straggling hand, distance between the lines & sentences spun out as long as possible that I have occupied more than three sides where one and a half would have answered every purpose. Love to Catherine & all relations & Compliments to all friends

I remain, Dr Manfield yours

Most sincerely,

T. M. HARDY.

P.S.—I shall write to my brother John tomorrow or next Day.

[1] Dorset ale and beer has been famous for centuries. It still maintains its old renown in the twentieth.

[2] Richard Travers of Loders, another of the Dorset Yeomanry Captains of the Great War. He was assigned the ninth division in the scheme of defence, which extended from the mouth of the Bride to that of the Brit, and thence westwards to Lyme Regis. Captain Travers' portrait, painted in his prime by Beach, is to be seen at Came. He is buried outside the chancel door of the interesting and picturesque church of Loders, near Bridport. The Traverses were allied by marriage to the Roberts family of Burton; and another picture of Richard Travers as an old man is in possession of Miss M. M. Roberts.

November arrives and still no Nelson. Hardy becomes more and more anxious and writes :—

9 DUKE STREET,
Novr. 8th, 1800.

DEAR MANFIELD,

  Notwithstanding all the Newspapers his Lordship is not arrived in town & when he will God only knows. His Father has lost all patience, her Ladyship bears up very well as yet but I much fear she also will soon despond. He certainly arrived at Yarmouth on Thursday last & there has been no letter received by anybody. Should he not arrive tomorrow I think I shall set off for Yarmouth *as I know too well the cause of his not coming*. Sir Thos Troubridge waits today for his arrival but sets off this evening for Torbay, he thinks my going to Yarmouth advisable. He has spoken to Lord Spencer for me & in short done every thing in his power to serve me.

I saw Ned Balston this Morning. He has not yet determined weather his health is equal to another Voiage but will write as soon as the Physicians give their answer. Bagster has recd the Game ; the Beer is not yet arrived—I dine with young George Bagster to-day therefore shall not close my letter till the Bellman comes to the dore however you may depend on hearing from me on Monday. I recd Catharine's order and shall not forget it. Give my Duty Love & Comps to all friends. I remain Dr Manfield

Yours most sincerely,

T. M. HARDY.

½ past 5 No News of Lord Nelson.

The last letter had not reached Dorchester before Nelson arrived. Hardy hastened to meet him, and their old friendship is at once renewed in spite of Hardy's outspoken sympathy for Lady Nelson, who finally separated from her husband a few weeks later—in the early

days of 1801.   On the 10th November 1800, Hardy writes
from 9 Duke Street to his brother-in-law as follows :—

DEAR MANFIELD,

I beg ten thousand pardons for not writing
by today's post but really his Lordship kept me till I had
not a moment to spare & then told me I must go with him
to dine at Guild Hall & as you will get a much better
description from the papers than I can possible give I refer
you to them.   All things go well here & in a day or two
you shall know more about it.   He is certainly to be
employed very soon and I leave you to guess the rest—On
Wednesday I go to Court and Thursday to make our bow
to the Queen—I shall not close this till tomorrow
afternoon therefore wish you a good Night as I am to
breakfast with his Lordship tomorrow at 8 o'clock Duty
Love &c

I remain Dear Manfield,

Yours most sincerely,

T. M. HARDY.

Tuesday 11th 5 o'clock.   I have nothing more to say
than you must *read* Hardy insted of *Gentleman* & Sir Edwd
Berry, as the Editors have not yet found out my name.

CHAPTER IX

HARDY ONCE MORE NELSON'S FLAG-CAPTAIN. HIS
COMMANDS OF THE "NAMUR," "SAN JOSEF," AND
"ST GEORGE." THE BATTLE OF COPENHAGEN.
[NOVEMBER 1800—APRIL 1801]

THE high hopes excited in Hardy by the advent of
Lord Nelson were speedily realised. Within a
week of his attending the Lord Mayor's banquet of 1800,
at the invitation of Sir William Staines, he obtained the
long looked-for appointment. Nelson realised the importance of the task before him, and knew that he could
have no better or more faithful a flag-captain than the
resourceful Dorset sailor, in whom he had placed entire
confidence during the whole of the Neapolitan and Sicilian
troubles. On the 13th November 1800, Hardy writes thus
from his quarters in Duke Street :—

DEAR MANFIELD,

I leave town in a few days for Dorsetshire,
where I shall remain 24 Hours (at most) in my way to
Plymouth & there to take the Command of the *Namur*
until the *St Josef* is ready which will be only a few days.
The former ship is then to be paid off and all the men go
to the other—I suppose the day for my departure will be
fixed tomorrow, if so I will let you know—I am this
moment come from Court where his Lordship was well
received & your Friend Tom cut no small figure as hat-

bearer to the Hero of the Nile. I saw Mr Damer,[1] but had not time to ask for my friends in Dorsetshire. My going out to Dinner I hope will be a sufficient excuse for not giving you more News as it is now ½ past five & the Bellman waiting, yours

Most sincerely,

T. M. HARDY.

P.S.—My appointment is not publick (tho' all the World knows it), say nothing about it but to my relations till you hear from me again. Doctor Bartlett must hold himself in readiness.

By a letter on the same day, Hardy wrote as follows :—

9 DUKE STREET, ST JAMES,
November 13*th*, 1800.

DEAR MANFIELD,

As I could not get a place in the Mail, I have taken one in the Mercury. I set off tomorrow morning at three o'clock. I believe we arrive at Dorchester about the same hour on Monday morning. If you will have the goodness to order a bed for me at the King's Armes, I will be much obliged and will breakfast with you at 8 o'clock. Captain Ingram is this moment arrived with his two jolly Weymouth friends. He is uncommon well, but how he will get over the Stone Expedition I know not,

Yours most Sincerely,

T. M. HARDY.

Mr MANFIELD,
     Attorney-at-Law,
          Dorchester.

---

[1] Mr Lionel Damer, M.P. for Peterborough, a brother to the second Earl of Dorchester. Came House, near Dorchester, still belongs to the Dawson-Damers, Earls of Portarlington. It is there that the portraits of the Dorset Captains of the Great War are preserved.

To face page 56.

DORCHESTER IN NELSON'S DAYS (*circa* 1797).
The King's Arms and All Sain s' Church.

Next day (November 14th, 1800) he writes from 9 Duke Street.

9 DUKE STREET, *Novr. 14th*, 1800.

DEAR MANFIELD,

I just received my Commission for the *Namur* & leave London tomorrow night & hope to see you on Sunday. I shall not take my place till tomorrow as my Admiral changes his mind every hour therefore cannot say by what conveyance I shall come but by the Mail if possible.

I have just recd the Beer but it has not been tasted yet. I remain

Dr Manfield, Yours sincerely,

T. M. HARDY.

P.S.—I fear I shall not be able see my friend Ingram [1] unless he comes to Dorchester.

The Christmas spent on board the *Namur* was little less festive than his previous one at Portisham. Both of them presented a striking contrast to that terrible Christmas Day (1798) between Naples and Palermo, when the six-year-old Neapolitan Prince died in Lady Hamilton's arms. Hardy's next letter to Manfield reads thus :—

"NAMUR," HAMOAZE, *Decr.* 11*th*, 1800.

DEAR MANFIELD,

I received my Books &c. the day I got your letter. Do tell the Girls at Possum I will not trouble them to get Mince Meat for me as my *acquaintances* here are so numerous I never dine at home. You did quite rite in putting my name to the Game you sent Lord Nelson. I wrote to Halford yesterday & did not forget to desire him to call on Mr Bryden & I will answer for it

---

[1] Then Captain, R.N., and a native of Burton Bradstock, where he died 3rd February 1826, aged 71. His tomb is still to be seen in the church there. It may be remembered that Hardy's first Captain, Francis Roberts, came from the same village at the western extremity of the Bride Valley.

you will hear from Mr B—— very shortly. You had better send Mrs Pitman's Papers to the Proctor and he will settle the remainder. I will thank you to pay Mr Yeatman & Mr Oakley, but for Gods sake send no more by land they are such d——d raskels here that they charged £1 : 2 : 6 : for the carriage of the Beer & 5s for the Brace of hares, which is double the price from Dorchester to London. I have heard nothing of Mr Wallis or young Hamilton but suppose they are doing very well. I am much obliged to the Weld[1] Family for enquirys give my best Compliments to them and say I shall be happy to see them whenever they can make it convenient. I also hope you will make one of the party. Everything goes on as I wish on board *San Josef* I have orders to prepare the *Namur* for paying off & I shall report her ready tomorrow. I had a letter from my *friend* Sir E. Berry yesterday where he Congratulates me on my promotion to *San Josef* & the happyness of serving with the Hero of the Nile. He hopes to keep the Pss Charlotte as that will give him a spell with *His Lady*. I partook of Part of the Mutton that was sent from Possum yesterday at Sir Thos. Pasley's[2] it was very good & the old Barontt was very much pleased with it.

Decr. 13th. I had not time to send this till today. Mr Wallis is arrived & I have got Martha's Letter which shall be ansd when I have an opportunity. If John is fortunate enough to get some game for my friends here do tell him to pay the Carriage of it as it will be no present at the Price I paid. T. M. H.

PLYMOUTH DOCK.

Hardy now transfers himself and his crew into the *San Josef*, where he witnessed the dawn of the nineteenth

---

[1] Of Lulworth Castle, Dorset. Mrs Fitzherbert'sfirst husband was a Weld, and the Captain Weld who commanded a troop of Dorset Yeomanry during the Great War, eventually became a bishop and car inal, and a candidate for the Papal throne.

[2] Admiral Sir Thomas Pasley, Bart. [1734-1808].

century. A few days before this he again wrote to his brother-in-law ·—

"San Josef," Hamoaze,
Decr. 29*th*, 1800.

Dear Manfield,

I enclose a letter to Martha in answer to one I recd from her yesterday. I am happy to hear you are got better. I thought you knew *better* than to allow the Merchant at Lothers[1] to *gull* you with so much Wine as lay you up for three Days. He was here the other day in very good spirits & said that you & Jos talked of coming to see me before I left Plymouth. I hope it is true & I advise you to be here within three Weeks or you will be too late. I have a very good Ships Company & everything got on very well. Give my Love to Catherine & the Children. I remain,

Dear Manfield,

Yours most sincerely,

T. M. Hardy.

As soon as you have payd Mr Yeatman & all the rest of my debts I wish you to draw on Cook & Halford for the amount as it is as well in your hands as theirs.

I believe I never paid my Aunt for the Lottery Ticket. Do it for me.

Hardy begins the new century with the following kindly letter to Mr Manfield :—

"San Josef," Hamoaze,
Jany. 7*th*, 1801.

Dear Manfield,

As you cannot spare time to come to Plymouth before the latter end of the Month after that period Torbay

---

[1] Loders, near Bridport. Sir Evan Nepean, Secretary to the Admiralty at the time of Trafalgar, lived at Loders Court, which he purchased in 1799. The merchant mentioned was probably Richard Travers, the genial Yeomanry captain.

will be sufficient as I think to sail for that place in 10 Days if His Lordship arrives as we are ordered there as soon as possible.

I am happy the Prints please. A Register Stove & Carpet, with the Hero of the Nile's Picture (which Jno Brown of course will get) cannot fail to make it the Handsomest Drawing Room in Dorchester. The King of Naples Picture will soon follow from Mr M'Arthur.[1] I have heard nothing of young Hamilton. Do send to his Father & say we are almost ready for sea.

Thank you for Harbin's[2] letters I have ansd it but I fear not to his satisfaction. Love to Catharine & the Childr.

                    I remain, Dr Manfield,

                              Yours sincerely,

                                   T. M. HARDY.

Nelson now made up his mind to join his ship; and Hardy writes the following characteristic letter to Mr Manfield:

                    "SAN JOSEF," PLYMOUTH DOCK,
                         Janry. 16*th*, 1801.

DEAR MANFIELD,

            I am sorry his Lordship passed through Dorchester so late in the evening which of course prevented my countrymen paying him the respect due to his merit. He arrived here last night, comes on board on Monday next and I believe we sail for Torbay the latter end of the week. He tells me that he was taken so ill just before they arrived at Dorchester that he thought he would have died in the carriage. You no doubt have seen Mr Hamilton and I trust he will give you so good an account

---

[1] These were probably the pictures of Nelson and King Ferdinand now at Portisham House, and which are now reproduced by permission of Mrs Manfield and her son, Mr W. Hardy Manfield.

[2] Of Newton Surmaville, Yeovil.

.

Lord Nelson

From a drawing by an unknown Italian artist

of my health that even Martha will be satisfied that Fagging agrees best with me. If any of my friends here have a wish to see *San Josef* they will find her at Torbay all the week after next as the Earl[1] has been good enough to say he will give us Seven days to put us to rights under his own eye. I recd a letter from Dr Sherive[2] the other day requesting I would take a Mr Tucker.[3] I wish Ingram[4] could advise him to keep the youth at home as it is a very unseasonable time to send a Boy to sea. I find he still laments the great loss he has sustained in our cousin Christopher.[5]

> With Duty Love and Compliments I remain
>> Dear Manfield
>>> Yours most sincerely,
>>>> T. M. HARDY.

On the 12th February 1801, Lord Nelson transferred his flag to the *St George* (the *San Josef* being considered too heavy for the Baltic service), and took Hardy with him. The following letter was written by the latter when the complications with Denmark were paving the way to the battle of Copenhagen.

>> "SAINT GEORGE," SPITHEAD,
>>> *Feby. 25th*, 1801.

DEAR MANFIELD,

I received your letter yesterday & am sorry to say that we have heard nothing of the Beer nor do I

[1] Earl Spencer was at the head of the Admiralty, 1794-1801. A keen appreciator of the genius of Nelson, whom he sent to win the battle of the Nile.

[2] Rev. Henry Sherive, LL.D., Rector of Bridport, Dorset, 1766-1791. Married T. M. Hardy's cousin, Martha Hardy of the Hyde, Bothenhampton, where Dr Sherive was living in 1801.

[3] Belonging to an old Bridport family.

[4] Of Burton Bradstock.

[5] Rev. Christopher Hardy Sherive, M.A., succeeded his father as Rector of Bridport, where he died 10th November 1800. Hutchins erroneously states that he resigned the living in 1801.

expect to unless you can find out the Vessel's Name and to whom consigned.   His Lordship left Portsmouth for Town on Monday last & we expect him the beginning of next Week.   He continues in good health but was rather low for a few days after quiting *San Josef.*   However we are to return to her as soon as the business in the North is settled which we trust will be completed by the latter end of May.   Sir Hyde Parker is expected down in a few days. The *London* waits here to hoist his Flag.   The change of Adminstration [1] was rather sudden.   We brought Sir Thos Troubridge from Torbay.   As I have nothing to ask of course nothing can be done for me.   Young Faddy is here & I wish I could say he was deserving of my notice, but I much fearful he will never do his Lordship or myself any credit.   He was with us in the *Vanguard* which ship he quited *not* for his good conduct.

Parker is gone to Southampton.   He returns on Friday next.

I saw the Thompson Family yesterday they are all well & desire their best compliments.—If I have an opportunity I shall not forget Mr Tucker in the Dockyard.   With Duty Love &c &c

I remain Dear Manfield,

Yours most sincerely,

T. M. HARDY.

Hardy's excellent seamanship was never more conspicuous than in the voyage to the Baltic, and the operations which immediately preceded the engagement before Copenhagen.   In all probability, he now profited by his five years' experience as a practical navigator while in the merchant service.   In the pitchy darkness of the night

---

[1] John, Earl St Vincent, succeeded Earl Spencer at the Admiralty, 19th February 1801.   Three weeks later, William Pitt resigned office, after a Premiership of eighteen years.   A new Ministry was formed by Henry Addington, afterwards Lord Sidmouth.

before the battle, he made soundings in the channel from an open boat, going so near to the enemy's vessels that long poles or rods had to be used lest the sound of the heaving of the lead should arouse suspicion. Had Hardy's calculations been relied on rather than the questionable information of the pilots, none of the English ships need have grounded, the loss of life would have been less, and the victory achieved more decisive. Unfortunately, the *St George* drew too much water for the shallows to be traversed, so Nelson shifted his flag to the *Elephant*, and Hardy's ship was unable to take an active part in the fighting of the 2nd April 1801. One of the most important letters ever addressed by Hardy to his brother-in-law gives a detailed account of the action :—

"ST GEORGE," COPENHAGEN ROADS,
April 5th, 1801.

DEAR MANFIELD,

This is the first opportunity I have had of writing to you since we left Yarmouth. Our passage was rather tedious and attended with bad weather. However, we arrived off Cronenburge Castle on the 30th of last month, when a plan of attack was formed against Copenhagen, and as the water is very shallow near that city it was thought necessary for Lord Nelson to shift his flag into the *Elephant* (Capt. Foley), and next morning we passed by Cronenburge where the 1st shot was fired at us from the Castle and a heavy canonading kept up on both sides on our passing, without the least effect, the distance being too great. The next morning his Lordship, with twelve sail of the smallest line of Battle Ships and all the Frigates, Bombs, Fireships, Gun Brigs, &c., &c., passed thro' what is called the middle ground, and the next morng made the most daring attack that has been attempted this war (the Nile not excepted) was made, and after a very heavy loss on both sides, he was completely victorious, having taken and destroyed every ship and vessel that was opposed to him, six of which was of the Line, the remaining twelve were Prames or floating Batteries.   Our ships were also exposed to the fire of more than eighty pieces of heavy Cannon from the shore.   The more I see of his Lordship the more I admire his great character, for, I think on this occasion, his Political management *was, if possible*, greater than his Bravery.   The water was so sh^{oal} [1] that two of the Line of Battle Ships got on shore before the action commenced, a third owing to the current and light winds was not able to get into Action, and his Lordship, finding his little squadron very hard pressed by the Batterys after the ships had struck, the wind not sufficient to take off his Prizes and crippled ships, he very deliberately sent a Flag of Truce on shore to say that his orders were *not* to *Destroy* the City of Copenhagen, therefore, to save more efusion of blood he would grant them a *truce* and land their wounded as soon as possible.   The Prince [2] thanked him for his great humanity and entered into a negotiation that moment which allowed him to get off all the Prizes that was not sunk or burnt, and his own ships, five of which at this time were on shore within gunshot of the Batteries.   His Lordship and myself was on shore yesterday, where, extraordinary to be told, he was received with as much aclamation as when we went to *Lord Mare's Show*, and I really believe it would not have been a very hard business to have brought on a revolution in Denmark. We dined with all the Court, and after Dinner he had an audience with the Crown Prince for more than two hours and I will venture to say that his Royal Highness never had so much plain trooth spoken to him in his life.

I shall not close my letter till the negotiation is concluded, which we expect will be to-morrow.   Tho' I could not be with his Lordship myself, I sent Messrs Gill & Walin, the former was slightly wounded, but Sir Hyde

---

[1] Shallow.

[2] Frederick, eldest son of Christian VII., and nephew of George III.   He was born in 1768, and declared Regent, April 12, 1784.

Parker has promised to promote him as soon as he can do his duty, which, I expect, will be in a few days. Mr Walin is appointed Lord Nelson's Secretary, and I hope soon to get him into a good Frigate. The young Doctor has written to his Father, and I suppose has given a very full account of the Action. I regret very much that Poor Parker was not with us, as I have little doubt but it would have gained him the other step. Young Roberts is very well as are the rest of the youngsters from Dorsetshire. Roberts, as is customary with them all, has lost almost all his clothes, however, he will do well enough by and by.

April 6th.—The Brig that takes Sir Hyde Parker's Despatches is now getting under weigh, and as his Lordship is on board the *London*, we do not know as yet * * (*torn*) the business is ended but hope for the best. Captn. Otway, Sir Hyde's Captn. is charged with the despatches. Domett is very well, but, I believe, very much tired with the Situation. As I have had but very little time to write this, I hope you will excuse the scrall. With Duty, Love, & Compts.

I remain, Dear Manfield,

Yours most Sincerely,

T. M. HARDY.

CHAPTER X

FROM THE BATTLE OF COPENHAGEN (2ND APRIL 1801) TO THE PEACE OF AMIENS (27TH MARCH 1802). HARDY, CAPTAIN OF THE "ST GEORGE" AND THE "ISIS"

HARDY'S next letters home are written two months later from the bleak and inhospitable shores of Kioge Bay, where the fleets had been anchored since the 25th April 1801. On the 6th June he commenced a lengthy epistle to Mr Manfield, which he only completed on the 17th of that month.

"ST GEORGE," KIOGE BAY,
June 6th, 1801.

DEAR MANFIELD,

I received your letter of the 20th of April the Day I received one from Jos & that of the 6th of the same Month I got yesterday by Mr Cox. I am sorry to say that his conduct on board the *Vanguard* has been so very improper that Sir Thos Williams[1] will not let him join the *St George* (at least for the present). As the *Vanguard* was but a short time with us Sir Thos had not an opportunity of explaining to me but I understand he feels that Mr Cox has been making a *convenience* of him & is actually borne on the *Vanguards* Books as Midshipman nor did he hint to Sir Thos his intention of quitting him till he had seen me & he informed me that he had his Captains permission to join the *St George*, & only waited my approbation; however when I next see the *Vanguard* I daresay I shall be able to get him & you may depend on my giving him

[1] Admiral Sir Thomas Williams, G.C.B. [1762-1841].

such a lecture as he will not forget these twelve Months. I had just time to inquire a little into his Character from one of my old Ship Mates who is with him, & I am informed that he acknowledges how much he is ashamed of his late conduct & promises fair to turn over a new leaf when he joins the Flag Ship. I think you had better apprise his relations of this & add that I will do everything in my power for him. *But he must alter his Conduct or quit the St George.*

12th.—I have not had an opportunity of seeing Captain Foley [1] of the *Elephant* but will not forget to enquire about Belninger when I do. I am sorry to hear of Mr Balstons illness but hope the Spring has quite brought him round. Give my best Compliments to my good friend Captain Ingram & tell him I Drank his health on the 4th and sighed when I thought of the Partner he introduced me to on that evening Twelve Months. The Weather is remarkably fine in the Country and I think nearly as warm as it is in the Mediterranean. The Crops of all description are remarkably fine & there is every prospect of a most plentiful Harvest. The export of Corn from this has been so great that the price of Bread is greater than in England. Lord Nelson is quite recovered but still anxious to go home & has again written to be superseded but we hope to be all ordered home very soon as we think it impossible that anything more can be done in this part of the World. His Lordship talks of sending the *Pylades* home soon therefore you will in all probability get this very soon. Parker is very well & desires his best compliments. I'll trouble you with my best compliments to Messrs Frampton [2] & Brown. It may

[1] Admiral Sir Thomas Foley, G.C.B., commanded the *Elephant* at Copenhagen [1757-1833].

[2] James Frampton, of Moreton, Dorset [1769-1855], married Lady Harriet Fox Strangways, daughter of the 2nd Earl of Ilchester, Colonel of the Dorset Yeomanry. In this year (1801) as Major he had charge of the 5th division of the Dorset coast defences, reaching from Worthbarrow Bay to Ringstead Bay.

not be unpleasant for the former to hear that his Relation
(by Marriage) Capt[n] Step[n] Digby[1] is well, a very good
young Man, much liked by Lord Nelson & I believe first on
the list for promotion.

June 17*th.*—The *Pylades* is just going to sail for England
with a fine easterly wind and I have little doubt that you
will receive this in less than a Week.   There is a Cutter
just come in sight which we think is from England but his
Lordship will not wait for her as the Wind is fair for
England & foul for the Cutter.   With Love to Catherine
& all the children

I remain

Dear Manfield

Yours sincerely

T. M. HARDY.

Doubtless, the cutter brought the news that his lordship had been superseded, for Captain Mahan[2] says that
on the 19th June Nelson left the Baltic in the brig
Kite, and landed at Yarmouth on the first of the following month.

A few days later, Hardy writes :—

"ST GEORGE," KIOGE BAY,
July 8*th*, 1801.

DEAR MANFIELD,

I wrote to Ann the other day requesting she
would make me two or three Dozen of Shirts; as letters so
often miscarry you will have the goodness to mention it to
her.   It is very immaterial weather the Linen is purchased

---

[1] Stephen Digby [1776-1820] was the son of the "Mr Fairly" of
Madame d'Arblay's *Memoirs* (see Mr Austin Dobson's Edition, vol.
ii., p. 411, etc.).   His mother, Lady Lucy Fox Strangways, was the
daughter of the first Earl of Ilchester.   He brought Lord Nelson
home in the *Kite*, and a characteristic letter written to him by Nelson
from Merton, on the 6th January 1802, is now in possession of his
kinsman, Admiral Noel Digby.

[2] *The Life of Nelson*, vol. ii., p. 117.

at Dorchester or in Town. Admiral Sir Thos Graves[1] sailed from here yesterday with a large detatchment of our Ships their destination is *not* yet *Publickly* known. Everything goes on well in this Quarter & I have little doubt but we shall all be in England very soon, & what is to become of me I know not ; however Lord Nelson says he never will be employed again, & I shall have a fine Frigate but it is as much impossible for him to remain at home as it is for him to be *happy at Sea*, therefore I expect soon to hear that he is gone to Egypt & I shall be ordered to follow him in the best way that I can. We learn by a Vessel that arrived from Yarmouth yesterday that his Lordship entered that Port on the 29th ulto. I am very Comfortable with Adml Pole[2] but I am not anxious to remain with him or any other Adml (except Lord Nelson) therefore I shall make all the Interest I can to get into a frigate when we get to England. I have not seen the *Vanguard* since, of course have not got Mr Cox & as It is probable I shall quit this ship very soon, I think he had better remain where he is however that shall rest with himself. As our stay here is so very uncertain I think you had better not write till you hear from me again which shall be the next opportunity.

With best Love to Catherine & the Children,

I remain Yours sincerely,

T. M. HARDY.

In August, reaches home two months later :[3]—

DR MANFIELD,

We arrived off Yarmouth this **Day** we are ordered round to Spithead where I suppose we shall not

---

[1] Admiral Sir Thomas Graves [1747-1814], second in command at Copenhagen, where he won his K.C.B.

[2] Admiral Sir Charles Maurice Pole, G.C.B. [1757-1830], succeeded Nelson in command of the English Fleet in the Baltic, 19th June 1801.

[3] This is the only undated letter found amongst the Hardy correspondence. It bears, however, the English postmark of 10th August 1801.

remain long therefore I hope to hear from you by return of post. As we have had no communication with the shore I know nothng of what is going on in England.

We have had a very good passage from Copenhagen & trust we shall soon be at Spithead. The Fishing boat that will take this on shore is now waiting I have therefore only time to wish you health &c. &c. With Duty love &c. I remain,

Dear Manfield,

Yours most sincerely,

T. M. HARDY.

I have not had an opportunity of seeing Mr Cox but shall not forget him when an opportunity offers.

Hardy's days on board the *St George* were now numbered. The news of his being superseded is thus conveyed to Mr Manfield :—

PORTSMOUTH, Augt 18th, 1801,
8 o'clock.

DEAR MANFIELD,

This day to my great astonishment Captain Nicholls received a Commission for the *St George* & I am ordered to the Downes Immediately, & what Ship I am to go to I have not the least idea. There is an order come by Telegraph for a Cutter to take my things on board as soon as possible, therefor in all probability I shall sail this eveng; however the Wind at present is not Fair. Everything as you may suppose is in a *happy confusion ;* however I shall leave my Servant Edward to take the greater part of my things to Mr Thompson's & Thos & I must do as well as we can till Edwd comes to us. To Make things better the *St George* is to sail this evening or tomorrow morning & I am obliged to leave all the youngsters behind in *St George* as I have no place for them. I am sorry to say that young Tucker's eyes are so very badd that he can scarcely see out of them & I very much fear he will be obliged to leave the

Service on account of it. I think Ann had better send my Shirts as soon as finished to the care of Mr Thompson as he will always have an opportunity of sending them to me.

You shall hear from me as soon as I can give you any more information about myself.

6 *o'clock*.—I can't sail this evening but should the Wind continue foul I go off by Land tomorrow morning. I am sorry to see by the Papers of to-day that his Lordship has met with the worst of it, and that poor Parker[1] is wounded ; however as it is not confirmed I hope there is no truth in it.

I recd Ann's letter to-day. I'll thank you to tell her that there is no great hurry for the remainder of the shirts. With love to Catherine the children & all Friends

I remain

Dear Manfield

Yours Affectionately

T. M. HARDY.

Hardy remained for some days in uncertainty as to his future. His next letter runs as follows :—

PORTSMOUTH,
August 20th, 1801.

DEAR MANFIELD,

I embark on board the *Vesuvius* Bomb at 12 o'clock this day for the Downes but strange to tell I have no orders from the Admiralty nothing but a private letter from Sir Thomas Troubridge desiring me to go to the Downes as fast as possible & that they would not *forget me.* I have not received the Shirts but it is of no consequence as we must call at this place before we go abroad (should we be ordered) I very much fear that my little friend Parker has lost his thigh & Langford (who was in the *Foudroyant* with us) I much fear is also wounded, &

[1] Commander Edward Thornborough Parker, R.N., Aide-de-camp to Lord Nelson. He died of wounds received on the 15th August 1801 in the unsuccessful attempt on Boulogne (see pp. 49, 73, and 114).

very singular to relate that they are the only two young men that I strongly recommended to his Lordship. Our Relation Mr Robt Budden came on purpose to see me yesterday & is returned to Leamington with Adml Man[1] this morning; he desires his Compliments to you & all friends.

10 *o'clock.*—I am this moment going on board & as the Wind is coming to the Westd I hope soon to write to you from the Downes.

With Duty Love &c. I remain

Dear Manfield

Yours affectionately

T. M. HARDY.

Mr MANFIELD,
Dorchester, Dorset.

Five days later, he writes thus on his way to join the *Isis* :—

"VESUVIUS" OFF DOVER,
August 25th, 1801.

DEAR MANFIELD,

We arrived off this Port last Night & are now Weighing to proceed to the Downes. We have had a very pleasant passage tho' a foul wind all the way. I see by the Papers of the 21st Int that I am appointed to the *Isis* but I have not heard a word about it; however the mystery will be unriddled before I close this letter. I saw a Horse the other Day at Portsmouth so much like the Roan, that I could have sworn it was that which I gave John even the No. 6 on the near Shoulder was not omited, but on inquiry I found it belonged to a Lord (I forget his name) in whose possession it has been more than Twelve months. I hear from the Fishermen that Lord Nelson sailed to the Eastward the Day before yesterday but his destination was unknown. I'll thank you to tell Mr Hamilton of Weymouth that I was very sorry to leave his

---

[1] Admiral Robert Man. He was in command under Hotham at the fleet action of 13th July 1795.

son in the *St George* but it was impossible for me to take any of the young Gentlemen with me as I did not know what was to become of me, nor do I at this moment; however Captain Nicholls has promised to take care of them & to advance any Money that may be necessary. They are all to return to me as soon as I am settled in a Ship. If you see Pearson of Steepleton & Roberts I'll thank you to tell them the same.

DEAL, *Augt. 26th.*—We arrived last night too late to save Post. This morning I received my Commission for the *Isis* & set off tomorrow to join her off Boulogne, & by Directing your letters at this Place they will be forwarded to me. Weather His Lordship is to Hoist his Flag or not with me I cannot learn but I should suppose not, as the *Isis* is but just Commissioned & I fear in rather a badish kelter. I am happy to say that I found my two wounded friends much better than I could have expected after the accounts we had seen, but I have often told you that there was no dependence on lampblack & oil. Parkers wound is certainly very bad. A Musket ball has passed thro' the Thigh very high up & completely broken the bone but he is in very good spirits & Doctor Beard[1] who is very clever Man says he is in great hopes of saving the Limb. Langford's[2] wound is a Musket Ball through the small of the Leg & it is hoped that the Bone is not Broken. I have been sitting with them all the Morning & they bear their misfortune like themselves. I suppose I shall see Lord Nelson in a Day or two when it is probable I shall know what is to become of me. With Duty love & Compliments to all Friends

I remain,

Dear Manfield

Yours Affectionately

T. M. HARDY.

[1] Dr Baird, *vide* Nelson's letters to Baird about Parker and Langford, *post*, p. 113.

[2] See *post*, p. 113.

Augt. 27th.—I missed the Post Last evening. Lady & Sir Wm Hamilton arrived last Night, & Lord Nelson Anchored this Mong; I hope he will not remain long; he says he is quite tired of his present Comand & hopes we shall soon return to *San Josef* I set off tomorrow morng for the *Isis.*

Hardy has now joined his new ship, the *Isis*, and writes again to Mr Manfield :—

" ISIS," DUNGENESS, *Septr.* 23rd, 1801.

DEAR MANFIELD,

I did not get your letter of the 11th Inst till yesterday. We arrived here last Saturday the Weather not allowing us to remain off Boulogne any longer & the Equinoctial gales seem to have set in, it having blown very hard these last four Days. We return to our Station as soon as the weather is settled. I am sorry for Mr Damer's [1] indisposition and trust he will soon get the better of it. I'll thank you to return my compliments to him & His Lordship [2] when you see them. You have heard of course that poor Parker has lost his Thigh & I am happy to hear from a Gentleman who came from Deal yesterday that he was much better and there was great hopes that he would do well but I very much doubt it. As Lady Hamilton has left Deal, we expect his Lordship here tomorrow should the weather moderate. The last time I saw him he told me he was determined to give up the Command on the 14th of this Month but the Admiralty has perswaded him to the Contrary, & I have no doubt but he will continue the Command all the Winter; he begins to think that Lord St Vincent has sent out Adml Pole to take the Comand from Lord Keith [3] if so It will be some time before the young Gentlemen from Dorsetshire can join me.

[1] Lionel Damer, M.P. (see *ante*, p. 56), died 28th May 1807.
[2] George Damer, second Earl of Dorchester, born 1746, succeeded 1798, died 1808, when the title became extinct.
[3] George Keith Elphinstone, Admiral Lord Keith [1746-1823].

I am much better pleased with the *Isis* than I was & I suppose in another Month I shall be quite sorry to leave her. The young Doctor is happy to hear that the Buggey is alive & I am sorry to hear of the Roans misfortune; however accidents will happen in the best regulated Families. I am astonished to hear that Bread still continues so Dear where it will end I am at a loss to guess. In this part of the Country Sheep are £3 apiece Turkeys S. 8 Gees 6. & Duck & fouls in proportion I think I have taken a very unfavourable time to begin housekeeping Mr Pearson's Money is to go in part to pay my debts. If my Cousin the Doctor [1] should offer you young Tucker's Money I'll thank you to take it £16 : 9 : is the sum but dont ask for it. With love to Catherine & the Children. Love & Compliments to all friends.

I remain Dear Manfield

Yours Affectionately

T. M. HARDY.

Three weeks later, he again writes :—

"ISIS," *October* 14*th*, 1801.

DEAR MANFIELD,

   I did not receive your letter and Jos' with one inclosed for Tom till three Days ago. I missed it in my way to the Downs to which place I went for Commodore Sutton & arrived here last night. It grieved me much to hear by Jos' letter the Melancholly account of the Poor Doctor's [1] Death; his loss must be felt very severely by Mrs Sherive & Miss Hardy [2] but his loss is quite irreparable in the neighbourhood as a publick Character & I know no

---

[1] Rev. H. Sherive, LL.D., of the Hyde, Bothenhampton, Bridport (see p. 61). Dr Sherive, who was some time Rector of Bridport, married, 5th Sept. 1776, Martha, daughter and co-heir of Joseph Hardy, Esq., of the Hyde, Bothenhampton, and was buried there, 26th Sept. 1801.

[2] Miss Anne Hardy, who died at the Hyde, Dec. 1839, aged 97.

Man that is equal to keep those Bridport Savages in order now he is gone. The Commodore was sent to me rather unexpectedly but I got so civil a Note from my friend Troubridge that nothing can withstand him; however the Commodore is a very good Man & we make it out extremely well. He expects as we do all to be ordered in within these ten Days & of course paid off as soon after as possible. I left Lord Nelson three Days ago very much displeased with the Admiralty for refusing him leave of absence, but I think they seem Determined to oppose him in everything he wishes. I begin to think Ld St V. wishes to clip his Wings a little & certainly has succeeded a little in the affair of Boulogne.[1] Troubridge like a true Politician forsakes his old friend (who has procured him all the Honor he has got) & sticks fast by the Man who is likely to push him forward hereafter.

My letters will come better if you will Direct them for me at New Romney as I have come here in preference to the Downes. I hope this will find you quite recovered & if any scolding would be of any service, you shall have it most heartily. I think bad eyes arise from cold & Cold from carelessness but Mrs Manfield must be to blame. I hope to be with you & then it will be time to think of my future residence. As yet I am quite undetermined what to be at. I think if I was to push hard I may get a Ship but I don't know whether it will not be as well to let it alone; however a short time will determine on what is to be done. With best love to Catherine & the Children

I remain Dr Manfield

Yours Affectionately

T. M. HARDY.

In September of this year, Lord Nelson obtained leave by royal license to use the foreign title of Duke of Bronté

---

[1] On the 15th August Nelson failed in his attack on the flotilla assembled at Boulogne. The British loss was 44 killed, 128 wounded (see Mahan's *Life of Nelson*, vol. ii., p. 137).

in Sicily, which had been some time before bestowed on him by the King of Naples. In November, Hardy writes thus from the Downs :—

"ISIS," DOWNS, *Novr. 7th*, 1801.

DEAR MANFIELD,

The Weather has been so very bad that I did not get your letter of the 1st Inst till the day before yesterday & have not had an opportunity of writing to you till now. The Papers has quite misinformed you respecting Lord Nelson's future destination as he has declared to me more than once that he was determined not to accept his Flag in Peace. Of Course you have seen His Lordship's speeches ; I only hope he will be guarded as we poor Sailors are quite out of our element when on Shore. As there can be no secret in my last letter to Jos I now come to an open explanation. Lord Nelson has given me one hundred Acres in any part of his Estate at Bronté that I chose to point out, with apartments in his House, a Knife & Fork &c. (he being determined to reside there in peace) the former part I certainly have accepted & intend to keep, but the latter I have not yet determined on, nor shall I till I know the Company that will attend him there. His Lordships leave is renewed a fortnight & I suppose at the end of that time it will be again renewed, therefore we do not expect to see him here again. When I got on shore yesterday after the Gale I was invited to Dine with Captain & Lady Charlotte Durham[1] & of course I could not refuse, her Ladyship was very pleasant and we had a long talk about Weymouth ; her Ladyship sets off today for Portsmouth & the *Endymion* sails for that place as soon as the Weather will permit.

The *Bombay Anna* Indiaman returned here the Day before yesterday with the loss of her Rudder & was very near lost off Margate. I am sorry for the sake of my friends Ingram and Festing that the Fencibles are

---

[1] Admiral Sir Philip C. H. C. Durham, G.C.B. [1763-1845], one of the few survivors of the Royal George accident at Spithead.

redused, but hope that Burton Bradstock will be as pleasant to our Friend as Weymouth was. I have no doubt of Mr Nepean's[1] success at Bridport particularly as our friends Travers[2] and Ingram[3] are the leading Characters in that part of the Country. I am happy to hear that Joseph Weld[4] is to settle so near us & I think the Staffordshire estate will suit Lord St Vincent very well. I am happy to hear your eyes are got Better & I trust with the care you take of yourself you will continue well. I have seen a letter from Hill to Lord Nelson before his Lordship left us, & that which appeared in the papers he received on his arrival in London, he has received several nearly to the same effect all of which he intends publishing at a future Day. With Duty to my Aunt who I suppose is a near Neighbour by this time & Love to the *Aldermans*[5] Lady Children &c. I remain

Dear Manfield,
Yours affectionately,
T. M. HARDY.

[1] Sir Evan Nepean (see *ante*, p. 59). He was duly elected as M.P. for Bridport in the place of Charles Sturt. He was again returned up till 1810. Sturt had also served in the Navy. When Prince William Henry was in the *Prince George*, under Rear-Admiral Digby, the future M.P. for Bridport was a brother midshipman with H.R.H. The Prince and Mr Sturt having had some misunderstanding on the quarter-deck, they agreed to go down to the orlop or cockpit to decide the matter, when after a long and very severe contest victory decided itself in favour of the latter, who was a greater adept in the art of boxing than his royal opponent. The generous prince did all in his power to conceal the affair from the admiral, and ever afterwards testified the warmest friendship for his victorious antagonist. See *The Naval Atlantis*, by Nauticus Junior, 1788.

[2] See *ante*, p. 52.

[3] Admiral Ingram, see *ante*, p. 57. Ingram House still stands at Burton Bradstock, a creeper-covered Queen Anne mansion of mellowed red brick, quite close to the Grove, the home of Francis Roberts and his descendants.

[4] Joseph Weld of Lulworth Castle, brother of Cardinal Weld [1777-1862].

[5] Mr Manfield now became Alderman of Dorchester, and served the office of Mayor three years later.

I see you know very little of the Service to suppose I can have much time on my hands. You have seen by the papers that Admiral Lutwidge has struck his Flag & is gone to Portsmouth to sit on Sir Wm Parkers Court martial.[1] The *Isis* is now the Commanding officiers ship & great part of the duty falls on me, however I shall always find time to answer your letters punctually & occasionally give you two for one. I got a letter to Day from Martha I find she is spending a few Days with our Relations in the East.

Hardy again writes :—

"ISIS," DOWNS, *Novr.* 15*th*, 1801.

DEAR MANFIELD,

Not having heard from you these ten Days I much fear your eyes are got worse ; however I can excuse you as business must be attended to. We continue here as usual anxiously waiting for the Definitive Treaty.[2] I see almost by every paper that Lord Nelson has been speaking in the House, I am sorry for it, and I am fully convinced that Sailors should not talk too much. You must not expect long letters now, for literally I have nothing to say. I suppose Martha is returned from Shapwick, if she is I will thank you to tell her she may expect a very long letter from me soon. I see by the Papers that Lord Fitzwilliam is one of the oppositionests to the Peace ; of course Lord Dorchester is of the same way of thinking, but if you have thought much on the subject I am of opinion you cannot agree with them, for I do not see any prospect of a better Peace being made had we continued the War for years to come. They appear to be getting too strong for Mr

---

[1] Admiral Sir William Parker [1743-1802]. His offence was only a technical one. He had sent two ships to the West Indies, when in command of the Halifax Station. He was acquitted of everything but indiscretion.

[2] The Peace of Amiens was not finally concluded till 27th March 1802.

Addington in the lower house, I do not know any man capable of taking his place but Mr Pitt. They have stopped Mr Tierneys mouth & Mr Grey is quite silent; you see we have all our Pluck. If John should happen to have a hare & a Phesant to spare, I will thank him to send it to Halford but it is of little or no consequence. As petitions will be presented to His Majesty as soon as the Peace is settled I expect to see that Alderman Manfield was the chosen Man from the Borough of Dorchester.

With Duty to my Aunt & Love to Catherine the Children & all friends I remain Dr Manfield,

Yours affectionately,

T. M. HARDY.

In the following month, Hardy is evidently a little nettled at not getting his news of Lord Nelson at first hand :—

"ISIS," SHEERNESS, *Decr.* 10*th*, 1801.

DEAR MANFIELD,

The *Isis* went into Dock last Monday & she is not found so bad as was expected. She leaves the Dock on the 21st & I hope to be at the Nore in about a Week after, from thence it is probable she will be ordered to Portsmouth as there is little doubt but Lord Radstock[1] is to hoist his Flag on board her. Captain Bligh who now commands the *Theseus*, will, I suppose exchange with me, as my friends at the Admiralty will not think it worth while to appoint another Captain for the short time she will be kept in Commission. I shall then have to pass accounts for five ships in about 10 Months, which will cost me nearly the amount of my pay for that time, therefore I fear I shall not add much to the 3 pr cent. Should any business or inclination bring you to Town I hope you will find a leisure hour to give me a call. I saw in the papers of yesterday that Lord Nelson had waited on the

[1] Admiral William Waldegrave, G.C.B., first Baron Radstock [1753-1825].

Admiralty previous to his taking the Command on a Foreign Station. I think it is not true as I had a letter from him three days ago, & I think he would have at least given me a hint; however there is nothing certain in this life but Death. I see Lord St Vincent is quite recovered & I think I may add that he will continue so only as long as convenient, Sir Thos Troubridge is very ill. Thank you for sending Halford the Game; & as he had got it, I think it but fair you should have the credit & thanks for it. I am sorry to hear that Mr Balston is so unwell but hope the Month of December will prove more favourable than that of November. As this will be received on Saturday Jos & perhaps John will be in Dorchester & will get the Sheerness News anxious as you.

   With Duty to my Aunt & Love & Comps to all friends I remain

Dear Manfield

Yours Affectionately

T. M. HARDY.

JOHN CALL. MANFIELD, Esqr.

A note on the above letter runs thus: " 3rd distribution of the Action of the Nile to be paid 4, 5, and 6 Jan. 1802. 2 William Tombs, *Minotaur.*"

Hardy, always mindful of his Dorset friends on the eve of the first Christmastide of the nineteenth century, writes :—

"ISIS," SHEERNESS, *Decr.* 21*st*, 1801.

DEAR MANFIELD,

   The *Isis* is found so bad that she is to remain in Dock till the 5th or 6th of January, therefore I trust that Business or Pleasure will call you to Town before that Period, & that you will have a Day to spare which I think cannot be better employed than coming to Sheerness, where I shall be very happy to see you. Of course you have seen by the Papers that Lord Nelson has taken leave of the Admiralty but it is all humbug as I heard

F

from him a Day or two ago & he says that he will not be employed if he can possible help it ; but I am of opinion that Old St Vincent will not let him remain at home if he can possible help it.   Peregrine Bingham of [Bingham's] Melcombe is Chaplain of the *Isis*, & I have not seen him since I have been in her, if you know where he is I wish you would tell him that I cannot continue him on the Books if he Does not join her.   The Son of Hawkins the Gunsmith is a Midshipman on board the *Waarzaamhind* in this Harbour, he has served his time & goes to pass the 1st of next Month ; his appearance is not much in his favour, but his Captain (Hall) speaks very handsomely of him ; however at present it is out of my power to do anything for him.   Lieutenant Hawkins of the *Alonzo* (late of the *Culloden*) is to be tried by a Court Martial in a Day or two I believe by the Pursur of the same ship for Quarreling.   I am sorry to say that his Captain does not speak very favourably of him ; he is very young which is the only thing which can be said in his favour.   I have seen him once or twice, & I think he has as little the look of a Gentleman as his Father.   I will thank you to give my love to the young ladies at Possum, and tell them that I have plenty of time on my hand & am ready to answer all their Letters.   I believe neither Ann or Augusta has written to me these six Months.   With Duty to my Aunt Love and Compliments to Catherine the Children and all friends and Wishing you the Compliments of the Season I remain, Dear Manfield,

Yours Affectionately,

.   T. M. HARDY.

The eventful year 1802 begins with the following letter ·—

" ISIS," SHEERNESS,
Jany 6th, 1802.

DEAR MANFIELD,

In consequence of your application from Mr Pitt & a very Polite letter I received from Mr Fane, I requested [1] Captain Hall of the *Waarzaamhind* to let young Hawkins come in this Ship with an intention (if possible) of recommending him to the next Captain who may join the Ship & to my great astonishment yesterday I received a letter from him to say he was arrested for a Mess Debt of Sixteen Pounds, at the same time enclosing a Bill on his Father for that amount, requesting I would endorse it however I have too often been taken in by those Gentlemen, & on inquiry to Day I am sorry to say his Character is by no means a good one, therefore his coming to the *Isis* is of no use as I cannot possible recommend him. The *Isis* does not come out of Dock till the 23rd; she is getting a very good repair and the report now is that Sir Thos Troubridge is to be made an Admiral to hoist his Flag in her & go to the East Indies; you know as much of the truth of the report as I do. Lord Nelson is determined not to be employed if he can help it. I think it by no means unlikely that they will make him hoist his Flag; particularly if the Bantry Bay business [2] is not quite stopped as he is a popular Man amongst us; however we have reason to believe it is all settled at least for the present. John will give you all the News & the manner in which we pass our time here.

With Duty to my Aunt & Love Catherine & the Children.

I remain, Dear Manfield,
Yours Affectionately,
T. M. HARDY.

Mr Hawkins still remains in the Spunging House (for that is the name of the Prison) & I hear from Pretty good authority that he is in Debt pretty largely in Sheerness. If his Father wishes more information I will get him the best I can.

[1] William Morton Pitt of Kingston Maureward [1754-1836], M.P. for Dorset, 1790 to 1809.

[2] In December 1801 the Bantry Bay Squadron, commanded by Admiral Mitchell, mutinied.

The following letters speak for themselves :—

"ISIS," SHEERNESS,
Jany 1802.

DEAR MANFIELD,

The *Isis* came out of Dock last Wednesdy. We are going on very well & I shall report her ready for Sea the latter part of this Week. What is to become of us is as yet quite unknown at least in this part of the World. Young Hawkins is out of Gaol; how he got out is not known nor has he as yet made his appearance on board the *Waarzaamhind.* Captain Hall is so much displeased with him that I think it more than probable he will be obliged to quit her very soon. I had applied for him, but have refused to take him as I could not possible recommend him. I have heard nothing of Pereguine Bingham nor do I ever expect to hear of him again. There is great talk of Sir Thos Troubridge having the Command in the Est Indies; *tho' a particular friend* of mine, I do not think we should make it out so well together in the same ship as he is extremely hasty on Duty. If Jos Tombs is very anxious to receive the prize Money for the Nile I think you may get it by applying to Halford. As it is only sixteen shillings I think he may as well wait till you go to London or till I am paid off. My share comes to £389 : 8 I understand there is to be another payment but it must be very small. The young Doctor recd a Letter from Thos Balston the other Day & I was glad to find that John was getting better. I hope he is quite recovered. I hope you will be called to town soon on a good errand that I may have the Pleasure of seeing you. I'll thank you to give my Duty my Aunt and Love to Catherine the Children & all friends.

I remain, Dear Manfield,
Yours Affectionately,
T. M. HARDY.

I forgot that Wm Tombs was Petty Officer his share will be between four and five pounds.

"Isis," Nore (Sheerness),
Feby 8th, 1802.

Dear Manfield,

We arrived here the Day before yesterdy our further destination is still a Secret, but I think it possible we shall be ordered round to Portsmouth & there be fitted for a Flag.   I see by the Papers that the *St George* is gone to the West Indies.   I suppose my Dorsetshire Friends are very anxious about their young relations which I left in her, & should the Yellow Fever carry any of them off, I fear I shall lose all my Credit at least amongst all the old Ladies. When I wrote to you last Mr Hawkins had joined his Ship & I find he behaves very well (at least for the present) ; he has not been to me & I have reccomend his Captain to advise him to save himself the trouble as my mind is fully made up.

Private letters from Town state that Lord Nelson is certainly going to the West Indies, but I have not heard a word from his Lordship nor do I believe he has the least intention of going.   It cannot be long before we shall get the Definitive Treaty & then all our destinations will be known.   Should they offer me a Frigate I do not think I shall refuse her but I do not feel very anxious about it.

, I conclude (as I have not heard from any of you lately) that John is quite recovered.   With Duty to my Aunt and Love to Catherine & Children.   I remain

Dear Manfield

Yours Affectionately

T. M. Hardy.

"Isis," Nore, *Feby 20th,* 9 o'clock at night.

Dear Manfield,

This afternoon, I recd orders to proceed to Spithead & tomorrow morning I shall sail for that place. What is to follow is yet a Secret, I have no doubt but we shall be ordered to be fitted for a Flag on our arrival. What is to become of me I know not (nor do I care); however I do not wish to sail under any other Flag but Lord Nelson's from whom I have not heard a word for some time, but I intend writing to him on my arrival at Spithead which I trust will be on Monday or Tuesday next.

With Duty to my Aunt & Love to Catherine the Children & all friends I remain,

Dear Manfield

Yours Affectionately

T. M. HARDY.

"ISIS," SPITHEAD, *March* 10*th*, 1802.

DEAR MANFIELD,

I have been waiting many days expecting to give you some news but nothing has yet transpired. Gore of the *Midusa* is arrived here & to fit with all expedition; the report is that Lord Nelson is to go in her to the West Indies however all is a profound secret at Portsmouth. My relation Colonel Moriarty is here in the *Standard* who desires his respects to all friends. Portsmouth is as Barren of News as Sheerness was; at least I find it so as I strictly attend to the Orders of the Admiralty (sleep on board) & of course am very little out of the Ship. William Pain I find is on Board the *Maidstone* & am happy to find his Captain speaks very well of him. Your old friend Dukey Prator is at Portsmouth & I think is fatter than ever. I saw Colonel Bingham[1] the Other day who was very civil, *Peregrine* is on board the *Rammillies*, at least he ought to be, but *Parsons* are privileged men on board Ships of War. Captain Meggs[2] wishes me much to Dine at the Dorset Mess but has not yet been able to prevail on me, as a trip

---

[1] Colonel Bingham of Bingham's Melcombe [1741-1824]. He commanded the Dorset Militia during the Great War. A fine mezzotint portrait of him is in existence.

[2] Captain (Thomas) Meggs (died 1819) belonged to the Meggs family of Bradford Peverel, but resided at Piddlehinton, where he is buried. He raised a troop of Yeomanry, and commanded in 1801 the eighth division of the Dorset Defences. His picture, by Beach, is to be seen at Came.

to Spithead is not very pleasant at 10 o'clock at Night.
My friend Harry Garnett is appointed to the *Jessel* as a
Troop Ship, which is not very pleasant at this moment.

With Duty to my Aunt & Love & Compliments to all
friends. I remain,

Dear Manfield

Yours Affectionately

T. M. HARDY.

Hardy appears to have greatly enjoyed the festive life
of Portsmouth. The following letter was dated the day
after the signing of the Treaty of Amiens, of which fact the
writer was, of course, unconscious :—

"ISIS," SPITHEAD, *March 28th*, 1802.

DEAR MANFIELD,

Literally for want of something to say has
prevented my writing to you before. We go on in the old
way expecting the Definitive Treaty Daily. I had a letter
a few Days ago from Lord Nelson, where he says he had
not the smallest intention of going to the West Indies ; the
other Day therefore (as I have often told you) lamplack &
Oil cannot always be depended on, I saw Mr Morton Pitt
& mentioned to him my reason for not taking young
Hawkins, he was in as great a hurry as usual & only
remained twenty-four hours at Portsmouth. After a
number of invitations from Meggs, I am to Dine to Day
at their Mess ; however as I alway sleep on board I shall
leave them at ½ past 7. If they push the Bottle fast I
shall not forget to mention my unfortunate Wound in the
head that always makes me mad after the first Bottle. I
recd an odd Letter from Tom Smith the other Day
requesting I would get him made a Purser, or take him in
any situation, as his liberty on shore was in Danger. I
told him I was sorry it was out of my power as I daily
expected to be paid off. I shall answer Martha's Letter in

a few days & give her the Chit Chat News of Portsea & Portsmouth Assembly where I was last Thursday & am to be again on Tuesday next ; she will be astonished to hear that Lady Charlotte Durham was my partner last but you know that Captains at Portsmouth are Nobbs. With Duty to my Aunt & Love & Compliments to all friends.

I remain, Dear Manfield,

Yours Affectionately,

T. M. Hardy.

CHAPTER XI

FROM THE PEACE OF AMIENS [MARCH 27, 1802] to
HARDY'S APPOINTMENT AS FLAG-CAPTAIN OF THE
"VICTORY" [JULY 21, 1803]

A FEW weeks after Portsmouth was ablaze with
illumination in honour of the delusive Peace of
Amiens, Hardy sailed for the Bay of Biscay to convey
H.R.H. the Duke of Kent[1] to the scene of his duties as
Governor of Gibraltar. The following letters need no
comment :—

"ISIS," SPITHEAD, *Apl 3rd*, 1802.

DEAR MANFIELD,

This Morning I recd orders to prepare the
Isis for the reception of the Duke of Kent who is going
Governor of Gibraltar. I am ordered to go to London to
wait on His Royal Highness & I leave Portsmouth this
evening for that purpose. You shall hear from me in a
day or two.

Duty, Love, &c.,

Yours truly,

T. M. HARDY.

[1] H.R.H. the Duke of Kent [1767-1820], fourth son of George III.
and father of Queen Victoria. He subsequently presented Hardy with
a magnificent silver soup tureen, now in possession of Sir Evan Mac-
Gregor, K.C.B. It bears his own arms on one side and those of Hardy
on the other.

LONDON, *Apl 5th,*
6 o'clock Eveng.

DEAR MANFIELD,

In about five Minutes I shall break my fast for the Day. I have been on the Leg ever since 7 o'clock this morning. I have now done all my business & shall leave Town in the Portsmouth Mail at 7 this evening. I was obliged to go to Windsor yesterday to wait on the Duke I was recd very politely & Dined with Genl Guinn &c. &c. I stole three hours today to go to Merton where I saw his Lordship Sir Wm & Lady Hamilton. They are all extremely well & her Ladyship was quite *angry* that I could not stay longer. It is settled with the Duke of Kent that the *Isis* is to leave Portsmouth on the 17th Inst for Falmouth where he is to embark on the 24th if possible. If anything should call you near Portsth before that time I shall be happy to see you.

My Dinner is now on the Table & I shall just have time to swallow it & Drink many happy returns of the Day to Jos &

Yours Affectionately,

T. M. HARDY.

"ISIS," SPITHEAD, *Apl 11th,* 1802.

DEAR MANFIELD,

By not hearing from you I conclude some of you intend visiting Portsmouth shortly; however you had better give me a line stating nearly the Hour of your arrival that I may be on the look out for you. I suppose you recd my letter of the 5th Inst which said I was to sail from Portsmouth on the 17th, & from Falmouth on the 24th Wind & weather permitting. I recd a Letter yesterday from the Duke's Aide De Camp saying that all the Servants Baggage &c. &c. would be at Portsmouth on Friday Morning (16th) therefore if I get my orders (which

I have no doubt but I shall) We shall sail that evening or early next morning.   The Thompson and Crone familys are well & desire their best Compliments.   Duty to my Aunt & Love to Catherine & the Children.

I remain, Dear Manfield,

Yours Affectionately,

T. M. HARDY.

"ISIS," SPITHEAD, *April 20th*, 1802.

DEAR MANFIELD,

   I have just received my Orders & shall sail as soon as the remainder of the Dukes things are on board which will be this evening or early tomorrow morning, & as the Wind is foul it is possible we shall not be off Portland before Thursday or Friday but I shall not put in there If I can possible help it, as my good friends at the Admiralty would say that I wanted to go home.

His Royal Highness is to be at Falmouth on Sunday, therefore I suppose he will pass thro' Dorchester on Saturday morning.

My stay at Gibraltar will be very short & I am to return to Spithead to be paid off, but I have applied for employment & am partly promised.   I hope it will be the Channel as I think to make some money by keeping a good look out after the Smugglers.

I have been lumbered a great deal in my time, but I think never so much as at present ; we have received twelve Waggon Loads of Cases Trunks &c. &c. however the bargain is made.   We must not grumble therefore but do as well as we can.   I was rather astonished to receive a letter from Martha in London, I hope by this Mrs Balston is well enough to return home as I suppose she will soon be tired of London.   If you wish to write to me at Falmouth the Letter must be there by Monday next as we sail as soon as possible after our arrival.

With Duty to my Aunt & Love to Catherine the Children & all friends I remain,

Dear Manfield,

a little Bothered,

Yours Affectionately,

T. M. HARDY.

On his return from his four weeks' voyage, he writes as follows :—

"ISIS," MOTHER BANK, *May 29th*, 1802.

DEAR MANFIELD,

After a passage of twelve Days we arrived at this Anchorage last Night at 10 o'clock. I remain under Quarantine (I suppose only for a few Days) Our Passage out was a very Pleasant one of thirteen Days & I had the satisfaction of landing my Royal Passenger in good spirits, & I believe much pleased with the *Isis* & her Captain. Our stay at Gibraltar was six days, the three last occasioned by Westerly Winds. As I found everything at Gibraltar nearly as I left it, & Providence has been so good to me since my departure from Spithead that I have no disasters to relate. What is to become of the ship or myself is as yet quite unknown to me, & you shall be made acquainted with our destination as soon as known. I see nothing but Frigates at Spithead & as we have no communication with anything but the Pratique Boat we shall get very little News till we have communication with the shore.

As the Boat is waiting for this I must conclude with Duty to my Aunt & Love to Catherine the Children & all friends

I remain

Dear Manfield

Yours Affectionately,

T. M. HARDY.

"ISIS," PORTSMOUTH HARBOUR,
June 5th, 1802.

DEAR MANFIELD,

The *Isis* this Day Paid off & I suppose by tomorrows Post I shall know what is to become of me. I expect to be offered to remain as Adml Gambier's[1] Captn which I shall positively refuse. Mr Bonnett (once the Hair Dresser now the Publican & soon to be the Gentleman, as he informs me he is to retire shortly on his fortune) has given me £5 : 10 : 0 which I shall be obliged if you will pay to Mr Thos Slade stone mason who I understand lives at the bottom of the Town.

I am sorry you did not take Portsmouth in your way from London the other Day as we were out of Quarantine on Tuesday Morng. If I am not employed of course you will see me soon. If I am and can with propriety ask leave I shall and give you a call for a few days.

With Duty Love &c.

I remain Dear Manfield

Yours Affectionately

T. M. HARDY.

PORTSMOUTH, *June 20th,* 1802.

DEAR MANFIELD,

I have just taken my place in the Mail for Tomorrow evg (Monday). I hope soon to hear what is to become of me. I intend going to the Spring Garden Coffee House, but my stay in Town shall be as short as possible, & I see nothing at present to prevent my being in Dorsetshire the latter end of the Week. I suppose the young Doctor arrived yesterday he will no doubt hammer out a long storey as to his Mother that will make her Hair stand on end on her head. I am just going to Dine with Mr Thompson.

[1] James Gambier, afterwards first Baron Gambier [1756-1833], distinguished himself on the " Glorious First of June," and in the second attack on Copenhagen.

With Duty to my Aunt Love to Catherine & the Children.

I remain

Dear Manfield

Yours Affectionately

T. M. HARDY.

Once more we find Hardy without a ship and an assiduous visitor to the waiting-room of the Admiralty.[1] He was, however, very soon appointed to the *Amphion*, his commission being dated 11th July 1802. The next letters speak sufficiently for themselves. They show that, notwithstanding the estrangement between Nelson and his wife, Hardy contrived to maintain friendly relations with both :—

SPRING GARDEN COFFEE, *June 24th*, 1802.

DEAR MANFIELD,

I saw Lord St Vincent yesterday & he has promised to give me a Ship very soon. I shall not remain in Town a moment longer than I am absolutely obliged to. I dine today with Geo Bagster tomorrow with Sir Thos Troubridge & if possible the Day after with Lord Nelson at Merton, & I think the Day after I shall take my departure in the Mail for Dorchester. I breakfasted this Morning with Lady Nelson I am more pleased with her if possible than ever ; she certainly is one of the Best Women in the World. As London is as barren of News as the Country I have nothing to add but Duty to my Aunt Love

---

[1] See *British Fleet*, p. 150. Captain Marryat is said to have written on the wall the following lines :—

"In sore affliction, tried by God's command,
Of patience Job the great example stands ;
But in these days a trial more severe
Had been Job's lot, if God had sent him here."

& Complts to all Friends & in hopes of seeing you in a few Days. I remain

Dear Manfield

Yours Affectionately

T. M. HARDY.

LONDON, *July 8th*, 1802.

DEAR MANFIELD,

Sir Thos Troubridge did not return from Yarmouth till this morning, & I find the *Amphion* is at Dungeness the nearest town to it is Dover for which place I set out this eveng. I am to write an official Letter to the Admiralty for permission to send a Gun Brig to Portsmouth, & Sir Thomas will manage the business for me. I will write to you as soon as I join the Ship & point out in what manner Tom is to proceed, my other Servant is waiting for me at Portsmouth but I shall not trust him with my things. I saw Ned Balston for a Minute I believe he dines with the Williams's tomorrow. There was a letter sent from the Coffee House for me the Day before I arrived I'll thank you to give me the heads of it in your next letter, as I understand it was from Mrs Walpole and she left Town before my arrival. You had better direct to me *Amphion* Dungeness Kent. With Duty to my Aunt & Love to Catherine the Children & all Friends. I remain

Dear Manfield

Yours Affectionately

T. M. HARDY.

I do not know where there is a Chaplain on board the *Amphion* but will tell you in my next. I fear it will be impossible to get my friend Geo Feaver into a Guardship.

I wish you Success at Weymouth.

"AMPHION," DOWNS, *July 12th*, 1802.

DEAR MANFIELD,

I arrived here yesterday & joined the same day; we sail tomorrow for Dungeness where your letters will always find me. Tell Tom Bartlett to go to Portsmouth & wait further orders. The Admiralty has promised me a Vessel to bring round my things, but is quite uncertain when she will be ready I shall direct to the young Doctor at Mr Thompsons where I think will be the best place for him to go. He had better go by the Coach as he may be wanted very soon you shall hear from me again very soon till then,

I remain, in haste,

Dear Manfield,

Yours Affectionately,

T. M. HARDY.

"AMPHION,"
OFF DOVER, *July 14th*, 1802.

DEAR MANFIELD,

The Admiralty has allowed me to send the *Bloodhound* Gun Brig to Portsmouth for my things I trust Tom is there; if not hurry him off as fast as possible, & should the *Bloodhound* be sailed before his arrival, he must make the best of his way to Lydd Kent about a mile from Dungeness Road.

Yours in great haste,

T. M. HARDY.

"AMPHION," DUNGENESS, *July 22nd*, 1802.

DEAR MANFIELD,

I am happy to hear (tho' not Victorious) you are so well pleased with your proceedings at Weymouth; but I trust you will be more successful against the Great Man at Dorchester, tho' I doubt not but you will have a very *strong fever* against you—I am sorry I had not an opportunity of paying my respect to Mr Weld & Family.

I'll thank you to give my Best Compliments to them when you see them ; I think there is but little chance of my being off the Isle of Wight. I inclose you a list of more expenses incurred by my young friend whilst off Cadiz. I have paid Captn Nicholls & will trouble you to receive the Money from their Friends. George Feaver has given up the thoughts of going to Sea as the emoluments (without trouble) do not amount to more than £100 a year ; with trouble I might safely add £50 ; however in those Days we all want to be Admirals or Bishops. I am rather astonished at not hearing from Portsmouth the *Bloodhound* left Deal the 15th. I suppose it is the D——d Custom-house that stops them. With Duty to my Aunt Love to Catherine the Children and all friends. I remain

Dr Manfield,

Yours Affectionately,

T. M. HARDY.

Tell John I have written to Captn Ganett & desired him to inform John how he would wish the Dogs to be sent. We have had very bad weather I fear bad for the Hay & Corn but good for Turnips.

This is the Ninth letter I have written toDay so much for being a Commodore however I believe it will do me a great deal of good.

More Dorset ale is now requisitioned for the table of the captain of the *Amphion*.

"AMPHION," DUNGENESS, *Augt 24th*, 1802.

DEAR MANFIELD,

I have not written to you before literally for want of something to say, & I believe if I wait till I have a long story to tell, it will be sometime before you hear from me. I find by Mr Nevill (now on board the *Amphion*) that my friend Mrs Walpole is only a Cousin to the Mr Walpole;

G

however I shall not forget to move her Interest with him when an opportunity offers. Young Hamilton of Weymouth is to join us soon (I believe by Water). If my Friend Mr Oakley should have any good Beer by him & Mr H. can take it without trouble, I will thank you to send me two Hampers. We continue Cruising as usual without much chance of success. The Weather has been very fine for this last Month & I suppose you have every prospect of a Good Harvest. I had a long letter from our Friend Captain Ingram; I find the Burton[1] Fish &c has been too good for him however a touch of Gout in September sometimes is a pleasant thing for the partridges. We met with a Gale of Wind last Night that drove us into the Downs; however it is moderate now & we are just arrivd off this place. The young Doctor has received a Letter from Tom Balston & I find John Manfield is with him & well. When you see Mr Weld I'll thank you to give my best respects to him & Family. I note you are in a fair way to beat the Great.

I'll thank you to give my Duty to my Aunt. Love to Catherine & the Children and all friends

I remain, Dear Manfield,

Yours Affectionately,

T. M. HARDY.

26th, Downs.—The Weather has been so bad that we bore up last night for this place.

Later in the autumn, Hardy was ordered to convey Lord Robert Fitzgerald to Lisbon, where he had been appointed Minister — (Hardy dubs him Ambassador). The Dorset ale had arrived, but, sad to relate, did not maintain its habitual standard of excellency.

[1] The future Admiral (see *ante*). There was evidently a great deal of conviviality at both Burton and Loders in those days.

"AMPHION," SPITHEAD, *Septr 25th*, 1802.

DEAR MANFIELD,

We arrived here this Morng per Telegraph from the Downs & I find my orders are to take Lord Robert Fitzgerald[1] to Lisbon as Ambasador; you see my friend Tom Troubridge[2] has not forgotton me. We are to be paid off on our return & reCommissioned. Thank you for the Beer I hope it will be up; I tasted a bottle the other Day & thought it rather Flat. I have not as yet learnt when his Lordship will be ready. I find the Possum people are to have a visit from the Thompsons in a few Days (Charles & Ann). I thank you to remember me to them.

With Duty Love & Compt. I remain (in haste)

Dear Manfield

Yours Affectionately

T. M. HARDY.

"AMPHION," SPITHEAD,
October 20th, 1802, 8 *ock morning.*

DEAR MANFIELD,

Lord Robert Fitzgerald & Family arrived at Portsmouth the Day before yesterday and the Weather had been so bad that they could not go on board. It is now very fine weather but the Wind still continues from the Westward. However I shall get them on board today and sail as soon as the Wind inclines from the Northd or Eastd. There are a few Ships gone with Dispatches to different Places, but I do not think there is the least prospect of a War at least for the present. The *Blenheim*

---

[1] Lord Robert Stephen Fitzgerald [1765-1833], sixth son of the first Duke of Leinster, and younger brother of the ill-fated Edward Fitzgerald. He married Sophia Charlotte, daughter of Captain Fielding, R.N. Hardy relates her troubles on shipboard with grim humour.

[2] Admiral Sir Thomas Troubridge, Bart. [1758-1807]. He has evidently now risen in Hardy's estimation (see *ante*, p. 84).

sails on Friday with Sealed orders.   It is supposed for the Mediterranean.   I am ordered to return to Spithead & that order has not been contradicted.   If the Winds should be foul we shall certainly put into Portland Road.

½ past 4.—The wind continues so strong to the Westwd that the Family do not think proper to venture on board, but I hope tomorrow will be more Favourable.   With Duty to my Aunt & Love & Compliments to all Friend I remain

Dear Manfield

Yours Affectionately

T. M. HARDY.

"AMPHION," PORTLAND ROADS,
October 25th, 9 o'clock Night [1802].

DEAR MANFIELD,

We arrived here about two hours ago as Lady Robt Fitzgerald realy could not stand the fatigues of the Sea any longer, & how she is to get to Lisbon God only knows, as we have literally had very fine weather ever since we left Spithead which was only yesterday at 3 o'clock in the afternoon.   The Wind is not fair but we could make a very good Slant could I prevail on them to allow me to proceed.   If ever married man was Blessed I think poor Lord Robert was last evening, and this Morning, out of a Wife eight Children, as many Female Servants a Secretary & Six Men Servants his Lordship had not a sole to put the Children to Bed & Dress them this Morng, but two Women belonging to the Ship[1]; however he bears it with the most Christian Fortitude & is worthy

---

[1] "The custom of carrying a certain number of seamen's wives to sea appears to have prevailed all through the eighteenth century. According to Marryat, Barker, Chamier, and others, the practice continued to exist, more or less, until the peace in 1817.   Captains often took their wives to sea with them."—Commander C. N. Robinson in *British Fleet*, p. 427.   Lady Hardy was often at sea with her husband after their marriage in 1807 (see *post*).

of being cald a good Husband & a good Father. I have written this in hopes some Portland Boat will call alongside of us in the Morning or should the Wind remain Westerly I shall send a boat to Weymouth for Fresh Beef but the moment the Wind comes from the Eastward (which I trust will be in the course of the day) We shall be off.

I shall write to Jos by the same Conveyance that takes this & for want of something else to say shall give him nearly a copy of this. With Duty to my Aunt Love to Catherine the Children & in hopes of an Easterly Wind in the Morning

I remain Dear Manfield

Yours Affectionately

T. M. HARDY.

PORTSMOUTH, *Decr* 10*th*, 1802.

DEAR MANFIELD,

We arrived at Spithead this morning after an 8 days Passage from Lisbon but I am sorry to say that we were thirty one Days going out, & the weather was not the most Pleasant in the World; at least Lady Robert Fitzgerald did not think it so, for she talked of departing this *Life* more than *once* but we landed her safe at last. What is to become of us I know not but suppose paid off in a few days. Mr Thompson (who I have just seen) desired me to say he had reced the game &c from Mr Balston & John & is much obliged. My stay at Lisbon was only six Days & I have brought no News from that part of the Country & have not been long enough here to learn any, but I learn from Mr Thompson there has been no news of us since we sailed, therefore determined to give you the earliest account possible of our arrival. With Duty to my Aunt Love to Catherine the Children & all friends. I remain Dear Manfield

In great haste

Yours Affectionately

T. M. HARDY.

The Hardy letters of 1803 begin here :—

"AMPHION," PORTSMOUTH HARBOR,
Jany 7th, 1803.

DEAR MANFIELD,

I have not written to you before for want of something to say, & I am truly sorry that the present subject is so unpleasant. Poor Ned Balston's accident of course was known here a few days ago ; it must be a very distressing thing to the Family. As the Papers did not mention his Death I conclude he is safe. I wish I had been in the Downs I could have then gone to his assistance he must have lost a great deal of Property & I much fear his Voiage will also be lost to him.[1] Let me know when you intend going to town & it is not unlikely but I shall meet you there. I expect we shall be paid off the latter part of this Month but it depends on the Shipwrights & their time is quite uncertain. Tell Augusta I recd her letter & shall write to her very soon. Miss Crone recd the Turkey, &c. & returns Thanks. With Duty to my Aunt Love to Catherine & the Children

I remain Dear Manfield
Yours Affectionately
T. M. HARDY.

"AMPHION," PORTSMOUTH,
Feby. 6th, 1803.

DEAR MANFIELD,

I could not answer your letter yesterday as there was no post. We get Men so fast that I almost despare of seeing you except you take Portsmouth in your way to Dorsetshire. Our 1st Lieut is now on leave of absence & I cannot possible quit the Ship till he returns, which I think will be in ten days.[2] I shall then try my

---

[1] Hardy refers to the shipwreck described in one of Tegg's illustrated pamphlets.

[2] This was partly no doubt attributable to his own popularity, and partly to the fact that when peace was declared thousands of

friends at the Admiralty for two or three Days.   If we are
not ordered to hold ourselves in readiness before that time,
but the Admiralty make it such a favor to grant leave that
I really do not like to ask them.   I learnt from a Captn
Pearce of the India Co Service that Poor Ned Balston was
still at Margate and that he was not yet out of Danger I
hope & trust his information was ill founded.   Did you
receive a Parcel for me some time ago from a Mr Pearce
(late of the *St George*) ; if you did I wish you would send for
it to London & give it to Halford to forward it to me the
first opportunity.   I hope Jos Ann & Augusta will remain
as long as you I will slip up & see you when Bennett
returns.   With best love to them all

> I remain Dear Manfield
> > Yours Affectionately
> > > T. M. HARDY.

> "AMPHION," SPITHEAD,
> *March 6th,* 1803.

DEAR MANFIELD,

To my great astonishment yesterday I recd
order to proceed to Cork without loss of time & I believe
we sail for that place either tomorrow or Tuesday.

Our Friend Capn Domett is taken so ill that he has
given up the Command, & who we are to have there I have
not yet learnt.   I conclude you are at Dorchester therefore
shall direct to you there.   I hope Ann got home safe &
trust she is getting better.   The Weather has been so bad
that yesterday was the first time I landed since our arrival

seamen were thrown out of employment, and were starving for want
of work.   As soon, therefore, as they began to commission ships in
view of a fresh outbreak of hostilities, the men flocked down, and it
was unnecessary to take the extreme measures for manning, which had
been necessary in the last years of the old century, to provide crews for
the Fleet.   Again Hardy says he "cannot quit the ship because the
first lieutenant is on leave of absence."   This was strictly according to
the regulations of the day.

at Spithead.   I think living on board a Week has done me
a great deal of good for I find myself quite recovered
except a little pain in the Back & as that is a Family
Complaint I must not Complain.   Everything here is so
barren of News that I have not a Word to say but Duty to
My Aunt Love &c &c

Yours Affectionately

T. M. HARDY.

"AMPHION," SPITHEAD,
March 30th, 1803.

DEAR MANFIELD,

We arrived last Night too late for Post.
We are ordered to be fitted for Foreign Service & what
follows is yet to be learnt.   The Papers I hear have
appointed me to the *Culloden* but all is unknown to me.   I
rather think Lord Nelson will hoist his Flag in this Ship
for a Passage to the Mediterranean should the War go on,
but to Day it is all Peace at Portsmouth.   Our Passage
from Cork was very tedious it was either a foul Wind or
Calm the whole way.   I was rather anxious as I feared old
Nelson[1] would have sailed before my arrival.   I am quite
recovered and was never better in my life than at present.
Young Roberts has joined but I have not seen him yet.   I
know you will excuse my scrall as you may suppose I have
but little time to spare.   I hope Ann Hardy is got well.
Give my Duty to my Aunt Love &c &c as Catherine says
is always the conclusion

Yours Affectionately

T. M. HARDY.

---

[1] The use of the endearing term "old Nelson" shows the strong
friendship which existed between them.   Although Nelson was only
ten years older than Hardy, the latter always looked after the health
and comforts of his chief with a paternal assiduity.

"AMPHION," St Helens,
Ap. 6th, 1803.

DEAR MANFIELD,

Here we are fitted for Foreign Service as full as an egg what is to follow is yet to be learnt. As you know I am not inquisitive I have not taken the trouble to ask but hold myself ready for the worst & then I shall be prepared for the best. The Papers (as you have seen I suppose) say Lord Nelson is to hoist his Flag here ; however that I suppose will be known in due time. I am sorry to hear Mrs Manfield has been so ill, give my love to her & tell her she must not gad about so much, Married Women are best at home. I am very sorry to hear poor Martha is so Ill, but trust this fine Weather will bring her round. If you see young Wallis remember me to him & tell him I hope soon to hear of his Ship being in Commission. My friend Sir Thos Troubridge is not worth one third of the Money that he was accused of selling out for, & he is the last Man in the world to do it. Our Friend Sir William Hamilton died on Sunday afternoon & was quite sensible to the last. How her Ladyship will manage to Live with the Hero of the Nile now, I am at a loss to know, at least in an honourable way. So soon as I know my destination (& am allowed to communicate it) you may depend on being informed. If you thought that I could receive my Shirts (that are at Possum) in 4 or 5 Days from this date I should like to risk it should we sail Mr Thompson will take care of them for me it would be as well to Direct them for me to his care. With Duty to my Aunt & Love &c &c

I remain

Dear Manfield

Yours Affectionately

T. M. HARDY.

"AMPHION," ST HELENS,
April 23rd, 1803.

DEAR MANFIELD,

I received my Shirts safe for which I am obliged. I am happy to hear you are all getting round again. I shall be happy to do anything I can for Mr Ferris but it appears by your letter he only wishes to be employed should the War go on. As I am not in the habit of making bargains I cannot give our Friend John Browne an answer till we know for certain how it is to be. I conclude Lt Ferris is married. I wrote to Colonel Bingham a few Days ago on the subject of his Son. If you see him, do ask if he received my Letter. Tho' I am extremely angry with his son yet I should be happy to serve the Father. I had a letter from Captain Digby yesterday requesting I would take a Son of Charles Strangeways[1] of Maiden Newton. I refused (in a handsom way) because I think Mr S. might as well a let it come thro' some of my relations as Captn D. Nothing has transpired relative to our Sailing since I wrote last, & what is to become of us is yet to be learnt. I am in hopes that matters will be made up but I fear a Peace cannot last long. With Duty to my Aunt Love &c to all I remain

Dear Manfield

Yours Affectionately

T. M. HARDY.

An unexpected slice of good fortune now falls to the lot of Thomas Hardy. Notwithstanding his loyalty to Lady Nelson and his unwelcome candour in the matter of Lady Hamilton, the Hero of the Nile, now on the point of starting in the *Victory* for the blockade of Toulon (the war which lasted for eleven years having been declared on the 18th May 1803), insisted that Hardy and no one

[1] A son of the Rev. Charles Fox Strangeways, B.C.L., Rector of Maiden Newton from 1787 to 1837.

else should be captain of the *Victory*, on which he had decided to hoist his flag. An exchange was accordingly arranged with Captain Sutton[1] as shown in the following letter ·—

"AMPHION," ST HELENS,
May 20th, 1803.

DEAR MANFIELD

I really have been so much employed that I have not had time to write & I can only tell you now that we are just getting under weigh. Lord Nelson is on board the *Victory*, but as it is not quite certain weather we shall not be obliged to leave her (the *Victory*) Off Brest, my change with Captn Sutton does not take place till we have passed Old Adml Cornwallis.[2] His Lordship looks remarkably well and is in high spirits. As the Boat is waiting I can only promise to write to you again by the first opportunity.

Yours Affectionately,

T. M. HARDY.

[1] Captain Samuel Sutton entered the navy in 1777; served in several general actions with Sir J. Rowley and Lord Rodney. Was Lieutenant of the *Culloden* on the 1st June 1795, and commanded the *Alcmene* at Copenhagen (1801).

[2] Admiral Sir William Cornwallis, G.C.B. [1744-1819], commanded the Channel Fleet in 1801 and from 1803 to 1806.

CHAPTER XII

NELSON AND HARDY ONCE MORE IN THE MEDITER-
RANEAN. THE BLOCKADE OF TOULON [18TH MAY
1803 TO 31ST DEC. 1804]

ON the 18th May 1803, Lord Nelson hoisted his flag
on board the *Victory* at Portsmouth. Two days
later, he sailed for Brest on his way to Gibraltar and the
Mediterranean. On the 10th July, however, he was on
board the *Amphion*, with Hardy, off Algiers. The following
important letter throws new light on the reason for this
change of ships. On the day in question, Hardy thus
writes to his relative at Dorchester :—

"AMPHION," OFF ALGIERS,
July 10*th*, 1803.

DEAR MANFIELD,

Our stay at Gibraltar was so short & I was
so much employed, that I had not time to give you a line, &
in short I had nothing to say but that we arrived there on
the 3rd Inst & sailed the 4th in the morning. We were
fortunate enough to capture a Dutch Ship off Plymouth
& should she be condemned (which at present is uncertain)
I suppose I shall get a Thousand pounds as the *Victory*
was the only Ship in Company. Since we left Gibraltar
we have taken another Dutch Man & a french Brig but
I believe their Cargoes are not Valuable. Mr Elliot[1]

---

[1] Hugh Elliot [1752-1830]. He eventually became a Privy Coun-
cillor and Governor of Madras.

Minister for Naples leaves us tomorrow Morning in the *Maidstone* for that place, by whom I shall send this Letter and wether you will ever get it or not is quite uncertain. We have a fair Wind for Malta where I hope to arrive in about two or three Days. William Payne is 1st Lieut of the *Maidstone* & is very well but complains he has not heard from his Friends for nearly twelve Months. We expect the *Victory* every Day & Captain Sutton is to have the *Amphion*. As Lord Nelson left England in the *Victory* you would be rather surprised to hear of his being in this ship, but the truth is it was necessary for her to make her appearance Off Brest with Adml Cornwallis, & as we were not fortunate enough to fall in with him, & the wind being fair His Lordship would not wait but thought it advisable to come on in this Ship. You may depend on hearing from me very often & I trust I shall not have reason to complain on your part. I shall write to Ann by the next conveyance which I think is Likely to be received before this. The Weather is very warm already I suppose it will be exceptionally hot at Malta however I trust our stay there will be very short. With Duty & love to all I remain

Dear Manfield,

Yours Affectionately,

T. M. HARDY.

It is not proposed to recapitulate in this volume the story of this period of Nelson's career, which has been so ably dealt with by Captain Mahan and other writers. The means of communication with England appears to have been far from satisfactory, or Mr Manfield was possibly over-occupied with his professional and municipal duties, and the cares of his coming mayoralty. Before the beginning of September, Hardy was evidently installed as captain of the *Victory* (his appointment dates from

July 31, 1803), for at the beginning of September he thus addresses Mr Manfield :—

"VICTORY" OFF TOULON,
Sept 5th, 1803.

DEAR MANFIELD,

I have written to some of you every opportunity since we left England, and tho' several vessels have arrived from Spithead lately, I have not heard a word from Dorsetshire, however I do not despair of a letter by the next arrival.   My hands have been pretty full as you may suppose but all is nearly to rights now, I have been very unwell but am quite recovered, in fact the N.W. Breeze off Toulon is so salutory that it is almost impossible to be unwell.   We get well supplied with beef, vegetables, &c from the Bay of Roses [Rosas] which is near our cruising ground and our men are all very Healthy, but I think there is every prospect of a war with Spain, when of course we must get our supplies from another quarter, which can be very easily done by sending to the Barbary States.   The French has made a move by sending two frigates out, and it was with some difficulty they got into Calvi in Corsica, and I trust the next attempt will be attended with better success on our part; and I have very little doubt but the fleet (which consists of 8 sail of the line) will make a Dust during the winter months. I hope the Business in Ireland [1] has not been of an alarming nature, and that government have taken strong measures to prevent a similar affair happening in future.   I think it necessary that every step should be taken in England to prevent the Enemy landing, but in my own opinion the Corsican never intended an invasion except he found parties run high, which I trust is not the case.   We have been very unfortunate since off Toulon in the way of Prize money, but upon the whole I have no reason to complain provided they condemn the Dutchman which we sent into

---

[1] Emmett's futile insurrection of July 1803.

Plymouth.   I long to hear that poor Ned Balston is again afloat; if he is at home do remember me kindly to him. The young doctor[1] is doing very well and I think very much improved; at present he is Lord Nelson's servant who is very fond of him, but I believe his attachment to his old master is such that he only considers himself as lent to his lordship.

This will be sent by the first opportunity that offers; till then God Bless you.

Off Toulon, October 24th.—The *Monmouth* leaves the fleet this day for Gibraltar by which I take the advantage of this.   This is so ·barren a spot for the pen that I really have nothing to say but that we are anxiously waiting for the French Fleet, as there is no prospect of going into port till they have been beat.

With Duty to my Aunt & Love to all

I remain Dear Manfield

Yours affectionately

T. M. HARDY.

P.S.—I have sent young Hamilton & Roberts with Captn Elliot of the *Maidstone*[2] in hopes of putting some money in their pockets as Capt E. is a very active fellow.

In December he writes :—

"VICTORY" OFF TOULON, *Decr 5th*, 1803.

DEAR MANFIELD,

I received your letter of the 21st of September by the *Excellent* which is the first from Dorsetshire since I left England.   If your Son John is determined to go to Sea the sooner the better I think.   It will be necessary for

---

[1] Edward Bartlett.

[2] Afterwards Rear-Admiral Elliot.   The second son of the Earl of Minto.   He died after seeing a great deal of war service in 1863.

you to point out to him all the inconveniences attending our profession, & that he must make up his mind to encounter numberless hardships ; with that & a good Constitution I have no doubt but he will do very well. If I can manage to put him on the Books (as John Callard Manfield) I will but I am not quite certain that I can do it. I will inclose you a letter to a Friend that I am sure will take care of him, which you can send or destroy as you judge fit ; if you prefer his coming out to this Country I would recommend your taking him to our Friend Mr Thompsons & he will get him a passage by the first opportunity that offers. I am happy to hear you have had so good a Harvest. If you see Colonel Bingham tell him his Son is with us in the *Victory*, & when we take the French Fleet he may depend on his being promoted. I am sorry to hear that Martha & Augusta continue ailing but hope this Winter will bring them quite round. Do give my best respects to the Weld Family & John Brown & condole or Congratulate him as you think proper. My kind Complements also to Captn Ingram & tell him we are all uncommon well here & only wait for the French Fleet to come out. I am sorry to hear they have not given Ned Balston a Ship but trust he will not be forgotten much longer. I have had a letter from Admiral Brine[1] & I find all I have done about his Son is quite right. This is written in readiness to be sent first opportunity.

AGINCOURT, SOUND ISLAND OF SARDINIA,
Decr 25th, 10 *o'Clock at Night.*

The *Phoebe* sails for Gibraltar tomorrow morning which is the first opportunity I have had since I recd your Letter. We hear there is a Cutter arrived off Toulon from England & I think I stand a fair chance of hearing from some of you. We have had some very bad weather,

---

[1] Admiral James Brine, who commanded the *Belliqueux* in the action with the Comte de Grasse on 5th Sept. 1781. He had two sons in the service, but which one is mentioned here it is impossible to say.

arrived here last Night to compleat our Water & proceed in a few Days for our old station.

I have not been on shore nor Do I think I shall, it is a poor miserable place not capable of furnishing us with fresh Provisions. .Wishing you all the Compliments of the season. I remain Dear Manfield

Yours Affectionately,

T. M. HARDY.

On the same day, he writes to Captain Langford[1] as follows :—

"VICTORY," OFF TOULON,
Decr 5th, 1803.

DEAR LANGFORD,

I am happy to see by the papers that the *Fury* is on so Active a Station and have no doubt but it will soon gain you the other step. I have a young Relation who is anxious to go to Sea ; if you can make room for him in the Class, I shall be much obliged should you be able to comply with my request, and will write to his Father (Mr Manfield, Dorchester, Dorset), he will send the Youngster to you. We are going on in the old way here. Sir William Boulton[2] joined us the other day, and of course, is first for promotion. Old Potterdale Commands the *Termagant*, Pearce, the *Halcyon* (a prize Brig), & Layman, the *Weazle*. You will have seen by the papers that George Elliott[3] has got the *Maidstone*, and I think

---

[1] Of Massingham, Norfolk. He was severely wounded in the attack on the Boulogne flotilla. (See Nelson's letters in *Nelson, His Public and Private Life*, by C. Lathom Browne, London, 1891, pp. 274-75. A portrait of Captain Langford is in possession of his descendant Mrs Chamberlayne of Maiden Bradley, Wilts.

[2] Captain Sir William Bolton, R.N., died 1st Dec. 1830. He married Catherine, niece of Lord Nelson (daughter of Thomas Bolton and Susanna Nelson). Her brother became second Earl Nelson on the 28th February 1835, and was the father of the present holder of the title (born 1823), who succeeded his father, 1st November 1835.

[3] Captain George Elliott (afterwards Admiral Sir George Elliott, K.C.B., 1784-1863) was placed in command of a ship by Lord Nelson on the 10th July 1803, and of the *Maidstone* frigate on the 1st August following. He was then only nineteen.

promises to make a very good Officer. I think Lord
Nelson looks as well as I ever saw him, he desires to be
kindly remembered to you. I am very happy to see that
Admiral Thornborough[1] has not forgotten to erect a Monument to our poor Friend Parker. Wishing you every
success,

I remain,

Dear Langford,

Yours very sincerely,

T. M. HARDY.

To Captn. F. LANGFORD,
H.M. Ship *Fury*, Downs.

Captain Langford writes thus to Mr Manfield :—

H.M.S. "FURY," DOWNS,
March 11th, 1804.

SIR,

I had the pleasure of receiving Captn. Hardy's
Letter from the *Victory* requesting I would receive your
Son to the *Fury*. If there is any Person in the creation
I could oblige—it would most certainly be him—to whom
I am under numerous obligations. I have frankly stated
to Captain H. there is at this moment no vacancy, neither
do I at present see a possibility of receiving Him. My
Complement of Men and Boys is and has been some time
complete. Indeed I have now a young Gentleman on
Board I am at a loss how to dispose of. If I can get any
of my friends on this Station to receive him till I have an
opportunity of entering Him on the *Fury* Book it will give
me great pleasure. If I succeed you shall hear from me.
In the Interval I am,

Sir, Your obt. Servant,

FRED LANGFORD.

Some months elapse. The tedious blockade still continues without any stirring events as far as Hardy is con-

---

[1] Admiral Sir Edward Thornborough, G.C.B. [1754-1834] (see p. 73).

cerned. Meanwhile, John Callard Manfield, the younger, joins the Navy. In August his uncle thus writes to the youth's father :—

"VICTORY," PALMA BAY,
ISLAND OF SARDINIA, *Augt 6th*, 1804.

DEAR MANFIELD,

I received your letter of the 12th of May one from Martha of the 19th of the same Month by John who joined us two Days before in the *Ambuscade* & Captain Durban has been good enough to take men for me into that ship which I consider a very fortunate circumstance as he pays particular attention to the education of his youngsters & is himself very clever in his profession. John appears quite satisfied with his situation & has got the better of the Sea Sickness. He Dined yesterday with Lord Nelson & his Lordship was pleased to say he was very much like his Uncle only the Chin was a little longer, you may depend on my taking every care of him, & you may make yourself quite easy about his Money concerns, all that I will strictly attend to. Captain Durban speaks very highly of his Disposition and I have no doubt but he will do very well. As I conclude you will be very anxious to hear of his safe arrival I take the opportunity of the *Childers* going to Rosas (in Spain) this afternoon of sending this by her, & shall write to you again by the *Kent*, who sails for England in about ten days & as the *Ambuscade* will not leave us before that time I shall make John Write to his Mother by the same Conveyance. We came here for the purpose of clearing the Victuallers & store ships that came with the *Ambuscade ;* the *Prevoyant* remained at Gibraltar at which place John joined Captain Durban ; our stay here will be but a few Days when we shall return to our old Station. I think this very extraordinary change in France [1] is likely to bring about Peace tho' I almost fear a

---

[1] Napoleon Bonaparte became Emperor in virtue of a decree of the Senate, dated 18th May 1804. He was crowned by the Pope at Paris on the 2nd December following.

good one cannot be made with Bonaparte. However it is not necessary to fight with every Rascal one meets but to be on our guard is incumbent on us.

I am sorry to hear from Martha that Aunt Hardy is not so well as she has been ; give my Duty to her & beg of her to make her self as comfortable as she can. With Love to Catherine & the Children. I remain,

Dear Manfield,

Yours Affectionately,

T. M. HARDY.

Hardy writes a week later ·—

"VICTORY," OFF TOULON,
Augt 17th, 1804.

DEAR MANFIELD,

I wrote to you some Days ago but knowing it to be quite uncertain whether you will receive it or not I take the opportunity of getting this ready as I know the *Kent* is to sail for England in a few Days. I shall now give you the heads of my last letter. John arrived safe in the *Ambuscade* on the 29th of July & did not make it known to me till our arrival in Palma Bay which was the 1st of August. I received your letter and one from Martha & I concluded John had remained at Gibraltar as the *Prevoyant* was detained there to deliver stores ; however Captn Durban informed me he had a young Gentleman on board by the name of Manfield who he understood was my Nephew & Mr John made his appearance soon after. He looks very well & says he is quite pleased with his profession. Captn Durban is quite pleased with him & has been good enough to keep him in the *Ambuscade*. He dined the next Day with his Lordship who was pleased to say my Nephew was very much like me except the Chin was rather longer therefore you will conclude mine is reduced a little. I have not seen the young gentleman since we left Palma but shall have him on board the first opportunity & I hope he has prepared a letter for his Mother ; if not I shall make him get one ready & inclose it with this. Make yourself quite easy about his Money Concerns. I will undertake it all & I would recommend you not to send him out any Cloths, as I can get every thing he may want in this Country. I consider it very fortunate his being with Captn Durban as he takes a great deal of pains with the Education of the youngsters & is himself very clever in his profession. I fear Mr Thompson is quite angry with me for not writing to him oftener however I wrote the other Day and shall write again by this conveyance. I believe he feels much for the loss of Poor William, & Steel's list has I see killed his Son John, but your Son John tells me there is no truth in it which I am quite happy to hear. I have written to Martha this Day & I am only sorry I have not more news for her but we are rather in a barren spot. The *Kent* is just going to sail & your Son John has forgot to send his Mothers Letter he was very well last Night you shall hear from him the next opportunity.

With Duty to my Aunt Love to Childn &c. I remain,

Dr M, Yours Affy,

T. M. HARDY.

On the 20th August in the same year, he writes thus to Mr Noble at Malta[1] :—

"VICTORY" OFF TOULON,
August 20th, 1804.

MY DEAR NOBLE,

I was favoured with your letter of the 22nd of May (*viâ* Madaline) by the *Belleisle* at which place I hear your vessel was at her departure. Should we fall in with her I shall be happy to pay every attention to her officers. I sent your letter by way of Rosas by our friend

[1] Mr Broadley's collection of Nelson MSS.

Sir Wm Boulton which I hope will be in England before the Convoy. I remain

My dear Noble

Yours most Sincerely

T. M. HARDY.

EDMUND NOBLE, Esq.,
    Malta.
    [Endorsed " Recd 31st Augt, Ansd 1st Oct."]

Now comes a charming and characteristic letter from Mary Manfield, the daughter of the Dorchester Alderman, to her brother John, serving with Captain Durban on board the *Ambuscade* off Toulon :—

DORCHESTER,
October 18*th*, 1804.

MY DEAR BROTHER,

I was happy to hear by your letters that you were well and liked being a sailor. My Mother hopes you will continue to write long ones every opportunity you have of sending them to England and I assure you I will always answer them equally long. We have not seen any account in the papers of the engagement you expected to have, I suppose you said it to alarm your Mother. William is gone to school to Mr Adams at Tiverton we have had one letter from him which was very well written for the first my mother wishes to go and see him before the vacation as he is very young to be sent 52 miles from home. I am happy to see you make good use of the Book I gave you ; it will amuse us to read your journal when you come home. The Yeomanry are come here to-day they are to be quartered in the town for a week we are to have Mr J. Browne the two Welds, Uncle Hardy, and Uncle John to sleep here. They expect to be reviewed by the King, if they should be I hope I shall go out and see them. I assure you I am very glad they are here, as it will make Dorchester a little gay, having such a number of soldiers in it. I shall be very much amused to see the gentleman going with their bags for corn which I understand they are obliged to do. I have been staying a fortnight at Weymouth, with Aunt Ann at Mrs Warne's. I spent my time very pleasantly, in walking on the Esplanade and sailing, I went to the ball and danced with an Officer in the Navy to whom Captain Ingram introduced to me : I was at a play which was very crowded and hot, but however I had a very good view of the Royal Family, as I sat opposite them. I went on board the *Royal Sovereign*, she is fitted up very superbly, covered with gold and scarlet velvet; the sea was unfortunately rough which made me uncomfortable the whole of the day. I can easily imagine what you must have suffered, from sea sickness at first : Weymouth has been extremely full for the first month the king was there, it was said there was not a bed to be got in the town, it is thining very fast now, the Royal Family are to leave it in a fortnight. My Mother wishes to know if you have written to Mr Thompson if you have not she desires you will do it, the first opportunity you have of sending a letter, Miss Ann Thompson has been in Dorsetshire this last two months, she staid a fortnight with us, then went to Weymouth, and is now at Portisham ; I saw her last Monday, she was very well and said she believed her Sister Eliza was married last week & Father, Mother, and Ann join me in love to My Uncle and yourself and believe me to remain

Your affectionate Sister,

M. MANFIELD.

After perusing the letter, the Alderman adds a postscript :—

P.S.—MY DEAR JOHN,

If you want anything apply to your Uncle who has been so good as to say he will furnish you with

everything you may want.   He speaks well of you continue to deserve it and no doubt you'll prosper.   God bless you
Yours affectionately
JNO CALL : MANFIELD.

The following letter is interesting as referring to the working of the impressment system[1] as late as 1804.   It is addressed to Mr Noble at Malta[2] :—

"VICTORY," MADALINA ISLANDS,
October 23rd, 1804.

MY DEAR NOBLE,
I was favoured with your letter of the 1st Inst by *Phoebe* & as yet have not seen the two men sent in lieu of Benjn Hambleton, but am quite satisfied with Captn Cassel's report of them, and have sent Hambleton on board *Active* for a Passage to Malta with a full discharge which I trust will be sufficient to prevent his being again impressed. I hope you have kept an account of the number of great-coats sent to me for I realy have no idea of the quantity as I disposed of them as fast as they arrived.

There is no doubt but his Lordship will leave us for England very shortly and our loss of course will be very great but we are in hopes he will return in the Spring. Should I see the Old Maid I shall be happy to pay her every attention for you must recollect I have not seen a female face these sixteen months.

Wishing you every Success
I remain Dear Noble
Yours very sincerely
T. M. HARDY.

EDMUND NOBLE, Esq.,   [Seal
Malta.   T. M. H.]
[Endorsed " Recd 1st Nov," Ansd 9th Do.]

---

[1] Many most interesting details about impressment and exemptions from it will be found in the *British Fleet,* pp. 104 and 412.   A man impressed might provide a substitute, and this is probably what Hambleton did.

[2] Nelson and Hardy MSS. in possession of A. M. Broadley.

A fortnight later Hardy writes :—

"VICTORY," OFF TOULON,
Nov. 6th, 1804.

DEAR MANFIELD,

The *Ambuscade* joined the Fleet the day before yesterday and I learn that John is well but the weather has been so bad I have not had an opportunity of seeing him ; and as it is probable he will not write by this conveyance I think it will relieve Catharine's mind to hear from this quarter as you doubtless have heard of the dreadful fever at Gibraltar.   However we are quite healthy here and I have little doubt but we shall continue so from the great care taken by our worthy and good Commander in chief.   His Lordship will certainly leave this country for England by the middle of this month and what is to become of me cannot be determined till it is known weather Lord Nelson gos home on leave or they supercede him.   If the latter, it is more than probable that I shall quit the *Victory* with his Lordship ; if the former of course I remain where I am till his return.   In the event of my leaving the Mediterranean I think I cannot do better than leave John with Captain Durban and all his money matters shall be settled by me.   Durban speaks very handsomely of him, and I have no doubt but he will make a good officer in due time.   We have had a great deal of bad weather and much more must be expected before the winter is over. We have had some little idea of a Spanish war but there appears no prospect of it now (at least for the present). The account we have just received from Gibraltar is extremely bad but we are in hopes that the cold weather and heavy rains that prevail in this season will soon stop the dreadful ravages.   Accounts from Malaga and Cadiz I am sorry to say are not less calamitous.   I will thank you to give my best compliments to Mr Jno Browne and Captain Ingram.   I hope the former will soon be one of the representatives of the borough of Weymouth.   The last letter I had from home was from Augusta ; it was answered by the *John Bull* cutter about the 13th of last month. You will know I hope that my relations do not trouble me with many letters.

With best wishes for all friends.

I remain Dear Manfield

Yours affectionately

T. M. HARDY.

Young Manfield in the following week thus writes to his father, now Mayor of Dorchester :—

"AMBUSCADE," OFF BARCELONA,
Novr 13th, 1804.

MY DEAR SIR,

I have been out on this Station very near six months and have received no letter from Home. I have wrote a great many to Mother and have expected answers but have received none. We have not been in port since I wrote you last but we have sent our boat ashore at Barcelona but they will not send us off any fruit. We expect to hear of a war with Spain every day as I suppose you have heard of the Engagement between four of our frigates and four Spanish Ditto.[1] We hear very little or no news so you must not expect a long letter I should not have wrote to you before I had received an answer, if Capt Hardy had not Commanded me. You promised to send me some newspapers but I have seen none yet, I hope in a little time the young Lawyer (William) will be able to write to me as I suppose he is the Officer already I assure him it will be better than going to sea. I suppose Mary is looking out for a Husband whoever marries her will have caught a Tartar I can assure him. Give my compliments to the members of the Club if it is met yet. Miss Cooper has left Dorchester I suppose and the Miss Thompsons Married, we are always at sea and have con-

---

[1] An engagement which preceded the actual declaration of war.

tinual gales of wind. Give my love to Grandmother and Aunt Manfield and to my Friends at Martinstown, Portisham and Corton[1] and my complyments all Friends at Dorchester. My love to Mother Brother and sisters

I remain Dear Father

Your affectionate Son

JNO CALL. MANFIELD.

Captain Hardy now congratulates his brother-in-law on his accession to the Mayoralty ·—

"VICTORY." OFF TOULON,
Decr 31*st*, 1804.

DEAR MANFIELD,

I received your letter yesterday of the 16th of October by the *Swiftsure* and I suppose you will not be a little surprised at the sudden arrival of your son John which I conclude took place about Christmas Day at last. I betted his Lordship a dollar that Admiral Campbell would dine in England on that day. As Captain Durban was good enough to put John on his books I thought it best for him to remain in *Ambuscade* and I am happy to say his Captain speaks of him in the handsomest manner.

However I hope Mama will not be —— enough to wish him to come home as the movements of Ships now a day are so sudden that he will run a great risk of losing his passage and of course his ship. I recommend you not to send him any clothes, or at least as little as possible. Shirts he is not the least in want of, as I procured him a dozen in addition to his former stock. I have every reason to believe the *Ambuscade* will be ordered again to this station immediately. I have given up all thoughts of returning to England myself & it is by no means clear to me that his Lordship will, but he has not yet given up the idea. You remark my old ship (*Amphion*)

---

[1] Corton is in Portisham parish.

has been lucky. I am glad of it. Should war be declared against the Spaniards the Fleet has done very well. It gives me great pleasure to hear that the King is so much recovered. I am sure we ought all to pray for a long continuation of his health. The Abby[1] must have been very much crowded. I think our friends Mr & Mrs Woodward must have had enough to do. I am sorry the poor Earl[2] has not recovered the use of his legs. I am happy to hear of Mr Bingham's safe arrival & that he will be able to give a good account of himself to his Father. I suppose the farmers expect all to be ruined; as ewes only fetch 50 shillings a head nothing can save them but Wheat getting up again to thirty pounds a load. I have written to Martha by this conveyance requesting her to try if my Aunt Hardy can make herself comfortable. I shall be happy to add anything to her income to enable her to do it. Sir John Orde is off Cadiz with 4 sail of the line; it is conjectured that he is to have the command here but it is quite unknown to our good Admiral.

I think since the thoughts of a Spanish War our Commander in Chief looks better & I conclude as troubles increase he will mend give my duty to my Aunt, Love to Catharine and the Children & all friends

I remain Dear Manfield

Yours affectionately

T. M. HARDY.

I see by the paper you are elected Mayor, I wish your Worship much Joy.

---

[1] This evidently refers to a wedding at Milton Abbey, Dorset, the seat of the Earl of Dorchester.
[2] George, second Earl of Dorchester, who died in 1808.

CHAPTER XIII

THE YEAR OF TRAFALGAR [1805]

IT is unnecessary to recapitulate the story of Nelson's tantalising pursuit of Villeneuve, first through the Mediterranean and afterwards to the West Indies. Two excellent maps showing the course of both fleets will be found in Mr Henry Newbolt's *The Year of Trafalgar*.[1] Captain Mahan deals exhaustively with the subject in his *Life of Nelson*.[2] Hardy's first letter home in this eventful year of his life is as follows :—

"VICTORY,"
OFF THE WEST END OF SICILY,
Feby 23rd, 1805.

DEAR MANFIELD,

We are now on our way off Toulon after a Trip to Egypt in pursuit of the French Fleet without the good fortune to fall in with them ; and yesterday we learnt that they had returned to Toulon a few days after they saild, which was on the 18th of last month in a very crippled state having met with a heavy gale of wind on the 19th.

Our good Commander in Chief's great zeal and activity pushed us in rather too fast ; however the error was on the right side (at least I think so) for by every account we can get, they were certainly bound to Alexandria, and if they

[1] *The Year of Trafalgar*, London, John Murray, 1905, pp. 8 and 18.
[2] *The Life of Nelson*, by Captain A. T. Mahan, London, Sampson, Low & Co., 1897, vol. ii., p. 267 *et seq.*

had not been TAYLORS instead of SAILORS it is more than probable we should have fallen in with them before they arrived at their destination. We have the satisfaction to hear that an eighty gun ship is wrecked at the entrance of the harbour of Ajaccio (in Corsica) and said to be totally lost. Some of their frigates are said to be missing and I trust some of our frigates will be fortunate enough to fall in with them, so that I think upon the whole the Emperor will not have much to brag of. How fortunate it is for us that he cannot cast sailors in a mould. We are not without hope that they will make another trial and we trust we shall have the good fortune to fall in with them. I think Bonaparte will not give up his favourite expedition for one failure. I see by the papers the arrival of the *Ambuscade* at Spithead of course you have seen John, and as Lord Nelson has written for her to be allowed to return to this country immediately, I conclude I shall soon have the pleasure of seeing the young gentleman. My friend John Harbin late Chaplain of the *Belleisle* is about to go to England and is good enough to take charge of a small box directed to you. It contains five gold chains one of each you will have the goodness to present to my five neices with their uncle's best love. If my sisters like them I will send an additional six the next opportunity but I am told they are only fit for *young* ladies.

March 11*th—off Toulon.*—We have just received the unfortunate news of the loss of the *Raven* Brig, Captain Layman[1] who was made out of this Ship into the *Weazle* about eighteen months ago, which brig he also lost six months after he took command of her. You might recollect him on board the *San Josef* a stout full faced man and you will agree with me he is D—— unfortunate. A cutter

[1] Nelson took a great interest in Captain Layman, whom he considered entirely free from blame in the matter of the loss of his ships. On the 10th March 1804 he wrote to Lord Melville, "Captain Layman has served me in three ships, and I am well acquainted with his bravery, zeal, judgment, and activity ; nor do I regret the loss of the *Raven* compared to the value of Captain Layman's services."

bound to the Fleet with despatches is also taken by the French Fleet and all the letters of both vessels are destroyed therefore I give up all hopes of hearing from you till the arrival of the *Ambuscade.* I conclude of course that my sisters wrote to me and that their letters are lost, I shall therefore write to them shortly. We have I am sorry to say received information that the *Arion* and *Acheron* (Bomb) are both taken. They had a valuable convoy under their charge. We have not yet learnt but I fear a number of them must have fallen into the enemy's hands.

Give my Duty to my Aunt Hardy who I hope is well. Love to Catherine the young folkes (I suppose I must not say children) and all Friends,

I remain,

Dear Manfield,

Yours affectionately,

T. M. HARDY.

Nearly three months later he again writes :—

"VICTORY,"
May 9th, 1805.

DEAR MANFIELD,

We passed thro' the Gut of Gibraltar yesterday and are now steering with a fair wind for Cape St Vincent when it is his Lordships intention to despatch a vessel for England.

I am sorry to say we have heard nothing of the French Fleet since they left Cadiz which was on the 10th of last month. It is therefore strongly believed by Lord Nelson that they are gone to the West Indies and of course we shall follow them, if we hear nothing of their destination from Lisbon from whence we expect the *Amazon* will join us tomorrow.

Thank God I am quite recovered from my late illness and was never better in my life than at present. I feel quite happy at going to the West Indies as I am convinced it will agree with me and at least it will vary the scene. I have not heard from you since last October but I conclude your letters are lost in the *Raven* Brig. I shall put you to an additional sixpence expense by enclosing a letter from you to John that you may have the satisfaction of destroying it. I think my nephew John has acted a very wise part in quitting the Navy, for I fear his delicate constitution would not have agreed with our very rough and uncertain service. I am sorry he was so much neglected on board the *Ambuscade* as he appeared quite clean when he came on board the *Victory* which made me think ourselves fortunate that he should be in so good a ship.

It is extremely unfortunate that the French Fleet should have so much the start of us. They were only nine days from Toulon to Cadiz and we were 26 from Sardinia (which is the same distance). However I recollect that poor Mr Thomas Russell recommended to my Aunt (or my Aunt to him) *Patience and Perseverance* which has and must be poor Lord Nelson's motto.

I wrote to you by my friend John Harbin of *Renown* and sent some trifles for my neices which I hope will be received safe. The *Renown* had a narrow escape of being taken but we conclude she is arrived in England by this time with Sir John Orde's Squadron which also was obliged to hasten from off Cadiz.

Lord Melville's business[1] of course makes us all stare and to say truth I am sorry for him for I believe it was much his wish to befriend the Navy in spite of his being a Scotchman. I think the opposition will push Mr Pitt very hard ; however I sincerely hope they will not succeed. I shall not close this till I know our destination.

May 10*th*, 10 *o'clock at night.*—A vessel leaves for England early tomorrow morning but I do not know her name. We are now off Cape St Vincent and his Lordship

[1] First Lord of the Admiralty, 1804-05. Erased from roll of the Privy Council, 1805. Subsequently impeached for malversation, acquitted, and restored to the Privy Council.

has made up his mind to bear up for the West Indies in the course of tomorrow. Our Fleet is in perfect health and spirits. We are all in great hopes that we shall meet the French Fleet. It will be needless for you to write to me till you hear from me again.

With Duty to my Aunt and Love to Catharine and the Children.

> I remain, Dear Manfield,
>> Yours affectionately,
>>> T. M. HARDY.

Just a month later he again writes :—

> "VICTORY," OFF ANTIGUA,
> *June 12th,* 1805.

DEAR MANFIELD,

As I think it probable that the Captains Friends will be more anxious about him than he deserves, I shall take the latest opportunity of closing this letter.

We arrived off Barbadoes on the 4th and there received accounts that the French Fleet had passed to the southward (supposed destined for Trinidad) on the 29th of May. We received on board Genl Sir William Myers and about one hundred and fifty Artilery men, and in the Fleet we have about two thousand soldiers. As the F. Fleet never passed to the southward of course we never saw them, and I am sorry to say that the different information we have received has as yet proved false. Yesterday we were informed by an American that he saw the F. Fleet at 5 o'clock that morning consisting of 18 sail of the line and 7 Frigates standing for Guadaloupe which I also believe to be a Lye, however we expect to hear something about them from this Island when we communicate with it which will be in the afternoon. Our squadron consists of 12 sail of the line which we think fully equal to twelve French and six Spaniards. I am quite recovered of the rheumatism and was never better in my life than at this moment. I think we have every prospect of very soon returning again to Europe but I realy have no great objection to remain in this country. I saw young Roberts of the *Jason* yesterday ; he is very well but I do not think he will ever set the Thames on fire.

June 13*th*.—We have just received information that the F. Fleet passed this Island (Antigua) on Saturday last steering to the northward and it is generally believed they are bound to Europe. We are now landing the troops and shall sail in a few hours for Gibraltar where you may direct to me as usual. I think we shall have had a pretty good round of it. We still hope to ketch the Rascals, (should they be bound to Cadiz) before they get there.

With best wishes for you all

I remain Dear Manfield

Yours affectionately

T. M. HARDY.

In his next letter, written a month later, he once more recurs to the old question of prize-money, and his business relations with Messrs Cooke & Halford.

"VICTORY," AT SEA,
July 15*th*, 1805.

MY DEAR MANFIELD,

I hope you will forgive my troubling you with this letter and I trust you will see it in the light I do.

I have directed Halford to answer your Bills on me for One hundred and fifty Pound, and I shall be thankful to you if you will present fifty Pound to each of my unmarried Sisters with my best Love. It will serve them as pocket Money for the present and should I be fortunate enough to receive half the Prize Money that is supposed will come to my Share, it will enable me to do something permanent for them ; however I never calculate on profits till they are in my Agents hands, and as yet he has not received any very large sums on my account. This letter will be directed by another hand and if it could be kept a secret from our relations I should like it better. I shall write another letter to you by the same Conveyance that takes this. From some little hints I have lately had I fear they are not more comfortable at Possum than they used to be. I am sure you will forgive my troubling you with this Commission and that you will believe

I am,

My Dear Manfield

Yours most Affectionately

T. M. HARDY.

On the same day he commenced another letter which may almost be described as a journal, and tells its own story of the return voyage to Europe.

"VICTORY," AT SEA,
July 15th, 1805.

DEAR MANFIELD,

We are now within fifty leagues of Cape St Vincent and as the wind is fair it is more than probable we shall be in sight of it tomorrow morning.

The movements of our good Commander in Chief are so rapid that I find it necessary always to be prepared with a letter, and I think it likely he will despatch a vessel to England in a day or two. Nothing has been heard of the Enemy since I wrote to you last, which was by way at Lisbon on the 17th of June. We are still in hopes that they are not arrived at the place of their destination, and should they be bound to Cadiz or the Mediterranean there is still a chance left of our getting hold of them.

We have had a very pleasant passage and our people continue excessively healthy notwithstanding the long time they have been without refreshments; none of any sort having been received since we left Sardinia.

His Lordship still talks of going home but so many events are about to take place that I give myself no thought on the subject, nor is it at all clear to me that I shall make one of the party as it is his intention to return again to this station.

July 20th.—We arrived at Gibraltar this morning and as yet have had no account of the French Fleet therefore we have little doubt but they are gone to some port in the Bay of Biscay. After our Water and provisions are compleat which will be in the cours of tomorrow we shall again sail for Cape St Vincent and I have no doubt but by that time their destination will be fully known.

Vice Admiral Collingwood with four sail of the line is off Cadiz so that we shall be fully equal to them should fortune at last favour us. I cannot say that I am sorry to find Sir John Orde [1] has struck his Flag, for in the first place he is senior to Lord Nelson, and in the next place he is a most unpleasant man to sail under.

I was on shore this morning for a few minutes, and I find it as hot and unpleasant as ever, and the greater part of my old acquaintance I am sorry to say are dead. If they do not take the greatest precautions I very much fear the fever will again break out in Septr.

July 25th.—We have just received accounts that the *Curieux* Brig passed the Enemy's fleet on the 19th of June therefore no doubt remains but they are gone to the northward, and I think it more than probable that you will (very soon after the receipt of this letter) hear of the *Victory* and Squadron being off Brest.

I am sorry to say that I have another attack of rheumatism tho' not quite so severe as it was last time. I shall therefore if possible procure leave to remain on shore a few weeks should we be ordered to England. We are now standing through the Gut and the *Pickle*

---

[1] Admiral Sir John Orde, Bart. [1751-1824]. Hardy evidently participated in Nelson's feelings of antagonism towards Orde. (See Laughton's *The Nelson Memorial*, p. 90.)

Schooner takes his Lordships despatches to England this afternoon.

With Duty to my Aunt and love to all,

I remain Dear Manfield,

Yours affectionately,

T. M. HARDY.

In three weeks' time what Hardy prophesied happened. Lord Nelson went home in the *Victory*, and his next communication to Mr Manfield is written well in sight of the coast of Dorset.   This letter runs as follows:—

"VICTORY,"
August 18th, 1805.

DEAR MANFIELD,

We are now standing in to Spithead and shall be at an Anchor in about an hour. As my health mends but very slowly[1] I have applyed to the Admiralty for leave of absence, therefore in all probability I shall have the pleasure of seeing my friends in Dorsetshire the latter part of this month.

His Lordship will strike his Flag so soon as we get Pratique which I trust will be in the course of the day.   As for news I know none, except that we fancy ourselves very unfortunate after so many anxious moments to have missed the combined squadrons, but when we come to consider that our force was 11 sail of the line and theirs 20 perhaps it will be as well to agree with Mr Pope "Whatever is is right."

Let me hear from some of you soon With Duty to my Aunt and love to all,

I remain Dear Manfield,

Yours most Affectionately,

T. M. HARDY.

[1] Hardy had been suffering severely from rheumatism.

Lord Nelson at once proceeded to Merton, and Hardy evidently lost as little time as possible in going down into Dorsetshire. Mr Newbolt does not share the somewhat despondent views entertained by the captain of the *Victory* as to the practical consequences of the great sea-chase. He says,[1] "On the 20th of August, Villeneuve ran south into Cadiz, unable to face the combination of Cornwallis's and Nelson's fleets. On the 25th, Napoleon, in bitter wrath, broke up his camp at Boulogne and marched against the Austrians. The British admirals had beaten the "Army of England.""

On the 12th of the previous month (July 1805) the court had migrated to Weymouth, the King, Queen, and the Royal Princesses taking up their quarters as usual at Gloucester Lodge, their favourite seaside residence ever since their memorable visit of 1789, of which Fanny Burney became the amusing chronicler. The homely life of George III. in Dorset had been the object of the gibes of Wolcot and the caricatures of Gillray, but heedless of ridicule, the British sovereign pursued the even tenor of his ways, making excursions by sea, announcing naval successes either at the theatre or on the esplanade, and indulging in the sea-bathing for the excellence of which Weymouth was, and still is, famous. In the audience chamber at Gloucester Lodge (now the dining-room of a hotel) George III. had conferred with Pitt and Addington ; with Loughborough and Eldon ; with Cathcart and Dundas, and with all the great personages of the time. It was in the same homely apartment that the mordant pen of "Peter Pindar" had, ten years before, thus pictured an audience between Pitt and his royal master :—

> "Lo, Pitt arrives ! alas, with lantern face.
> 'What, hee, Pitt, hee what, Pitt, hee, more disgrace ?'
> 'Ah Sire, bad news ! A second dire defeat !
> Vendée undone, and all the Chouans beat.'

---

[1] *The Year of Trafalgar*, Henry Newbolt, p. 22.

> 'Hee, hee, what, what?—beat, beat? what, beat agen?
> Well, well, more money—raise more men, more men.
> But mind Pitt, hee mind, huddle up the news,
> *Coin* something, and the growling land amuse:
> Make all the *sans-culottes* to Paris caper,
> And Rose shall print the vict'ry in his paper.'"

Times had changed since then, and Bonaparte had succeeded the revolutionaries of 1793 as our national bugbear and standing terror.   Tradition says that Hardy (with Lord Nelson's knowledge) had paid a hurried visit to Lady Nelson, before setting out for "Possum," where he would be the near neighbour of the king, whose loyal and faithful servant he was.   The sojournings of King George in Dorsetshire ended for ever in 1805.   On the 7th of August their Majesties had given a gala dinner at the Royal Hotel (then as now one of Weymouth's principal hostelries), in honour of the twenty-second birthday of the Princess Amelia. A few days later much excitement was occasioned by the passing of a homeward-bound West Indian convoy, and on the 27th August the news arrived of the death, on the previous day, of the king's brother, the Duke of Gloucester, at whose earnest recommendation Weymouth had first been patronised by the English court.   It is recorded that grief kept the king and queen indoors for several days, but an intimation must have reached "Possum" that His Majesty, at any rate, desired to hear all the details of Nelson's voyage from the lips of the captain of the *Victory*.   *The Morning Chronicle* now makes the following announcement :—

"*Weymouth, Tuesday Sept.* 3, 1805.—Captain Hardy, Lord Nelson's captain, was waiting the return of his Majesty (from his ride), and had a long conversation with him."

Even then Hardy had earned the name of "Nelson's Captain," and so he is likely to be known for all time.

CHAPTER XIV

TRAFALGAR, OCTOBER 21ST, 1805

THE news of the arrival of the combined fleets at Cadiz reached London the very day before Hardy's interview at Weymouth with George III., but the captain of the *Victory* could hardly have been cognisant of it.[1] Probably the intelligence was communicated by signal-telegraph to the King,[2] who may have at once summoned Hardy from Portisham only 7 miles away. Pitt's Government at once determined either to blockade the enemy's ships in Cadiz effectually or to compel them to give battle the moment they came out. Nelson, and nobody else, could strike the longed-for blow. By the 6th September, three days after his visit to Gloucester Lodge, Hardy is back at Portsmouth getting the *Victory* ready for the admiral's arrival. On that day he writes to Dorchester:

PORTSMOUTH, *Septr 6th*, 1805.

DEAR MANFIELD,

I arrived at Portsmouth at 6 o'clock on Wednesday therefore too late to save the Post on that day.

---

[1] See Mahan, vol. ii., p. 328 ; Newbolt, p. 25.

[2] The telegraph of 1805 was an elaborate arrangement of slabs of wood encased in a framework on the principle of a Venetian blind, so that each slab could be moved at will. Corresponding machines on various eminences connected London with the principal naval ports. In view of the constant visits of the Royal Family to Weymouth, that place had been included in this primitive system of signalling.

Yesterday I was on board the *Victory* and it Blew so fresh I could not get on shore time enough to save post. As Lord Nelson is expected on Saturday, I thought it not worth going to Town therefore wait patiently his arrival. I continue to mend as fast as can be expected, and my friends here are surprised to see me look so much better in so short a time. I find by a letter from our Friend Davison[1] that *Orion* (a Dutchman)[2] will be paid on Sunday I hope to Touch £2000 at least.

I have a small parcel I wish to send Mary Masterman but I fear sending it by the Cross Post. It may be lost therefore Shall put it in the hands of Mr Thompson to have sent the first opportunity.

I remain in haste

Dear Manfield

Yours Affectionately

T. M. HARDY.

I think we shall sail Monday next.

A week later he again writes :—

PORTSMOUTH, *Septr* 13*th*, 1805.

DEAR MANFIELD,

The Letters Parcel &c all came safe to hand for which accept my best thanks. The *Victory* is gone to St Hellens and his Lordship is expected tomorrow morning at 9 o'clock of course we sail the same Day. I continue to mend as fast as can be expected and am in hopes that the Salt Air will again agree with me. My Cousin Budden has been to see me and dines here toDay. Roberts of Burton

---

[1] Alexander Davison, clothing contractor to the Army. One of Nelson's closest friends, and a very frequent correspondent. He was the donor of the Nile medals, and acted as agent for the prizes taken at that battle. He caused a reliquary to be made of the eighty-four guineas found in Nelson's purse after Trafalgar, for the reception of a lock of Nelson's hair in a glass tube. This has recently been sold in London.

[2] Prize-money due for the capture of the Dutch ship *Orion*.

has brought his Son who seems a fine lad. He is to be in the Pursing line.[1]

Give my Duty to My Aunt and love to Catherine and Mary.

I remain, Dear Manfield,

Yours Affectionately,

T. M. HARDY.

On the following day, as Hardy expected, Lord Nelson arrived and hoisted his flag. They did not sail till the 15th September, and on the 29th of that month (Lord Nelson's forty-sixth birthday) joined the English fleet off Cadiz. On the 9th October, Nelson had issued his famous memorandum as to the order of sailing being that of the order of battle.[2] Hardy evidently realised that the supreme moment they had so long looked forward to was now near. The letter he wrote home a few days after the informal conferences of the British commanders on board the *Victory*, breathes the old spirit of affection and solicitude for others. There was no blinking the gravity of the situation.

"VICTORY," OFF CADIZ,
Octr 13*th*, 1805.

DEAR MANFIELD,

I enclose you a Codicil to my Will but trust it will not be opened by my relations for many a year. We are in daily expectation of the combined Fleet coming out but I fear they will think us too strong for them.

[1] This certainly refers to Richard Francis Roberts, the eldest son of Richard Roberts of Burton Bradstock, and therefore the nephew of Hardy's first captain, Francis Roberts. He had probably already had some years' experience in the merchant service. According to the archives of the Public Record Office, he volunteered as an A.B. in the *Victory* on the 10th September 1805, at the age of 20. Hardy promoted him to the rank of Midshipman two days before the battle of Trafalgar, and he finally quitted the Navy from the *Gannet* fifteen months later (December 8th, 1806).

[2] See Mahan, vol. ii., p. 340 *et seq.*

I am happy to say that my leg is getting much better and the Surgeon is in hopes of making a good Job of it and I am of the same way of thinking. I saw Mr Plow man yesterday. He is very well and says he has not heard from home for nearly twelve months, tho' he writes every opportunity. He appears to be a very good young man and his Captain speaks very handsomely of him. Perhaps it would be satisfactory to Colonel Bingham to hear that his son John is made a lieutenant into the *Prince* (Capt Grindall) but he is at Gibraltar in the *Canopus* and is not yet acquainted with his good fortune. I shall not write to his Father on the subject tho' I have assisted in the promotion of his son. I am sorry to say that my good friend Sutton late of the *Amphion* is so unwell that he is invalided and is returning to England by the same conveyance as takes this (the *Prince of Wales*) I hope poor Sir Robert Calder will get well over that unfortunate business. I heard from Martha the other day and shall write the next opportunity. I have seen John Browne's friend in the *Prince,* Mr Ferris and will be useful to him if it lays in my power.

With every good wish for you all

I remain Dear Manfield

Yours affectionately

T. M. HARDY.

In the "remark-book" of Midshipman Roberts,[1] one finds the following entries as to what occurred on board the *Victory* during the days immediately preceding the battle:—

"*Saturday 19th October.*—At 10 A.M. a ship was discovered to leeward in a calm or but very little wind

[1] This book is now in possession of his kinswoman, Miss M. M. Roberts of Burton (see Preface). It seems probable from its contents that "young Roberts," evidently a man of superior education, although rated first as A.B. and afterwards as midshipman, was employed as Captain's Clerk or in some similar capacity.

(supposed to be a frigate), firing minute guns and making signals, but could not make out what they were.

"At 10.30 observed her signal, which communicated that the combined fleets were coming out of Cadiz. The signal was immediately made by the Commander-in-Chief, and two guns fired to leeward for a general chase. Cadiz then bore of the fleet S. 88 E. dist. 16 leagues. Every ship immediately made all sail and chased accordingly, with very little wind which was from the westward.

"At 11.30 another signal was repeated to us from the frigate (repeated to her by ships which were stationed for that purpose betwixt Cadiz and the fleet) that the enemy were out and had been three hours.

"Employed on board the *Victory* getting up a thousand shot on each deck, stowing away chests, etc. etc., clearing for action.

"At 12 P.M. a little more wind, nothing particular going on but preparing for action.

"At 12.30 another signal was repeated to us from the frigate, communicating that the enemy were still at sea, steering S.S.E. The *Defence* made the signal which was repeated to us, saying that she was within 4 miles of the Enemy's fleet.

"In the evening a little breeze from the southward, going 3 or 4 knot; made sail all the night. Sunday morning at daylight the fleet were upon the point of entering the Gut with a fine breeze, when we observed a frigate to leeward firing guns and making signals which was repeated to us by the *Royal Sovereign*, that the enemy's fleet were north. The Commander-in-Chief made the signal immediately to tack and shorten sail.

"At 9 A.M. we lay too with a fresh breeze. Enemy's fleet steering for Cadiz. *Victory* tellegraphed to the *Africa* to paint the hoops of her masts yellow.

"At 12 part of the Enemy's fleet anchored off Cadiz (or in Cadiz, which I am not positive of). The remaining 9 sail did not anchor.

" At 1 P.M. filled and made sail to the westward.

" At 4 the enemy put again to sea steering N.E. ; made sail and stood towards them. Hazy weather with a fresh breeze from the S.W., dist. from Cadiz 7 or 8 leagues. *Euryalus* tellegraphed 'that the Enemy appeared determined to push to the westward.' *Victory* tellegraphed 'I depend on your keeping sight of the Enemy during the night.' The whole of the Enemy's [Ships] were at this time at sea.

" At 7.30 saw two of the enemy's ships from the deck on our starboard bow. Fresh breezes and lightening.

" *Sunday Evening.*—Our look out ships showed their blue lights and sky rockets signifying that they were still in sight of the Enemy. English fleet to windward of the Enemy.

" At 8.40 wore and stood away from them. Wind W.N.W. drawing them off from Cadiz as much as possible, they continuing on the same tack in our wake. Our lookout ships continued showing their blue lights, rockets, and firing guns (making signals of the Enemy's position in the night).

" *Monday morning.*—At daylight saw the Enemy's fleet in line of battle laying too the leeward. Dist. 10 or 11 miles, consisting of 33 sail of the line, 5 frigates, 2 brigs. A very fine morning, but little wind. Enemy's fleet bearing E. by S. extending from N.N.E. to S.W.W. The signal was made by the Commander-in-Chief to bear up, and set all sails, even steering sails. English fleet in two lines consisting of 27 sail of the line and frigates schooner and cutter. *Victory* Commander-in-Chief leading the weather line and *Royal Sovereign* second in command leading the lee line cleared away everything for action.

" At 10 A.M.—Beat to quarters.

" At 11.—Dinner and grog.

" *Victory* telegraphed *General* 'England expects that every man will do his duty.'

" At 11-30.—*Victory* telegraphed to *Royal Sovereign* 'If

the *Tonnant* cannot close, order other ships between,' when the *Mars* took her place in the line, and the other ships closed. *Royal Sovereign* tellegraphed to the *Victory* ' The enemy's Chief appears to command in a frigate.' "

Roberts here breaks off his own narrative with the words, " The remainder of this was taken from the *Victory's log.*"

It is not proposed to tell once again the now familiar story of the great naval battle of the 21st October 1805. All writers on the subject are in agreement as to Hardy's honourable share in the laurels won, and the occurrences preceding and following the death-wound of Nelson in which he, as captain of the *Victory*, played an important part. These incidents may be conveniently summarised as follows :—

Soon after the fighting began, Nelson and Hardy were walking on the deck of the *Victory* when flying splinters passed between them, cutting Hardy's left foot, and taking off the buckle of his shoe.[1]   " This is too warm work, Hardy, to last long," said Nelson. And so the two friends continued on deck in the thick of the fight, Nelson conspicuous with his four stars, an object for the marksmen in the enemy's rigging. At about half-past one, Nelson turned suddenly as he walked, and before Hardy could reach him, fell on his knees and hand. Hardy bent over him in tender inquiry. " They have done for me at last, Hardy," said Nelson. " I hope not," answered Hardy. " Yes," replied the other, " my backbone is shot through." A sergeant-major of marines and two seamen, at Hardy's orders, carried him below into the cockpit of the *Victory*, and thither the flag-captain came in the intervals of the crisis of the fight, to tell his admiral how the fortunes of the day inclined. It is significant to note that one of Nelson's chief anxieties as he lay dying was as to how Captain Hardy

[1] *Vide illustration.* The broken buckle is still treasured by Mrs. J. C. Thynne, Sir T. M. Hardy's descendant.

WATCH worn at Trafalgar.

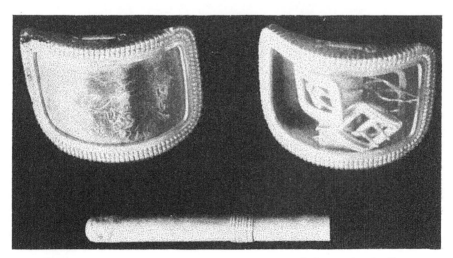

SHOEBUCKLES, one of which was damaged by a Splinter of a Shell at
the Battle of Trafalgar.
PENCIL CASE used on board the *Victory*.

[*To face page* 142.

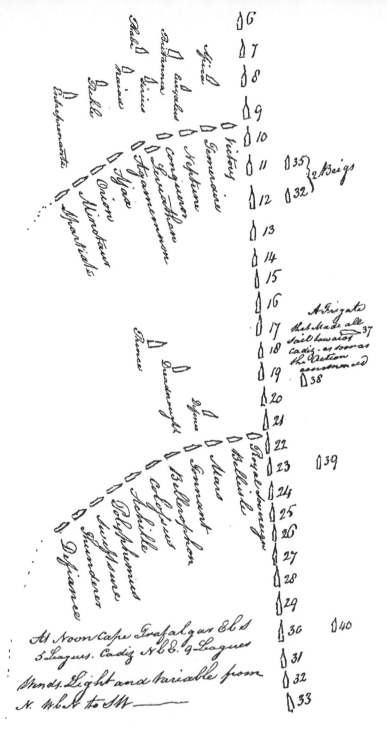

SKETCH-PLAN of the Battle of Trafalgar from the "Remark-Book" of
R. F. Roberts, Midshipman on board the *Victory*.

[To face page 143.

fared, and when his flag-captain came to report the progress of the fight, and to say that twelve of the enemy had struck, Nelson said, "I hope none of our ships have struck." "I am a dead man, Hardy, I am going fast, it will be all over with me soon. Pray let my dear Lady Hamilton have my hair," and Hardy went to his post on deck again. When he returned to the dying hero he was able to report that 14 or 15 ships had struck, Nelson replied, "That is well, but I bargained for 20." And then Nelson went on to say, "Anchor, Hardy, Anchor," and when Hardy asked whether Collingwood ought not to make the necessary signal, he answered, "Not while I live, Hardy. No, do you anchor, Hardy; if I live I'll anchor." As Hardy left to return on deck, the final parting between him and Nelson, which was touching in the extreme, took place. "Don't throw me overboard, Hardy," said Nelson; "take care of my dear Lady Hamilton, Hardy, take care of poor Lady Hamilton. Kiss me, Hardy." The flag-captain kissed him, and Nelson murmured, "Now I am satisfied. Thank God I have done my duty." Then Hardy, taking one last look at his friend, bent over and kissed his forehead. Nelson asked who it was, and on hearing that it was Hardy, said, "God bless you, Hardy," and the two friends parted for the last time. The scene is realistic, the pathos of that parting is something too deep to be described by words.

In the course of his lengthy extract from the log-book of the *Victory*, Roberts interpolates the words, "This is incorrect," after the much-quoted phrase, "Partial firing continued until 4.30, when a victory having been reported to Lord Nelson, K.B., he died of his wound."[1]

For an entire week Hardy had no leisure to take up a pen. He had no rest day or night. The *Victory*, with

---

[1] Roberts probably means that firing continued some time after 4.30 P.M. In his remark-book is a roughly drawn but perfectly comprehensible diagram of the order of battle, which is now reproduced.

Nelson's body on board, was riding out the gale, which sprang up as soon as the last shot had been fired. It was not till the 27th October that Hardy was able to give his friends at home the following modest account of the greatest sea-battle of naval history.

"VICTORY," OFF CADIZ,
Octr 27th, 1805.

DEAR MANFIELD,

We have on the 21st Inst obtained a most Glorious Victory over the Combined Fleets, but it has cost the Country a Life that no Money can replace, and one for whose Death I shall for ever mourn. Our Dear and ever to be lamented Lord fell in the Action and as it fell to our lot to lead the Fleet into Action, our loss has been rather great (54 killed and 80 wounded), however I have come off unhurt. The weather ever since the Action has been so bad that we have had some Difficulty to save our shattered ship, and have had no communication with any of the Fleet. I realy cannot say the exact number of ships taken but twelve we are certain of, tho' I much fear many of them are since lost and one or two taken into Cadiz as the gale for thease last 5 Days has not ceased blowing directly on that shore. Thos Bartlett is well and has written by this conveyance. It will also be satisfactory for Sam Clark (of Possum) to know that his son is well. The *Victory* is in so nude a state that she must be ordered to England, at any rate you will soon see me and I am determined to remain on shore some months. You will suppose my mind is not very easy and I am sure you will excuse this hasty scrall. We are this moment ordered to Gibraltar by Telegraph and I have only time to say that in hopes of seeing you soon,

I remain, with good wishes for all,
Dear Manfield,
Ever yours most Affectionately,
T. M. HARDY.

Midshipman Roberts, Hardy's Dorset compatriot, had meanwhile contrived to add the following notes to his narrative of what happened after Trafalgar :—

" *Tuesday October 22nd.*—Fresh breezes and cloudy. Employed knotting and splicing the fore and main rigging, etc. Cape Trafalgar bore S.E. 2 E. dist. 11 leagues.

" *Wednesday 23rd*—Employed clearing the wreck of the mizen mast. Strong gales and heavy squalls from the westward. Sounded in 70 fms. Cadiz bore E. by S. dist. 5 leagues. Mustered the ships company, carpenters employed stopping the shot holes. H.M.S. *Polyphemus* took us in tow. The high land of Rota bore E. b. S. 5 or 6 leagues. Winds this day S. b. W. and S.

" *Thursday 24th.* — Fresh breezes and squally. Employed setting up the fore rigging. Got up a Jury fore top mast and a main top gall. yard for a fore top sail yard, and bent the mizen top sail for a fore top sail. Sounded in 60 fm. Observed a ship on fire astern. At 9.45 she blew up. Strong gales and squally with rain at intervals. Winds this day S.W. and S. b. W.

" *Friday 25th.*—Strong gales and squally with rain. At 4.15 P.M. heavy squalls. At 5.10 carried away the main yard. Split the main top sail and main sail all to pieces. Cleared away the wreck, sounded every hour with 100 fm. no bottom. *Polyphemus* increased her distance from us supposing the hawser had parted. Hard gales and a heavy swell from the W.S.W.

" At daylight saw the *Royal Sovereign* in the N.E. with signal 314 flying, made the signal to the *Polyphemus* with the *Royal Sovereign* pendts. At 7 wore ship. At 8 more moderate. Heavy squalls at intervals. *Africa*, N.N.E. with the signal of distress, all her masts being gone. At noon, moderate breezes and squally, heavy swell from the W.S.W. Several sails in sight around us. Winds S.W. b. W. and W.S.W.

" *Saturday 26th.*—Fresh breezes and hazy. Employed

rigging the jury main yard and fitting a main top sail yard. *Neptune* took us in tow. Bent the main sail. Sounded in 50 fm. Mud. Saw the land bearing E.b.N. p. compass. Fleet E.S.E. Winds this day W.S.W. & W.

"*Sunday 27th.*—Moderate and hazy. Fleet in sight E.N.E. At 9.40 carried away the tow rope. Tried for soundings every hour; no bottom. Saw the land over Conil Bay E.S.E. Squally with rain. *Neptune* carried away her fore top mast. Made and shortened sail occassionally. At noon Cape Trafalgar bore N.E. 2 E. dist. 7 miles. Sounded in 29 fm. Winds this day W. by S. and W.S.W.

"*Monday 28th.*—Fresh breezes and cloudy. Steering for Gibraltar. At 7, anchored in Rosia Bay, Gibraltar. Found lying here H.M. Ships *Prince, Tonnant, Thunderer, Revenge, Colossus*, and several men of war. Rear-Adml. Knight's flag flying on board the *Endymion. St Juan* Spanish prize at anchor here. Departed this life, Mr A. Palmer, Mid., of his wounds."

It was not till five weeks later that the *Victory* reached St Helens. Hardy said to Capt. Parker of the *Amazon*, who was one of the first to come on board : " Parker, you and Capel have often talked of your attacking a French line - of - battle ship with two frigates. Now, after what I have seen at Trafalgar, I am satisfied it would be mere folly, and ought never to succeed."[1] The news of the arrival of the *Victory* was thus conveyed to Mr Manfield by Hardy's Portsmouth friend, Mr Thompson.

PORTSEA, *4th December* 1805.

DEAR SIR,

It is with infinite pleasure I communicate to you the safe arrival of the *Victory* at St Helens this Morning she cannot get further to Day it being a Lee Wind and Tide. I could not learn at 3 o'clock that any

---

[1] *Life of Admiral Sir William Parker*, by Rear-Admiral Augustus Phillimore ; London, Harrison, 1876, vol. i., p. 308.

Capt. Ha.
Action off

Octr 27, 1805

Dear Mansfield

We have on the 21st inst
obtained a most Glorious Victory of
over the Combined Fleets but it
has cost the Country a life that no
Money can replace and for whom death
Sorrow in vain place and for whom death
would for ever hymn our Dear
Gallant ... lamented Lord fell in
and over it the lamented Lord fell in
the action), as it fell to our lot to lead
the Fleet into action our loss has been
rather severe / 54 killed and 612 wounded)
Remember I have come off unhurt the
... immense the Action has been so
made that our loss has more de officially
to save

[Nicolas pp. 146-47.]

our Railways (this end) have no determine) to remain in some new
communication with any of the sub-Divisions — You will continue to
greatly cannot say the slow ... members is not very easy and) I am
... rather but twelve ... are within your will of ... this reply
of the) ... from many of them are ... thinner ... of ...

... as the guide for these and
5-6 days the most careful ... time ... to say that this ...
... to that them. Mrs. Bartlett ...
is mild and) has written by this ... woman.

... It interests ... satisfactory
... from Clark (of Clapham) to them
that this has ... the history
... in so much a ... that the most
... ordered) to England) it very much

I am ... field
every yours most ...

27ᵗʰ Octᵃ 1805.

...ʳ Hardy—after the
...ᵉⁿ off Trafalgar —

RETU

Boat is yet from her,
worthy Friend to Mo
a most fatiguing and
and the loss of his mo
distressing sight to n
half Mast on the mela
of someones writing a
    With sincere Res
family and all around

    You will of cour-
the Family.

ᵗ The following note,
7th December 1883, is a
possession of Earl Nelso

    "This chair is the las
was given by the Capt
father, Anson Thompso
Isabella Thompson, a
Trafalgar, and taken to
After various removals it
that my aunt did twit Ca
and gave her the one he
her, and with a nautical
*was not the Admiral's ch
broken in clearing the sh*
is to be given at my dece
Lord Nelson has added,
the matching, the coveri
from the *Victory* cabin, a
on the right arm of the c

ENGLAND   14?

God to meet my good an
he must have experience
y time of it since the Actio
nd gallant Friend. It is
: Ships Flags and Pendan
casion; you may be assure
orrow.
ourself Mrs Manfield an
ain,
nost truly,
    GEO. A. THOMPSON ¹

icate the Contents of this

enry Thompson of Andover
lmiral Nelson's chair now in t
r House near Salisbury:—

:eat Lord Nelson ever sat in.
M. Hardy (to whom my gra
a friend in his youth) to my an
it of the *Victory* in 1805,
er's house in Chapel Row, Port
by my aunt to me. I would
that he kept the Admiral's cl
f, upon which Sir Thomas assu
ed it, that '*he'd be d——d if*
:llow, in which he himself sat,
' It has never been repaired,
resent Earl Nelson and his he
further proof of its authentici
of the sofa I already posse
e is a soft place covered with
tump of his arm to rest on."

27ᵗʰ Octᵃ 1805.

day after the

Trafalgar —

IPLE...

Dorchester

Dorset

Boat is yet from her.   I hope in God to meet my good and worthy Friend to Morrow well, he must have experienced a most fatiguing and melancholy time of it since the Action and the loss of his most brave and gallant Friend.   It is a distressing sight to now see the Ships Flags and Pendants half Mast on the melancholly occasion ; you may be assured of someones writing again to Morrow.

With sincere Respect for yourself Mrs Manfield and family and all around you I remain,

Yours most truly,

GEO. A. THOMPSON.[1]

You will of course Communicate the Contents of this to the Family.

[1] The following note, written by Henry Thompson of Andover on 7th December 1883, is attached to Admiral Nelson's chair now in the possession of Earl Nelson at Trafalgar House near Salisbury :

"This chair is the last chair the great Lord Nelson ever sat in.   It was given by the Captain Thomas M. Hardy (to whom my grandfather, Anson Thompson, had been a friend in his youth) to my aunt, Isabella Thompson, and landed out of the *Victory* in 1805, after Trafalgar, and taken to my grandfather's house in Chapel Row, Portsea. After various removals it was given by my aunt to me.   I would add that my aunt did twit Captain Hardy that he kept the Admiral's chair and gave her the one he used himself, upon which Sir Thomas assured her, and with a nautical oath confirmed it, that '*he'd be d——d if that was not the Admiral's chair, and its fellow, in which he himself sat, was broken in clearing the ship for action.*'   It has never been repaired, but is to be given at my decease to the present Earl Nelson and his heirs." Lord Nelson has added, "*N.B.*—A further proof of its authenticity is the matching, the covering, and legs of the sofa I already possessed from the *Victory* cabin, and also there is a soft place covered with silk on the right arm of the chair for the stump of his arm to rest on."

CHAPTER XV

AFTER TRAFALGAR [1806-1816]

THE moral effect of Trafalgar throughout England was very great. On the Dorset littoral it can only be described as tremendous. For eight weary years the word invasion had been on everyone's lips, for it was very generally thought (on shore at any rate) that Bonaparte would in all probability endeavour to effect a landing at some point between St Alban's Head and Thorncombe Beacon. Between 1797 and 1805, the staple topic of conversation had been of wars and rumours of wars; there had been constant marching and counter-marching of Yeomanry and Militia; elaborate plans of supply in case of emergency had been frequently distributed amongst the farmers, and, as has already been mentioned, a chain of beacon-signals had been planned on the summits of all the highest cliffs and hills.

It was then (and for years afterwards) that Dorset nursemaids overawed their refractory charges with the refrain :—

> " Baby, baby, naughty baby,
>   Hush, you squalling thing, I say ;
> Hush your squalling, or it may be
>   Bonaparte will pass this way.
>
> Baby, baby, he's a giant,
>   Tall and black as Rouen steeple ;
> And he dines and sups, rely on't,
>   Every day on naughty people.
>
> Baby, Baby, he will hear you
>   As he passes by the house,
> And he, limb from limb, will tear you
>   Just as pussy tears a mouse."

By a felicitous coincidence it has fallen to the lot of another Thomas Hardy (like the captain of the *Victory*, a man of Dorset), whose vivid pen-pictures of Wessex life have, during the past thirty years, been read and admired by millions on either side of the Atlantic, to describe in soul-stirring verse the condition of the country he loves so well in the dark time of the Great War. Captain Hardy, as might be expected, figures prominently in *The Dynasts*.[1] While Nelson lay wounded in the cockpit of the *Victory*, Captain Hardy is made to say in response to Nelson's query, "What are you thinking that you speak no word?"

> "Thoughts all confused my lord—their needs on deck,
> Your own sad state, and your unrivalled past,
> Mixed up with flashes of old things afar—
> Old childish things at home down Wessex way,
> In the snug village under Blackdon Hill
> Where I was born. The tumbling stream, the garden,
> The placid look of the grey dial there,
> Marking unconsciously this bloody hour.
> And the red apples of my father's trees
> Just now full ripe."

In the thick of the fighting on board the *Victory*, Hardy's mind doubtless went back to "Possum," for he knew full well that his brother Joseph had charge of the beacon on Blagdon Hill, which he had so often gazed at when going up or down channel. With Hardy's letter describing Trafalgar, was tied up the following memorandum :—

To Mr Joseph Hardy,
Portisham.

June 23rd, 1804.

Sir,
       I am directed by Lord Dorchester to desire that you will without delay, send me an account of the whole expense of erecting, and also watching the beacon

---

[1] *The Dynasts*, a drama of the Napoleonic Wars, by Thomas Hardy, part i. London : Macmillan & Co., 1904.

on Blagdon Hill from the beginning to the present time according to the form below, in order that the same may be discharged forthwith.

(Signed) EDWARD BOSWELL,

Clerk to the Lieutenancy.

May 2nd, 1804.—Received of Mr Hardy £1, 16s. for attending to the beacon four weeks at 9s. a week.

WILLIAM BOYT X his mark.

It would be curious to learn if Thomas Hardy, the Poet, was aware of the existence of honest William Boyt, who could only make his mark, although his family possibly vied in antiquity with that of the Turbervilles of Bere Regis, when he planned the following graphic scene as taking place on one of the neighbouring heights :—

First old man.—" Now Jems Purchess once more mark my words. Black'on is the point we've to watch, and not Kingsbere ; and I'll explain for why. If he do land anywhere here about 'twill be inside Deadman's Bay and the signal will straightway come from Black'on.[1] . . . The words of my Lord Lieutenant was whenever you see Kingsbere Hill beacon fired to the eastward or Black'on to the westward light up and keep your second fire burning for two hours. Was that our documents or was it not ? "

[1] The following contemporary letter throws considerable light on the organisation of these Dorset beacons in and before 1805. Lord Dorchester, writing to Henry Bankes of Kingston Lacy, 12th October 1803, says :—" I beg of you that you will give directions for an assemblage of faggots, furze, and other fuel, also of straw to be stacked and piled on the summit of Badbury Rings so as the whole may take fire instantly, and the fire may be maintained for two hours. It is to be fired whenever the beacon of St Catharine's is fired to the eastward, or whenever the Lytchett or Woodbury Hill beacons are fired to the westward ; but it is not to be fired from any demonstrations of any coast signals." *The Story of Corfe Castle,* by the Right Hon. George Bankes, M.P., p. 278. London : John Murray, 1853.

Second old man.—" I don't gainsay it. And so I keep my eye on Kingsbere because that's most likely o' the two says I."

In the interval of the news of Trafalgar reaching England and the arrival of Nelson's remains at Portsmouth, few of those who had taken part in the battle were as much talked of as Hardy. The following letter, written within a fortnight of the victory becoming known, speaks for itself:—

MR EDITOR,

In no great action in this or any preceding war has the Captain of the Comm^r-in-Chief's Ship been forgotten, when the honours of our Sovereign have deservedly been conferred on the Flag Officers of the Victorious Fleet. The public are anxiously expecting that the brave Captⁿ Hardy, who was the immortal Nelson's Captain, and indeed he may be called the Captain of the Fleet, will not be forgotten, and will "receive soon the honours due to his gallantry." England expected that he would do his duty, and "he has done so."

I am, Sir,

Your humble Servt,

A FRIEND TO THE VALIANT,

AND A CONSTANT READER.

London, *Nov. 19th*, 1805.[1]

On the 8th January 1806, the day before the final consignment of Nelson's "honoured remains" to their last resting-place in St Paul's, Sir Isaac Heard, Garter King of Arms, confirmed to Thomas Masterman Hardy and his heirs the ancient "coat" of the Jersey Hardys, with a difference of colour and the substitution of the heads of dragons instead of "wyverns."[2] On the next day Hardy, carrying

[1] *Naval Chronicle*, vol. xiv. (1805), p. 383.
[2] See Appendix, p. 287.

"the banner of emblems"[1] just before the members of the Nelson family, was the observed of all observers, in the greatest funeral pageant which London had witnessed for centuries.

On the 28th January, Hardy received, with the rest of the Trafalgar officers, the vote of thanks awarded them by both Houses of Parliament, and only two days later he was further honoured with the presentation of the freedom of the City of London, accompanied by a sword of the value of one hundred guineas. The civic address is now amongst the Hardy relics at Portisham. A month later (4th February) Hardy was created a baronet. The patent, a very formidable document indeed, with the Great Seal pendant, is still preserved at Portisham. The preamble to it runs as follows :—

"Know ye that we of our especial grace, certain knowledge and meer notion have erected, appointed & created our trusty and well-beloved Thomas Masterman Hardy, Esquire, Captain in our Royal Navy, a man eminent for family inheritance, estate and integrity of manners to and unto the dignity, state and degree of a Baronet."

About this time the last will and testament of Lord Nelson, with its various codicils, was proved. Amongst the numerous bequests to friends was the following :— "To my worthy friend, Captain Thomas Hardy, all my telescopes and sea-glasses and a hundred pounds." The shorter of these telescopes, employed by Nelson at Trafalgar, now belongs to Lady Helen MacGregor, the widow of Hardy's grandson. The longer, used by Nelson prior to the loss

---

[1] The nature of the flag borne by Hardy at St Paul's is seen in the accompanying contemporary illustration. This banner was evidently regarded as the one of the greatest importance, for the official ground plan shows Hardy's position in the ceremonial to have been just behind the chair of state occupied by the Prince Regent as principal mourner at the foot of Nelson's coffin.

LORD NELSON's

BANNER OF EMBLEMS,

*As carried in the Funeral Procession on the 9th of January, 1806
from the Admiralty to St Paul's.*

THE BANNER OF EMBLEMS.

[To face page 152.

of his arm, was given by Hardy in 1837 to his nephew by marriage, Lord Frederick Fitz Roy. Hardy also received from Lord Nelson's family a handsome memorial ring, with the initials "N. B." coroneted, and the word "Trafalgar" in enamel.

Hardy's war medals are in possession of Lady Helen MacGregor, by whose permission they are now reproduced for the first time. She also possesses the silver pencil-case he used to note the signals at Trafalgar, and which still shows the marks of his teeth, made while he held it in his mouth.

It was apparently Hardy's task to convey to Lady Hamilton the incomplete letter begun by Nelson before the commencement of the battle. It is endorsed in her handwriting—"This letter was found open on his desk and brought to Lady Hamilton by Captain Hardy." He also brought with him to Merton the coat worn by Nelson when he fell, and which afterwards, by the generosity of the late Prince Consort, became the property of the nation.

Sir T. M. Hardy's town residence was now at 16 Buckingham Street. Thence he writes to Manfield on the 10th March :—

16 BUCKINGHAM STREET,[1]
March 10th, 1806.

DEAR MANFIELD,

Thank you for your letter and its inclosure which I got this morning, my trunk also was received in due time. Mr John Browne left us yesterday and will give you an account of our proceedings. I have had so much to do since my arrival that I have not yet had an opportunity of paying my respects to Lord Dorchester, but intend calling tomorrow, if possible. I have not yet seen Mr Guy nor shall I be in a great hurry. I did not forget to speak to Miss Crone and I think it all right.

---

[1] As this house still stands, the attention of the London County Council is respectfully called to it as a fitting site for the erection of a commemorative tablet.

Prosser of Charing Cross by my side and talks so fast that I can only say God bless you all.

T. M. HARDY.

'A few days later he writes :—

16 BUCKINGHAM STREET,
March 20th, 1806.

DEAR MANFIELD,

      Mr Nayler wants to know who was the Father of My Grand Mother Hardy, of course my Aunt can tell and then I believe the Pedigree will be finally settled, at least I hope so. My Friend Travers[1] has breakfasted with me almost every morning since his arrival in Town, and is, I assure you, in very high spirits. It is almost feared that Digby will not stand his ground as he has not arrived in Town according to promise. I have had an interview with Mr Grey and conclude I am soon to be employed, I dine with him next Wednesday. I have called three times at Lord Dorchester's, and he has always been out in his Carriage, therefore I conclude he is much better. Tell Jos when you see him that his Plows, &c., left London by Russel's Waggon on Feby 22nd, therefore I conclude they are save arrived at Dorchester. I have sent, directed to you, a small Clock for them at Possum. Bridge and Rundell has promised to send the Watches I took from Lulworth to their proper owners in a few days.

    I hopes of seeing you soon in this part of the World, I remain with Duty to my Aunt and Love to Catherine and Mary,

Dear Manfield,

Yours affectionately,

T. M. HARDY.

The Money is already for Jos.

---

[1] Richard Travers of Loders (see ante).

MEDAL to Celebrate the Victory of the Nile.

MEDAL to Celebrate the Victory of Trafalgar.

The Trafalgar medal is of pure gold, $1\frac{7}{8}$ inches in diameter, and covered with glass. It was suspended from a gold bar $1\frac{5}{8}$ inches wide by a white ribbon edged with navy blue. On the reverse is a figure of Britannia, standing on the prow of a galley; her shield bearing the Union Jack is behind her; her right foot rests on a helmet, while a winged Victory crowns her with a wreath. The inscription on the obverse reads:—"Thomas Masterman Hardy, Esquire, Captain of H.M.S. *Victory* on the 21st October MDCCCV. The combined Fleets of France, Spain, and England."

Hardy had already received a very splendid gold medal on account of the Nile, now also in the possession of Lady Helen MacGregor. It is 2 inches in diameter, and is covered with glass on either side. On one side are engraved two ships of the line in dead gold relief, with the sun setting on the horizon. Round the upper part, in block capitals, runs the words:

ALMIGHTY GOD HAS BLESSED HIS MAJESTY'S ARMS

below the sea, in two straight lines,

VICTORY OF THE NILE
AUGUST 1, 1798.

The other side has a figure of Britannia in relief, standing on a rock, holding out in her right hand an olive branch, and leaning her left arm on an oval shield, with bust portrait of Nelson in further relief, and round the shield is the legend:—

EUROPE'S HOPE AND BRITAIN'S GLORY.

Above the figure, also in relief, are the words:

Hardy's Dorset friends were now desirous that he should enter the House of Commons, and he accordingly offered himself as a candidate for Weymouth, where he had seen the King the year before, and which was then described as one constituency "with two names (Weymouth and Melcombe Regis) sending four members to Parliament." Notwithstanding the heroic exertions of Mr Manfield and others, and despite all the glamour of Trafalgar, Hardy was seventh on the poll.   In the following year he again entered the lists, but with no better results.

On the 27th March Hardy became Captain of the *Sampson*, and a few weeks later of the *Triumph* (15th May). Meanwhile, he wrote the following letter to his brother :—

PLYMOUTH DOCK,
May 12th, 1806.

DEAR JOS,

I suppose before you get this you will see by the papers of my appointment to the *Triumph*, so that I trust my friends will not allow that I was not in the wrong to accept the *Sampson*.

We sail in a few days under the Command of Sir Richd Strachan,[1] I believe, off the Western Islands.   If I had been offered my choice of any Ship in the Navy, I should have taken the Ship I now have, and had they given me my choice of a Cruise, I should have chosen that which we are now going on, therefore, you will see I, as usual, fall on my Legs.   As we are to sail so very soon, you may suppose I have not much time to spare, therefore, in hast, I remain, with Love to all,

Dear Jos
Yours Affectionately,
T. M. HARDY.

The object of Sir Richard Strahan's expedition, in which Hardy was now to take part, was the pursuit of Admiral Willaumez, who was reported to have sailed for American

---

[1] Admiral Sir Richard Strachan, Bart. (born 1760, died 1828).

waters. A fairly full account of the movements of the squadron will be found in the life of the late Admiral Sir William Hargood, who was then captain of the *Bellisle*.[1] Strahan's force consisted of seven ships of the line, two frigates, and a brig. After cruising for some time between the Cape de Verde Islands and the Azores, the news reached Strahan at Funchal, on the 20th July 1806, that Willaumez was in the West Indies. They at once started in pursuit, but encountered some days later (18th August) a terrible hurricane, in which both fleets experienced the most serious damage, and a fight became impossible. Hardy's trusty weather-glass warned him of the coming storm, and Hargood ascribes his safety to having followed Hardy's example in shortening sail, being aware, as his biographer tells us, of the superior quality of Hardy's marine barometer. The Admiral, however, in his eagerness to come up with the enemy, continued to fly the signal "make more sail," and his vessel, the *Cæsar*, being dismasted in the gale, his flag was transferred to Hardy's ship the *Triumph*.

Sometime in the summer of the following year (1807), Hardy in the *Triumph* joined the squadron of Vice-Admiral Sir George Cranfield Berkeley, then in command of the North America station. From Chesapeake Bay he wrote the last letter ever addressed to his brother-in-law, Mr J. C. Manfield, who died on the 21st June 1808, at the early age of forty-six:

"TRIUMPH," CHESAPEAKE, AMERICA,
August 4th, 1807.

DEAR MANFIELD,

I am really at a loss to know the reason that I have not heard from you every Packet. Letters reach me from people who I am not anxious to hear from, but

[1] *A Memoir of Sir William Hargood*, by Joseph Allen, Esq., Greenwich. Printed for private circulation only, by Henry S. Richardson, 1841, pp. 158-165.

none from Dorsetshire except one from Richd Roberts some Months ago. I have written frequently to you I therefore conclude they must all have miscarried. I got a letter from Halford dated 1st of April he told me he had seen you a few Days before the date of that Letter. Our Blocade[1] has been rather tedious, and now to mend the matter the President of the United States of America has interdicted all of us and will not allow us the smallest sort of refreshment and I really begin to think that war with this Country is inevitable. You will have seen long before

[1] The "blocade" Hardy refers to, was that of a portion of the French Fleet shut up in Chesapeake Bay by the presence of the *Triumph* and her sister ships in these waters during the latter part of 1807 and the commencement of 1808. The following certificate, given by Hardy to Francis Roberts, speaks for itself:—

"These are to certify the Right Honble. the Lords Commissioners of the Admiralty that Mr Francis Roberts[2] served as midshipman from 1806 to 1811 on board his Majesty's ships *Triumph* and *Barfleur* under my command. He was promoted to the rank of lieutenant in 1811 for his good conduct by Admiral the Honble. Sir George Berkeley from the latter ship. During the time the *Triumph* was assisting to blocade a French squadron in the Chesapeak in 1807 Mr Roberts was entrusted with the command of the *Hamilton*, tender to the *Triumph*, where he was very active particularly after the affair of the *Leander* ["Say *Leopard*" in another hand written below], and the United States frigate *Chesapeak*, he with great perseverance got up to the town of Norfolk in a very dark night and made the result of the action known to Captain, now Vice-Admiral Douglas of H.M.S. *Bellona* then the senior officer in the *Chesapeak* who was on shore at that place. He received Captain Douglas on board the schooner before the account of the action was known at Norfolk and conveyed him to the *Bellona* in Chesapeak Bay.

Lieutenant Roberts is the nephew of the late Captain Roberts who died on board the *Success* in the West Indies early in the war. I consider him a very deserving officer and beg to recommend him to their Lordships' notice.

Given under my hand in London this 18th day of September 1830.

T. M. HARDY,
Rear Admiral."

[2] A younger brother of Richard Francis Roberts of the *Victory* (see *ante*).

you get this the affair that happened between the *Chesa-*
peake frigate and the *Leopard*.[1]   One would hardly suppose
that the Jonathans could be so blind to their own Interest,
but their Insolence is not to be borne with and they will I
suppose oblige us to take and destroy the whole of their
Trade.   It will be a mellancholly thing for me to increase
twenty or thirty thousand Pounds which I can easily do in
a fortnight.   I literally write this to tell you I am well and
in hopes of drawing a letter from you.   I shall be at
Halifax in October if you write by the Packet there is no
doubt of my getting it.   All the youngsters from Dorsetshire are well except young Dampier[2] who I think gets
worse every Day.   I wrote His Father on the subject a
long time ago but no answer.   I think If I had told him
that his Son had made a Thousand Pounds I should have
had an answer.   Give my Duty to my Aunt who I hope
continues as well as usual Love to Catherine the Young
Ladies and all Friends.   I remain

   Dear Manfield,

    Yours Affectionately,

      T. M. HARDY.

His projected visit to Halifax had important consequences, which he evidently did not foresee when he wrote
to Dorchester, for on the 17th November he there married
Miss Anne Louisa Emily Berkeley, the eldest daughter of
his chief,[3] who was, as might be expected, considerably his
junior.

[1] On the 22nd of June 1807, Captain S. P. Humphries of the *Leopard*
(fifty guns) asserted the right to search for deserters, by causing the
surrender of the American ship the *Chesapeake*, after an action of
ten minutes, because the latter refused to give up some British seaman, who had deserted to his ship.   This action caused much tension
between the two Governments, and was one of the causes which led
to the war which broke out five years later, 18th June 1812.

[2] The Dampiers were a very old Dorset family of Huguenot origin.
They possessed two residences in the Isle of Purbeck, Leeson House
in Langton, and Morton's House, Corfe Castle.

[3] Sir George Cranfield Berkeley, G.C.B., Admiral in the Royal Navy,

Lady Hardy has left behind her some amusing notes of their early married life. "We spent," she writes, "from December 1807 to April 1808 in that gloomy desolate bay (Chesapeake), not allowed to land, as the Americans were in such an exasperated state that they might have been very disagreeable. At last we were released, and I returned to Bermuda where my parents were." She often vividly described the incidents of those weary days to her grandson, Sir Evan MacGregor. During the whole winter there was no fire in the cabin, and the ship was kept perpetually ready for action; but she always stipulated with the Captain that should there be any fighting she was to come on deck and not remain below. She was a true Berkeley, whose courage was hereditary and traditional. She also proved a clever diplomatist. On her husband telling her she must never refuse to take wine with any particular officer, lest it might lead to quarrels, she accordingly quietly substituted a decanter of toast and water for the orthodox sherry, and so never shirked the ordeal thus imposed upon her.

At this point the Manfield correspondence ceases. He died 21st June 1808, and was buried in the Hardy vault, beneath the chancel of Portisham Church. Hardy, however, was not unmindful of his other Dorset friends. In the year of Mr Manfield's death he once more returned for a short time to England, and in September wrote to Mr Richard Roberts at Burton Bradstock, whose younger son Francis was now serving with him as midshipman, the following characteristic letter :—

"TRIUMPH," PORTSMOUTH,
Septr. 22d in the Evening
1808.

DEAR SIR,

It was not till this afternoon that I received your letter sent me by your son Frank owing (I believe) to

and some time Lord High Admiral of Portugal, born 1753, second son of Augustus, fourth Earl of Berkeley ; married, 1784, Emily Charlotte, daughter of Lord George Lennox. Died 25th February 1818.

his having mislaid it.   He now is in perfect health but you
may rely on it that he shall not be allowed to go aloft or
to do any duty that may in any degree indanger his health.
May I beg of you to give my best compliments to Admiral
and Mrs Ingram.   I request also you will give my best
regards to Mrs Roberts.

I remain, Dear Sir,

Yours very faithfully,

T. M. HARDY.

While cruising in lat. 47.3 and long. 4.25, during the
early days of 1809, Hardy captured the *Jonge Fanny*, galliot,
bound from Bordeaux to Bergen laden with good French
wine.   Young Francis Roberts was sent home with her in
command of the prize crew, he being rated as master's
mate.   The galliot, however, was caught in a storm, and
made shipwreck in Whitesand Bay on the 25th January.

Meanwhile Sir John Borlase Warren had relieved Sir
George Berkeley on the North America station, and the
latter, accompanied by Lady Berkeley, had returned
home on the *Leopard* flag-ship.   Admiral Berkeley had
already (December 1808) been appointed to the chief
command "on the coast of Portugal and in the Tagus";
on the 17th May 1809, Hardy became captain of the
Barfleur, and in her, with Lady Hardy on board, proceeded
to join his father-in-law in Portuguese waters.   On Hardy's
arrival the Admiral's flag was transferred to this ship, from
which the Captain thus writes to Burton :—

"BARFLEUR," TAGUS,
Septr 23*d*, 1809.

MY DEAR SIR,

Your letter of the 3d of August I found here
on my arrival at this Port, and mentioned its contence to
your son who is now so far recovered that he seems quite
equal to do his Duty and has declined accepting of your
offer.   Should a relaps take place and the surgeon

To face page 160.

THE GROVE," BURTON BRADSTOCK.
The Home o Francis Roberts Hardy's first Captain.

recommend it I shall most certainly advise his trying his native air, and he shall have leave of absence for that purpose but we have every reason to hope that he will do very well. I beg of you to offer my very best compliments to Admiral and Mrs Ingram and I shall be most happy to give him an account of his nephew's promotion which I hope is not far distant. Lady Hardy joins me in best compliments to Mrs Roberts and yourself.

I remain, Dear Sir,

Yours very sincerely,

T. M. HARDY.

RICHARD ROBFRTS, Esq.,
Burton, Bridport.

Hardy remained with Sir George Berkeley for about three years, receiving in 1810 the rank of Commodore in the Portuguese Navy.[1] On the retirement of Sir G. C. Berkeley from active service in the autumn of 1812, Hardy came with him to England, and on the 8th October received a commission as captain of the *Ramillies* (seventy-nine guns), and proceeded to reinforce the North America squadron, war having been declared against the United States, 10th June 1812. Nearly a year later he writes to his brother as follows ·—

"RAMILLIES," OFF BLOCK ISLAND,
NOT FAR FROM NEW YORK,
May 1st, 1813.

DEAR JOS,

We are cruising off this Island to prevent if possible the Sailing of the *United States* and *Macedonian*

[1] Under date September 1810, the *Naval Chronicle*, vol. xxv., p. 437, makes the following announcement :—

"Notice that the Portuguese Government had conferred on the Hon. Admiral Berkeley and Captain Sir Thomas Hardy, the former the rank of Commander-in-Chief, and the latter of a Chief of Division, in the Royal Armada of Portugal, and had recently doubled the pay attaching to those appointments."

Frigates they are both ready for sea and laying at New York; however I rather wish they would put to sea for the chance of our falling in with them.   We have been fortunate enough to take several prizes tho' not valuable, yet they will all turn to account, but I never reckon on Prize Money till I have received it.   As young Burgis is a constant correspondent with Sister Thresher I have no doubt but you will get all the News of the *Ramillies* from him ; at least much more than I can give you.   He is a very fine Boy and I have no doubt but he will turn out very well.   I hope Mr Crawford will get Prize Money sufficient to repay me, for his friends have not supplied him with Sixpence and literally he could not walk the Quarter Deck without my assistance and he really behaves so well that I continue to advance him Money at my own risk.   Fortunately for us Block Island has no Guns in it, therefore we get plenty of Water and Stock from it and we also get our Linen washed there.   The inhabitance are very much alarmed and of course they are most completely in our power, but as long as they supply us we shall be very civil to them.   I have not heard from any of you since I left England and my last letter from Louise[1] was Dated Jany 5th and we are quite out of the way of all News.   However I will dispense with that for the sake of some good Prizes, and there are two or three India Men expected which we are looking out very sharp for.   As it is possible Edward Bartlett might not hear from his Son, tell him that he is very well and goes on much to my satisfaction and Doctor Plowman is very well pleased with young Hodder.   My Steward had the misfortune a few Days ago (whilst loading a gun) to blow a piece of his left Arm off and I very much fear if he will ever get the better of it; he is a most excellent Servant and will be a very great loss to me.   I have heard nothing of poor Thos Bartlett but much fear that he died soon after we left Portsmouth for I think I never

---

[1] Lady Hardy.

saw any Creature look worse than he did the last time I saw him.

With best Love to all.   I remain,

My dear Jos,

Yours most Affectionately,

T. M. HARDY.

About two months later (25th June 1813), Hardy in the *Ramillies* was off New London in command of a squadron of ships of the line.   He captured an enemy's schooner making for that harbour, and the boarding officer reported her to be laden with provisions.   The crew, however, had escaped in the boats after planning a carefully-contrived arrangement of clock work and gunpowder, which they hoped would have destroyed the English ships.   Hardy was not to be taken in; he did not bring her close to the *Ramillies*, but ordered her to be secured alongside another prize, and sent a prize crew of thirteen men under Lieutenant Geddes to take possession.   They had no sooner got on board than an explosion took place, and the officer with ten of his men perished.

Another attempt to blow up the *Ramillies* a month later is interesting, from the fact that it shows that submarine warfare was contemplated by the Americans at a much earlier date than is generally supposed.   In July 1813, whilst lying at anchor off New London, the deck sentinel suddenly sang out, " Boat ahoy," on seeing an object rise to the surface like a porpoise a few feet astern of the ship. The thing immediately disappeared ; so the sentinel fired an alarm gun ; all hands were called to quarters ; the cable was cut and the ship got under weigh with all possible dispatch.   Once more the mysterious stranger rose to the surface, and before any guns could be turned on her, dived again and fastened herself on to the keel of the British ship, remaining there for half an hour, during which time a man within her succeeded in drilling a hole through the copper of the *Ramillies*, but whilst engaged in attaching a torpedo, the screw broke and the attempt failed. It turned out to be a diving boat "the invention of a gentleman living at Norwich, U.S.," who by means of paddles could propel himself in her under water at the rate of three miles an hour, ascending to the surface and descending at pleasure. Commodore Hardy thereupon withdrew his squadron from New London, and issued orders to his ships to keep under weigh the whole time instead of lying at anchor.[1]

On 7th July 1814, Hardy in the *Ramillies* with two transports, having on board the 102nd Regiment, joined with a land force under Lieut. Col. Pilkington, Adjutant-General, and proceeded up the Passamaquaddy Bay, anchoring off the town of East Port on Moose Island on the 11th, whence the following summons was sent to the officer commanding Fort Sullivan :—

> ON BOARD H.M.S. "RAMILLIES,"
> OFF MOOSE ISLAND, *July* 11.
>
> SIR,
>
> As we are perfectly apprised of the weakness of the fort and garrison under your command, and your inability to defend Moose Island against the ships and troops of his Britannic Majesty placed under our directions, we are induced from the humane consideration of avoiding the effusion of blood, and from a regard to you and the inhabitants of the island, to prevent, if in our power, the distresses and calamities which will befall them, in case of resistance. We, therefore, allow you five minutes, from the time this summons is delivered, to decide upon an answer.
>
> In the event of your not agreeing to capitulate, on liberal terms, we shall deeply lament being compelled to resort to those coercive measures which may cause destruc-

---

[1] *Gentlemen's Magazine*, 1813, ii., p. 285.

tion to the town of East Port, but which will ultimately insure us possession of the island.

T. M. HARDY,
Captain of H.M.S. Ramillies.

A. PILKINGTON,
Lieut.-Colonel Commanding.

To the OFFICER COMMANDING THE
UNITED STATES TROOPS ON MOOSE ISLAND.

On the refusal of the Americans to surrender, Hardy made every preparation for an attack, but as the boats filled with soldiers were approaching the shore, the American colours were hauled down, and the garrison became prisoners of war. The Allen and Frederick Islands were also subsequently occupied. In these last operations not a single life was sacrificed. The terms of the summons to surrender are curiously characteristic of Hardy's decision of character. In his dispatch of July 12th, 1814, Lieut.-Col. Pilkington writes: "To Captain Sir Thomas Hardy I consider myself under the greatest obligations, having experienced every possible co-operation, with an offer to disembark from his squadron any proportion of seamen or marines which I considered necessary."

Having satisfactorily disposed of the islands in Passamaquaddy Bay, Hardy was able to turn his attention to the town of Stonnington, the inhabitants of which had excited his wrath by their activity in preparing the torpedoes which had so narrowly missed destroying his ship. On the 9th August the *Ramillies*, with the *Pactolus* (dispatch-brig) and *Terror* bomb, anchored off Stonnington. Two days later (an attempt at "boarding" the fort having failed on account of the shallowness of the water), the town was partially destroyed by bombardment.

The Second American War, terminated by the Peace

of Ghent, concluded on Christmas Eve 1814. A month later (January 1815) Hardy was made a K.C.B., and returned to England in the eventful month which witnessed Wellington's crowning victory at Waterloo, the *Ramillies* being paid off five days before that battle.

CHAPTER XVI

HARDY IN COMMAND OF THE "PRINCESS AUGUSTA" YACHT AND THE "SUPERB" [JUNE 23, 1815— AUGUST 11, 1819]

AT last the captain of the *Victory* was to obtain the brief respite from foreign service he had lately been looking forward to. By this time Lady Hardy, to whom he was devotedly attached, was the mother of three engaging daughters, viz., Louisa Georgina (who died unmarried), Emily Georgina (afterwards the wife of Mr William Chatteris of Sandleford Priory, Newbury[1]), and Mary Charlotte (who became Lady MacGregor), and survived both her sisters, dying on the 29th April 1896.

Ten days after the *Ramillies* had been paid off, Hardy was appointed to the captaincy of the *Princess Augusta*, the royal yacht, generally stationed at Deptford. This command lasted very nearly three years. During the first part of that time Sir T. M. and Lady Hardy lived at 3 Montagu Square, but towards the end of 1847 they went to reside at Teignmouth in Devonshire. The first letter of Hardy's in the Dorchester collection, belonging to this part of his career, is addressed to his brother Joseph, and relates to a now forgotten lawsuit in which the gallant captain, as usual, scored a signal success over his

[1] Once the home of Elizabeth Montagu, Queen of the Blue Stockings [1720-1800].

enemies, who did not dare to face a trial, but allowed judgment to go by default. Hardy writes :—

> MONTAGUE SQUARE,
> *June 5th,* 1816, 5 *o'clock.*

MY DEAR JOS,

I am just returned from Serjent Best.[1] The business was brought before the Sheriff and as the party pleaded guilty the Damages are given at a Thousand Pounds[2] you will see by the papers of Tomorrow all that transpired and all who were present seemed quite satisfied.

> In haste I remain,
> Yours Affectionately,
> T. M. HARDY.

I was not in Court.

The slanders, though obviously ridiculous, did not end here. Hardy's next letter speaks for itself :—

> 3 MONTAGUE SQUARE,
> *June 17th,* 1816.

MY DEAR JOS,

I wrote you a long letter yesterday which would have reached you if I had had the misfortune to have fallen in an unpleasant affair which took place at 4 o'clock yesterday afternoon between Lord Buckingham and myself.[3] His Lordship is the person whom I suspected to have been the author of the Anonymous letter,

---

[1] Afterwards Lord Wynford, and one of Hardy's contemporaries at Crewkerne School (see *ante,* p. 20).

[2] *The Times* of Friday 7th June 1816 alludes to the matter in the following terms :—" In the Sheriff's Court on Wednesday, Sir Thomas Hardy obtained a verdict with £1000 damages against the proprietors of the *Morning Herald* for a libel contained in various paragraphs last winter, insinuating that Lady Hardy had eloped with the Marquess of Abercorn." [John James, first Marquess of Abercorn, born 1756, died 1818.]

[3] Richard Temple Nugent Brydges Chandos Grenville, first Duke of Buckingham, born 1776, succeeded his father as Marquess 11th February 1813, died 1839.

and in fact all my domestic troubles. After exchanging a Shot the seconds would not allow us to proceed, so that it has ended nearly as it began, and I still suspect his Lordship to be the person, however now the eyes of the World will be on him, and most probably he will cease to trouble us. On Tuesday last I was taken into custody by the Peace Officers, owing to an anonymous letter having been written to Marlborough Street Office stating that a Duel was to take place on the following day between Lord Abercorn and myself, his Lordship was also brought up from the Priory (12 Miles from London) and bound over to keep the Peace, and as I had strong grounds to suspect Lord B—— to be the Writer of the letter, I took an opportunity of saying something to him in strong language, which was the occasion of our meeting. I am certain that you will do me the justice to believe that I would not have brought my name under the discussion of the public if I could possibly have avoided it, but the infamous attacks which have been made on my Wife left me no alternative, and I hope by following it up with moderation & firmness, that I shall soon get the better of our enemies. Louisa of course is very much annoyed but she has born up against it with the greatest fortitude. Our three children have got the Measles but it is very favourable and they are doing remarkably well. I forgot to Say that Mr Fremantle[1] attended Lord Buckingham & Lord March[2] was my second; it will of course occasion a great deal of conversation and of course it is very unpleasant. My time of late has been so much occupied that I have not seen Captain or Mrs Balston lately, but I purpose calling on them in the course of the day. I am getting a rough case made to hold a Dozen of Shirts which I will forward to you by

[1] Afterwards the Right Hon. Sir William Henry Fremantle, M.P., Treasurer of the Household (born 1766, died 1850). In 1816, M.P. for Buckingham.

[2] Charles, Earl of March, subsequently fifth Duke of Richmond and Lennox (born 1791, died 1860).

Russell's Wagon in a Day or two to remain at the Waggon Office Dorchester till called for, I am joined by Louisa in best love to you all.

I remain,

My Dear Jos,

Yours most Affectionately,

T. M. HARDY.

Five days later he writes :—

3 MONTAGUE SQUARE,
June 22nd, 1816.

MY DEAR JOS,

Many thanks for your kind letter and I assure you that I should not hesitate one instant in requesting of you to come to Town if I saw the least necessity for it, but it is pleasant to see that the greater part of London espouses our cause. I have put the business in the hands of Lord Sefton [1] who is indefatigable in our cause. Positive Proof we certainly have not, but everything short of that is in our possession and we have just learnt that the suspected person is laid up with a fit of the gout. We have not been troubled with any more annonnymous letters & I now hope that we shall in future be allowed to rest quiet. My Rheumatism has troubled me very much, but as the cause is now removed, I have no doubt but I shall soon recover my health. Louisa has also been very unwell but I think she is getting better, the children are all doing remarkably well and in a few days will I trust be quite recovered. Sir George Berkeley has got a house at Moulsey about 12 miles from Town. We are going there on Tuesday next for a short time but if you should have occasion to write to me you might as well direct London, as

---

[1] William Philip, second Earl of Sefton (born 1772, died 1838). As "Lord Dashalong," he is depicted in one of the best of Dighton's caricature portraits. He was a great dandy, and moved in the most fashionable society.

I shall frequently be in Town. I sent off the Shrub by Russell's waggon on Thursday so that most probably it will be at Dorchester on Monday. I am quite sorry to hear so bad an account of poor Mrs White but hope the fine weather will soon restore her to health. I occasionally see the Balstons, Edward is very much taken up with his Ship, as she is to sail again very soon he purposes going into Dorsetshire only for one day. Pray give our best love to all, I remain,

My Dear Jos,

Yours most affectionately,

T. M. HARDY.

JOSEPH HARDY, Esq.

In September he writes:—

3 MONTAGUE SQUARE,
Septr 9th, 1816.

MY DEAR JOS,

I am again put off by the Admiralty till the 18th with a promise, if the person is not then ready to try his experiment,[1] I shall be allowed to proceed into Dorsetshire, so that I hope to be with you by the 20th & which I suppose will be quite soon enough for shooting, as I conclude the corn will not be down before that time. We have not been in the least troubled by our Anonymous friend, but he has now made an attack on my friend Lord Sefton & I have been much alarmed fearing that a Duel with him could not be prevented, but I am happy to say that it is settled without comeing to that horrible extremity. The worry again brought on my complaint in my leg, but I am now quite well again, Louisa & the

---

[1] This refers to one of the many projects for new departures in marine construction brought at this time to the notice of the Admiralty. Hardy was always anxious to encourage inventors, as he already felt the time for great improvements and radical changes was at hand.

children are quite well she joins me in best love to Mrs Hardy and all the family I remain,

My Dear Jos,

Yours affectionately,

T. M. HARDY.

Early in the following year Hardy writes to his brother :—

3 MONTAGUE SQUARE,
Febry 7th, 1817.

MY DEAR JOS,

I received your letter yesterday & should have answered it but I was in hopes of getting a Frank for to-day but no member has happened to come this way. I met Mr John H. Browne who told me that Sir William Oglander[1] & Mr Purling[2] had both written to request that they might not be named as Sheriffs, I hope you have also written as Lord Bathurst[3] told me, that he had but one voice, but it was the custom to name the first on the list & which I sincerely hope will be the case. My expenses this year has been rather more than I expected, which has put me a little behind hand with Halford, therefore I should feel thankful if you would remit the money to him to be placed to my credit. I was at Court yesterday & it was the most crowded one that I ever remember to have seen. The Prince was looking remarkably well & I think that the late attack[4] on him will be strengthening the Ministers more than anything they could possibly have done. I made use of the Heal-all, at the time I

[1] Sir William Oglander, sixth Bart. of Parnham, Dorset (born 1769, died 1852). Sheriff of Dorset, 1818.

[2] George Purling of Bradford Peverel Manor, Dorset (died 1840). Sheriff of Dorset, 1820.

[3] Henry, third Earl Bathurst, K.G. (born 1762, died 1834).

[4] The revelations of Tierney as to the extravagance of the Prince of Wales since becoming Regent. It was at this time that the ominous words, "Bread, or the Regent's head," were written on the walls of Carlton House.

wrote to you last, and in three days the pain was quite removed, nor has it in the smallest degree since returned. Lady Hardy strained her ankle about the same time and after using it a few times the pain was completely removed, so that she swears by it as well as myself. When you see any of the Possum Family will you thank them for the butter[1] which is so good that we are using it for breakfast in preference to the London fresh butter. Louisa & the children are all well, they join me in best love to you all, I remain,

My Dear Jos,

Yours affectionately,

T. M. HARDY.

JOSEPH HARDY, Esq.,
Dorchester, Dorset.

In 1818 Sir T. M. and Lady Hardy went to reside at Teignmouth, while Joseph removed from Dorchester to Charminster, where he lived till his death. In February of this year Sir T. Hardy writes:—

TEIGNMOUTH, Feby 27th, 1818.

MY DEAR JOS,

I am sorry to acquaint you that I have this day received an account of the death of poor Sir George Berkeley[2] He was seized with violent spasms on Wednesday last, and expired almost immediately, I am excessively glad that Lady Hardy is in Town as she will be a great comfort to her Mother, who is in a most deplorable state, as she never would allow herself to believe that he was in the least danger. I do not know if I shall be wanted in London as I can be of no use I shall not go unless they particularly desire it; however

[1] "The real Dorset" of *Our Boys* sixty years later.

[2] Lady Hardy notes in the diary she kept at intervals, now in the possession of Mrs Thynne, that after the funeral, which Sir T. M. Hardy attended, she went to stay with her grandmother, Lady Louisa Lennox, at Woodend, and in returning to Teignmouth, slept on the night of 18th May (1818) at Mrs Manfield's house in Dorchester.

should they wish it I will go by the Mail and will give you notice of the Day which I pass thro' Dorchester, and if you are not otherwise engaged, I might hope for the pleasure of shaking you by the hand. I received William Manfields letter this morning and will attend to his directions respecting his chimney piece, I am sorry to hear that he has had a fall from the Grey, until the horse has had more practice in leaping I hope my Nephew will be more careful. I am happy to hear better accounts of Mr Balstons health, the children are all quite well & join me in very best love to you & Mrs Hardy, I remain,

My dear Jos,

Yours very affectionately,

T. M. HARDY.

In May, Hardy resigned his command of the *Princess Augusta*, and remained without any appointment till the following November, when he returned (Nov. 30, 1818) to active service as captain of the "old" *Superb*, the same vessel which had accompanied the *Victory* home to England just before Trafalgar. During the interval it seems that Sir T. M. and Lady Hardy for a time lived at Plymouth,[1] from which town, beloved of all naval men ever since the days of Drake and Hawkins, he wrote the following letter on Midsummer Day :—

42 DUNSFORD STREET,
STONE HOUSE, NEAR PLYMOUTH,
June 24th, 1818.

MY DEAR JOS,

My reason for going to Plymouth before I first intended was the danger I should run of getting a house in August, & as I had an opportunity of giving up that which I had at Teignmouth, I thought it advisable to

[1] In Lady Hardy's diary, mention is made of numerous social gaieties at Plymouth, including eighty-five receptions as well as balls, dinners, and other festivities. She and her husband were amongst the guests who stayed at Mount Edgcumbe during the Grand Duke Michael of Russia's visit.

do so, I have taken this for a fortnight, to give Louisa time to suit herself, she & the children are not yet come, but I expect them this evening. Will you say to Admiral Ingram that I shall be most happy to do all I can for Lieut. Pitfield,[1] but I have already made application for two, & I fear their Lordships will only give me one, however, I will try, I recollect his Father very well, I have had already several applications from Chaplains, but I do not like to take one that is not known to me, or strongly recommended by some friend, now it appears by your letter that you have only seen him, Mr Brice, once or twice.[2] Will you, therefore, make enquiry about him & let me know in what ships he has served, so that I might know a little more about him before I reply to his request, as I am very anxious to have a respectable Clergyman if possible. I have not written to John Ward, but if you see him will you say that I shall give him timely notice. I expect to be commissioned about 1st of September, which I hope will not prevent my paying you a visit, as I feel myself quite equal to a little partridge Shooting. I was not in the least hurt by my overturn in the Subscription,[3] I fortunately fell on my head, and whether I partake most of the Hardy or the Masterman Breed, I know not, but I believe the brains that ought to have fallen to my share are transferred to some other branch of the family, as my head must be composed of a much harder substance.

5 *o'clock*.—Louisa & the children are all arrived, they are quite well & join me in best love to you all. I remain,

My Dear Jos,
Yours most affectionately,
T. M. HARDY.

[1] Joseph Pitfield [1790-1858], of Symondsbury, Dorset. Taken prisoner in the *Proserpine*, 28th February 1809 ; escaped 4th February 1811. Distinguished himself at the bombardment of Algiers.

[2] Rev. Edward Brice, B.A., Wadham Coll., Oxford [1785-1873], son of the Rev. George Tito Brice, Vicar of Canford Magna, Dorset. He married the sister of Francis Roberts of the *Triumph*.

[3] A well-known coach.

Hardy, however, did not join the *Superb* till November. Four months later he writes :—

"SUPERB," PLYMOUTH DOCK,
March 27th, 1819.

MY DEAR JOS,

I am very much obliged to you for yours of the 15th instant. I am truly sorry to hear so bad an account of Mrs Balston, but sincerely hope the Spring will bring her about again. I am also sorry to hear so bad an account of Martha & Augusta, but I look forward to the fine weather for their recovery. I am much obliged to your County Member[1] for his good opinion &c & pray return him my best respects when you next see him. Captain Gambier, Nephew, (I believe) to the late Mrs Pitt, is going to reside near Dorchester, he is married to a daughter of General Browne, Lieut Governor of Plymouth. I am much obliged to you for a very fine Cheese it is remarkably good. Mr Colston was good enough to bring it to me[2] I have sent you by the Balloon of this day (I hope) a fresh cod with a hund^d of oysters & we have taken the precaution to embowel it & I hope it will arrive good, it was alive when I bought it. The weather of late has been so unfavorable that no terbits have been caught. By todays conveyance I have also sent Mrs Thresher a cod & Trimmings. I hope it will arrive in time for the Wedding,[3] but to say the truth I am not in the Secret but I wish them all much happiness, & should the purchase be made at Charminster I shall be enabled to visit my brother & Sister without the assistance of a horse ; however I do not think it possible that such an arrangement is likely to take place. I never before knew that Matrimony was

---

[1] W. Morton Pitt, M.P. for Dorset. His first wife was Margaret, daughter of John Gambier.

[2] The "blue vinney" cheese of Dorset, like the Dorchester ale, has been famous from time immemorial.

[3] The marriage of Miss Thresher, Hardy's niece, of Corfe Hill to Tom Nicholls of Weymouth.

good for a Paralitic stroke, & I always have remarked that our old Admirals with young wives soon leave their spouses in quiet possession of their prize money : however I hope Tom Nicholls will be more prudent. Louisa & her eldest Daughter are going to Town, the second week in April. Lady Emily has expressed a great wish to see them & I see no objection to their going ; as the new road is so much better than the old, as well as ten miles shorter they will go that way. If you see Admiral Ingram will you say that I am very sorry that I could not get Mr Cox with me, but Sir Henry Hotham has put him into the *Lee* on this Station, so that at a future day I do not despair of getting him with me. I am joined by Louisa & the children in best love to you all I remain,

My dear Jos,

Yours most affectionately,

T. M. HARDY.

I hear Mary Manfield is still at Exeter.

On the 12th August 1819, Sir Thomas Hardy, K.C.B., was appointed Commodore and Commander-in-Chief on the South America Station, and hoisted his broad pendant on the *Superb*. Next day he writes to Nelson's old friend, Sir Benjamin Hallowell, K.C.B., as follows :—

PLYMOUTH DOCK,
August 13th, 1819.

MY DEAR SIR,

I will take out your son the moment the *Owen Glendower* joins & place one of mine (if I have no vacancy) with Spencer. I can only repeat what I hastily stated to you at Lord Spencers "that your son shall be the first promoted by me," & I do assure you that it will give me the greatest pleasure to prove to you that I have never for a moment forgotten your kindness to me in former times, & I do not think you will feel greater pleasure in hearing of his promotion than I shall in communicating

M

it to you which I hope will be the day after he has served his time and is of age. I have got the duplicate of his time which I will take care of. I am quite glad you have communicated to Sir Geo. Cockburn[1] how things stand & I sincerely hope something will soon be done for you. Lady Hardy joins me in best regards I remain My dear Sir

Yours most truly and sincerely

T. M. HARDY.

Rear-Admiral
    SIR BENJAMIN HALLOWELL, K.C.B.,[2]
      Ealing, Middlesex.

Shortly after this (Sept. 9, 1819) Hardy set out for his new sphere of usefulness on the east coast of South America.[3]

---

[1] See *ante*.

[2] (Born 1760, died 1830.) Assumed the additional name of Carew, 1828. It was Sir B. Hallowell who gave Nelson the coffin made out of the timbers of the *Orient*.

[3] Lady Hardy says the house they rented from General Desborough, in Durnford Street, Stonehouse, was at once given up, as she had settled to go abroad with their children. "There were no leave-takings. Sir Thomas hated them. He would never even allow anybody to see him off, saying that at such a time he was completely absorbed by his duties to his ship."

CHAPTER XVII

HARDY COMMODORE AND COMMANDER-IN-CHIEF ON THE SOUTH AMERICA STATION [1819-1824]

THE selection of Hardy for this particular command speaks volumes for the high opinion of his discretion and ability, which must have been entertained both by Lord Liverpool and Robert, Lord Melville. Whenever he had been placed in a position requiring a combination of tact, foresight, and courage, he had always made his mark for good, raising, when the exigencies of the situation required it, the prestige of the English flag by some bold stroke of firm insistance. He had also more than once given evidence of diplomatic talents of no mean order. Hardy's biographer in Colbourne's *United Service Journal*,[1] gives a very lucid description of the situation with which Hardy now had to deal and the difficulties he was expected to grapple with "This command," he writes, "was one of the greatest possible importance."

The War of Independence, or as the Spaniards termed it, the Revolutionary War, had generated anarchy and confusion everywhere: the interests of all parties had to be consulted, British trade to be protected, and a strict neutrality to be observed. At such a time the arbitrator required to have a clear head and a vigorous arm, both of which were found in Sir Thomas Hardy: his conduct was the theme of universal praise; the loser and

[1] *United Service Journal* for 1839, part iii., p. 385 *et seq.*

the gainer equally allowed the justice of his awards, and he had the additional satisfaction of receiving the thanks of the Admiralty on his return from the station. In Marshall's *Naval Biography*, Captain Basil Hall says :—

'Hardy was trusted everywhere, and enjoyed in a wonderful degree the confidence and esteem of all parties. His advice, which was never obtruded, was never suspected, and a thousand little disputes were at once settled amicably, and to the advantage of all concerned, by a mere word of his, instead of being driven into what are called national questions, to last for years, and lead to no useful end. When this respect and confidence had once become fully established, everything went on so smoothly under his vigilant auspices, that it was those only who chanced to be placed near the scene who could perceive the extent, or appreciate the importance of the public good which he was silently dispensing."

The following correspondence between Hardy and his brother throws some light on this portion of Hardy's life.

"SUPERB," RIO DE JANEIRO,
Novr 20th, 1819.

MY DEAR JOS,

I wrote you a hasty letter a day or two after our arrival at this place I now take advantage of the Packet who sails tomorrow to say I like the climate very much & I think the Country by far the most beautiful I ever saw. I have seen a great deal of Mr & Mrs Cunningham, they are good enough to give me a Bed when I sleep on shore, but I prefer living on board. I am sorry to say the climate does not seem to agree with young Ward ; altho' he is not absolutely ill, yet he is constantly unwell, & is troubled with a very unpleasant cough. He is however better now than he has been for some time. I forgot if I told you in my last letter the best mode of writing to me, but if you will enclose your letters to John Hay Esqr, Admiralty London he will forward them to me. I meet occasionally with some of my old friends (Portuguese) who I knew at Lisbon & I receive the greatest civility from them all. We had a most excellent passage here from England & I landed all my passengers in high good humour. I am very much pleased with Mr Thornton & as we shall have some business to transact, it is very fortunate for us both, that we seem to understand each other. There is a Son & Daughter here of our old school fellow Dampier, She is married to a Mr May who is a Merchant here, & the Brother is a Clerk with him, She is really a very nice woman & I believe her Husband is making money very fast, I frequently see him & of course talk of our Dorsetshire friends. Pray offer to Mrs Hardy my best love as well as to all my relations.

I remain,

My Dear Jos,

Yours most affectionately,

T. M. HARDY.

In the spring of the following year :—

BUENOS AYRES, *March* 24*th*, 1820.

MY DEAR JOS,

I send by the *Blossom* who takes despatches to England tomorrow morning. This Country is in a sad troubled state having experienced three complete changes of Government, in as many months. The last which took place on the 12th of this Month was attended with a great deal of confusion & some alarm. A strong party, called the Montoneros entered the City by force, drove the then Governor from his Post & he took refuge on board some of the Ships in the Road. Some firing took place a Lieut Colonel was killed and another Officer badly wounded. Many robberies were committed & Houses broken open & Plundered. The Montoneros Bivouacked close to my Quarter, and as the English families living close to me were dreadfully allarmed, I took three ladies and seven children under my protection, so with my own family which amounts to seven, and about a dozen servants I think we were pretty well filled.

Three of my Officers were robbed & their horses taken from them & an attempt was made to treat Mr Ward in the same manner, but he resisted with great firmness, galloped off & saved his horse & money for which he has gained great credit.   We are now very quiet but I will not vouch for its long continuance as the parties are nearly of the same strength and their annemosity is very great ; however we must expect those things till a regular form of Government is established.   The present people in power have published a secret correspondence with France which you will see in the English papers, it is making a great noise here & I have no doubt but it will gain strength by going to England.   Mr Ward like myself complains very much at not having heard from Dorsetshire since we left England ; however we hope to hear by the next Packet which is expected from Rio de Janeiro in about a week ; our last accounts from England was 7th of Decr.   They appear to be in a very troubled state in some parts of the Country, but I sincerely hope that the new Laws will keep you all quiet & those who are not satisfied with our Government should come to this nice Republican Country, where liberty is enjoyed only by the strongest & we live nearly by Club Law.   Pray offer to Mrs H. & all the family my best love.

I remain,

My Dear Jos,

Yours affectionately,

T. M. HARDY.

The next letter is written four months later :—

"OWEN GLENDOWER," BUENOS AYRES,
July 9th, 1820.

MY DEAR JOS,

I was much gratified yesterday by the receipt of your letter of the 16th of Febry & I hope the fine weather which you have now got, has put you all to rights. This is the finest climate I was ever in, this is your January & we have the Thermometer at night down to about 30 & the Day tho' a little cold it is quite delightful, but from the sad quarrels in the Country we cannot take the exercise we otherwise should. A Battle was fought on the 28th of June between what is called the Federal Troops & those of Buenos Ayres about 3 leagues from the City. The Buenos Ayrians were completely beaten. We are now blockaded by the Federals. The Town is so strong that they are afraid to enter it. Skermishes daily take place, & of course we keep out of the way. How it is to end we have yet to learn, but I hope the Federals will not enter the City for the sake of British property which is very considerable. I am very glad Mr Hay has written to you as I shall hope to hear from some of you occasionally. I shall reply to William Manfield's request & shall be very happy to do as he desires when I can find out who he means, but we have no such Midshipman on the Station as "Robinson" but I have no doubt some young man will soon let me know that he is recommended to me by Mr Cowper. I have not been at Rio de Janeiro since I first left it but I hear frequently from there. Mrs May & her family were quite well on the 21st of last Month; one of her children had been unwell but it is quite recovered. I am in regular correspondence with Cunningham, I sent him the other day two horses & four Mules we having them very cheap here & at Rio they are very dear. He is now acting Consul & his son is Vice Consul; I shall give him an account of the poor Admiral in my next letter. How he must have regretted the loss of so many good dinners. Tell him when you see him, that his friend Mr Cox is very well but has not *grown* in the least. I much fear that I cannot promote him for no one will die. As the River Plate is very much exposed for ships of the line, I have sent them to Rio de Janeiro & they will return again in August. I am quite happy to hear so prosperous

an account of Mrs Henning, before you get this I hope
we shall have added a cousin to our family. Pray offer
to her and Mrs H. my congratulations.

How fortunate it is for our Service that all our wives
are not so fond of us as our Niece is of Captn Balston,
I should be quite wretched if mine was to take it into her
head to keep me at home. She writes me a very good
account of our children they are the Beauties of Geneva,
& I find Emmy still bears the Bell; Lou the most graceful
& Mary is now become very good.

I remain

My dear Jos

Yours affectionately

T. M. HARDY.

There is a silence of six months, and then he writes :—

BUENOS AYRES,
Jany 14*th*, 1821.

MY DEAR JOS,

We are all very busily employed packing up,
as I am going to embark tomorow on board the *Creole*,
and I purpose passing round Cape Horn, to see that part
of my Station. The voiage is said to be very boisterous
but I have no doubt but we shall do very well. I have
not heard from you for some time; my last letter from
Louisa is dated 17th of August she was then at Lousanne
near Geneva, and where she purposes remaining twelve
months. The children were quite well and improving very
much.

Everything remain very quiet at Buenos Ayres, I
sincerely wish that things looked so well in England, but
I am sorry to see that the Radicals seem daily to gain
strength.

I hear frequently from Colonel Cunningham but I have
not seen him since my first arrival in South America. Mr

and Mrs May are quite well; one of the children was unwell but is now quite recovered. I hope Mrs Hardy and all our Family continue in good health. Young Ward still continues with me; not having had an opportunity of promoting him, he is a very good young man and I should be much pleased if I had an opportunity of providing for him. You will not hear from me again for some time, as my passage round, in all probability will be six weeks, and the conveyance of letters from the other side of the Andes to England is quite uncertain. We hear that Lord Cochrane has been very successful and has taken one of the Spanish Frigates. Most likely I shall have the pleasure of seeing him and I have no doubt but we shall agree very well. Pray offer my best love to Mrs Hardy and all our friends, I remain,

My Dear Jos,

Yours affectionately,

T. M. HARDY.

In the following November he again writes :—

"CREOLE," CALLAO BAY NEAR LIMA,
Novr. 29th, 1821.

MY DEAR JOS,

I have not heard from you for a long time but probably I shall by the next opportunity.

You will long ago have heard of the sad accident which Louisa and our Eldest Daughter met with; however I suppose we must thank God that it was no worse, I heard from Little Lou three weeks after the accident, and she was doing very well her Mother was very much bruised but no bone broken, my wife was so anxious about her daughter that she quite forgot to mention herself.

I am going to reside at Lima for two months when I purpose returning to Valparaiso, and shall pop round Cape Horn, for Rio de Janeiro in April.

Peru is now nearly in possession of the Patriots, and

our trade in Lima is very considerable.   As there is no
return for our Manufactories but Dollars and Bullion, a
good proportion falls to our share to carry to England.   The
Superb will sail tomorrow with about a million and a half
dollars, and this ship probably will take to Rio de Janeiro
about the same sum, which will be forwarded home by
some other ship of War ; I am doing very well, in fact
much better than could have been expected.

Young Cox is quite well as is Mr Ward, the latter complains much of not hearing from his family, do mention
them when you write.

My time of service will expire in October, and I expect
to be relieved immediately.

Give my best love to all my friends, I remain,

> My Dear Jos,
>
> > Yours most affectionately,
> >
> > > T. M. HARDY.

I hope Mrs Hardy is well give my love to her.   I have
never seen our Weymouth friend but I hear he made a
very bad passage round Cape Horn.

On New Year's Day 1822 his thoughts travel back to
"Possum" where his brother John lay on his deathbed.
He writes home thus :—

> LIMA, *Jany.* 1*st*, 1822.

MY DEAR JOS,

I received your letter of June 10th a few days
ago, and one from Mary Manfield at the same time.   I am
quite sorry to hear so bad an account of poor John's health,
but sincerely hope that the abcess will take a favourable
turn, or the consequences I much fear will be fatal.   The
summer season I hope will be found favourable for his
complaint, and I trust long ere this that he is again
restored to health.

John Ward is very unwell the climate does not agree with him so well as it does with me, as I have enjoyed remarkable good health. Owing to the death of a Mr Lambert late Purser of the *Alacrity*, I have appointed John Ward to the Vacancy, and he is now certain of being confirmed which I am much pleased at, as it will give him with care, an independence for life. He is not seriously ill, but he was confined to his bed the last time I heard of him. He is at present on board the *Creole* at Callao, but the *Alacrity* is daily expected.

Young Cox is under some alarm, for the fate of some of his money as he says he has seen in the Portsmouth paper, the failure of the House of Cox Patterson & Co. I own I have not seen it in the Paper and I sincerely hope it is not true. I am not surprised to hear of the death of poor Mr Edward Balston, the last time I saw him I did not think that he would have lived six months the sum he has died worth is something enormous. The Captain (Balston) I think has not chosen a good time to turn Farmer, however I hope it will only be on a small scale. I think you are quite right to have a little business, as it will be an amusement to you. I am rather astonished that Captain Thompson should have spoken so highly of the Buenos Ayres Pigs, they originally come from Spain, they are quite black, and in my opinion of the coarsest kind ; however I will take some of them to England and if the breed is approved of you shall have some of them. I am anxious to hear from you again, for your last account of poor John is less favourable, however we must hope for the best. With best love to all, I remain,

My Dear Jos, Yours most affectionately,

T. M. HARDY.

I expect to be at Rio de Janeiro by the 1st of May.

His next letter is one written six months later :—

BOTAFOGO, NEAR RIO DE JANEIRO,
July 3rd, 1822.

MY DEAR JOS,

A few days ago I received your letter of the 11th April, and I am truly sorry to hear of the distressing state that poor John appears to have been in at the time you wrote, and from your account of him I much fear that there is very little hope of his recovery. Independent of the loss of a Brother, it will be a most distressing thing for our Sisters, and from the badness of the times I am at a loss to know what is best to be done, but I shall be most happy to do everything in my power for them. Thank God I have enjoyed my health and have sent home about fifteen thousand pounds, but I fear that my golden harvest is nearly at an end.

I have left things tolerably quiet in the Pacific, but I fear that our troubles are about to commence in the Braziles, as the Government here seem determined to shake off the Mother Country.

Young Cox is my acting Flag Lieut. and I sincerely hope that I shall be able to get him promoted. Poor fellow, I find that he has lost his Father, and a large proportion of his money was in hands of Cox, who it appears by the Papers has failed, and I hear that he is on his passage to Lima. He will arrive there at an unfortunate time, for all the mines are now filled with water, and for many months to come, there will be very little silver got.

Colonel Cunningham (for that is the name he goes by) is quite well and Mrs C. as gay as ever. He was Deputy Consul General, but Mr Chamberlain is arrived which is a bad thing for our Piddle Town friend.

As I have reason to believe that I shall be here for a few months I have taken a house near Cunninghams, and we are living very comfortable, having a whist party most evenings. I hear my little friend Plowman is doing very well, and I am quite sorry to learn that he has made so bad a choice. I have not heard from Lady Hardy since

December but I am told that she is gone with her family to Florence which probably is the cause of my not hearing from her. Pray offer my best love to Mrs Hardy and all the family, I remain,

My Dear Jos, Your affectionate Brother,

T. M. HARDY.

Hardy had now shifted his broad pendant into the *Creole*, from which ship he writes :—

"CREOLE," RIO DE JANEIRO,
Sept 7th, 1822.

MY DEAR JOS,

I have not heard from you since last April, but I have seen in the Portsmouth Paper that Poor John died on the 25th of that Month. In common with you all, I very much lament his being taken from us, his loss I fear will be very much felt.

My troubles have again just commenced. The Brazil Troops at Bahia have resisted the King's forces, and that City is in great confusion. As we have a considerable Trade there, I feel it right to go there, and shall sail for Bahia in a day or two.

My time of service on this Station has expired, and I expected to be relieved, but as yet I have not heard who is to be my successor. Thank God I continue to enjoy my health, and I wait with patience the Orders of the Admiralty.

I have got a house close to Cunninghams, and as I have been at some expense in fitting it up, of course I am sorry to quit it. Mr Hetherly son to Mrs Cunningham who you might recollect at Piddle Town[1] is going to Bahia with me for change of Air, he has been very unwell and I hope the change of scene will do him good, he is the Vice Consul at this place.

Mrs May has been in England some time, and is

---

[1] A village six miles from Dorchester, now called Puddletown.

expected out again very soon; her Brother Mr Dampier is here, and is a very fine young man. I have lent Mrs May my house during my absence which I should hope will not exceed two months. Young Cox still continues my Flag Lieut he is not yet confirmed, but I am in great hopes that I shall be able to get him Promoted when I arrive in England. Pray offer my condolence to all our family, I remain,

My Dear Jos,

Yours affectionately,

T. M. HARDY.

A month later he again writes :—

"CREOLE," BAHIA, COAST OF BRAZIL,
October 6th, 1822.

MY DEAR JOS,

I did not receive your letter of the 3rd of June until a few days ago owing to my having left Rio de Janeiro sooner than I first intended, but my letter to you of the 7th of September will have shown that the death of Poor John had reached me thro' the Portsmouth paper. From the account you give of his late illness and sufferings, it must have been a happy release, both for him and our Sisters. The account you gave of Augusta's health is very uncomfortable, but I hope she will bear up against the loss we have all sustained. I think his Will has been judiciously made, and I hope the Ladies will take your advice, and give up, at the least, one of the Farms, altho' their loss in the sale of stock will be considerable, yet probably the first loss may be the least.

Fortune has been very kind to me, and I shall be most happy to make my Sisters an annual allowance of £50 each, which I feel I can afford out of my present income. I have sent home about Eighteen Thousand Pounds, and I hope to increase that to Twenty before my return.[1]

[1] Hardy here refers to the freight of treasure by a ship-of-war, then a legitimate source of gain to everybody concerned, from the

I have left the Pacific and Buenos Ayres tolerably quiet, but I fear we shall have some trouble in the Brazil. This place is in Latitude 13 South, and very hot it is, but thank God I continue to enjoy excellent health.

I have not heard for some time from John Ward, but he was quite well in June and on his way to Valparaiso from Lima, in the *Alacrity*.

Young Cox is still acting as my Flag Lieut., and I shall do all I can to get him confirmed, he is a very clever fellow, and a great favourite of mine.

I have not yet had the pleasure of seeing the Reverend Mr Penny, you will have heard that he quitted the *Doris*, and is residing at Pernambuco, which place is between three and four hundred miles to the North of Bahia.

I am quite sorry at what you tell me about Tom Nicholls, but am not much surprised at it.

I find I have got a Weymouth young man on board as my Secretary's Clerk, his name is Edward Thorne,[1] I am very much pleased with him, and shall give him the first vacancy as Purser should one occur during my stay in South America.

The accounts I get of my children are very flattering, and I am very anxious to see them. I was always of opinion that Emily would be the handsomest, but her Mother would not allow it. Louisa is a Berkeley and Emily a Hardy; little Mary is between the two, and I understand is very much improved, Louisa has quite recovered the fall she had, it happened in April 1821. Her Mother is so partial to Lusanne that she talks of remaining there until my return. I hope Mrs Hardy is recovered of her

Admiralty downwards. Greenwich Hospital also had its share of the profit. At this particular time it added materially to Hardy's income. It was then regulated by a Proclamation, dated 12th July 1819. This, with other enactments, has since been modified by a "Proclamation respecting the conveyance of public and private treasure," issued on the 10th August 1888.

[1] See *post*, chapter xx., p. 222.

Rheumatism.   Pray offer to her my best love as well as to all my Relations, I remain,

My Dear Jos,

Yours affectionately,

T. M. Hardy.

Once more the broad pendant of Commodore Sir T. M. Hardy is shifted to the *Doris*, from which he writes :—

"Doris," Bahia,
Jan. 1st, 1823.

My Dear Jos,

I have been in daily expectation of the arrival of a packet from England, but as she is not come, the *Conway*, which takes this letter, will sail early tomorrow morning for Spithead, with a tolerable good lot of Dollars. I have not heard from you for some time, but I hope that "no news is good news."   Probably the papers will alarm our friends for the safety of the British in this quarter, and I own that our situation is not enviable as we are completely surrounded by the Brazilians, who almost daily attack the Portuguese, but the ground is very strong and can be defended with great ease.

Provisions are very scarce and dear, a couple of fowls cannot be purchased for less than thirty to forty shillings sterling, and other necessaries in proportion, but I manage to get a little from Rio de Janeiro, where I have sent the *Creole* to refresh her Crew.   I was in hopes to have finished my troubles, when I left all quiet in Spanish South America, but this new Emperor of Brazil[1] seems determined to drive all the Portuguese out of this Country, and the Butes[2] Interest is so connected with Lisbon that individuals must suffer.   I wrote to you on the 6th of October, and I think

[1] Pedro I., crowned Emperor 1st December 1822.   He abdicated 7th April 1831.

[2] The meaning of this phrase is not clear, unless the "Butes" describe some commercial house of business.

I told you that I was to remain out a little longer. Of course I feel grateful to my friends at home for their good opinion of me, and I sincerely hope that I shall continue to give satisfaction, but I find it very difficult to please my Countrymen. As probably you will see by some of the papers, Dan. Cox now stands first on my list for Promotion, and I hope he will soon be provided for, I continue to enjoy good health, but I do not like the climate of Bahia. I have not had an opportunity of seeing the Reverend Mr Penny, but I hear that he is quite well at Pernambuco. Pray offer to Mrs Hardy and all the family my best love, I remain, My dear Jos,

Yours most affectionately,

T. M. HARDY.

John Ward was quite well at Valparaiso when I last heard from him.

CHAPTER XVIII

HARDY REAR-ADMIRAL. HE RETURNS HOME, ESCORTS
THE EXPEDITIONARY FORCE TO LISBON, COMMANDS
THE EXPERIMENTAL SQUADRON, AND STRIKES HIS
FLAG [1824-1827]

IN January 1824 Hardy reaches England in the *Creole* to
which once again he has transferred his pendant.
Lady Hardy is now living at Florence with her daughters,
and the Commodore, who now makes the United Service
Club his headquarters, acquaints his brother with the news
of his arrival in the following letter :—

> GODALMING, on my way to London,
> *Jan. 24th*, 1824.
>
> MY DEAR JOS,
>
> I left the *Creole* off Cowes assisting to get off
> the *Seringapatam* which ship we found on Shore yesterday.
> We experienced some bad weather on our way to Ports-
> mouth, but kept clear of accident. I shall get thro' my
> business in Town as soon as I possibly can and then pay
> you a visit, but I fear it will be nearly a month before I
> can possibly go into Dorsetshire.
>
> My address for the present is United Service Club,
> Waterloo St., London.[1]

---

[1] The first United Service Club was in Charles Street. Hardy
either refers to Waterloo Place, or Charles Street may in 1824 have
been known as Waterloo Street.

With best love to all, I remain, in haste,
>> My Dear Jos,
>>> Yours affectionately,
>>>> T. M. HARDY.

My Wife and Girls are all well at Florence.[1]

His next letter is written on his way home to
"Possum" :—

PORTSMOUTH, *Febry 19th*, 1824.
MY DEAR JOS,
>> I am at last thus far on my way to Dorset-
shire. I was obliged to come here, as I have many things to
settle, but I purpose quitting Portsmouth on Sunday morning and if possible will be at Dorchester on Sunday evening.
I shall write to Mary Manfield tomorrow as it is possible
that William might be out of Town. I have had a great
deal to do in London and began to fear I should never get
away.

I have heard from Louisa ; they are all well and at Florence, and as the oldest girl is rather delicate the Mother
does not like to remove her for the present. In hopes of
seeing you on Monday morning and with best love to Mrs
Hardy, I remain,
>> My Dear Jos,
>>> Yours affectionately,
>>>> T. M. HARDY.

Now intervenes a silence of more than two years (19th
February 1824 to 4th August 1826). On 27th May 1825
he became Rear-Admiral. Sir T. M. Hardy now ceased
to be a Colonel of Royal Marines, having held that rank

---

[1] Lady Hardy, in her diary for May 1824, mentions a visit paid to
Florence and Leghorn by her husband. On returning together from
Leghorn to Florence, a ball was given by them at their house in the
Piazza San Maria Novello, "in return for much civility." Long rides
were also constantly taken in the neighbourhood of the city, and the
sojourn in Italy was ever after referred to as a most enjoyable
experience.

ever since the 19th July 1821. In that capacity his pay was £80 per annum. In the autumn of 1826 he is apparently living with his family in Regent Street. The following gossipy letter speaks for itself :—

8 REGENT STREET, *August 4th*, 1826.

MY DEAR JOS,

I had the pleasure of receiving your letter a few days ago. I hope the Claret will be found as good as Mr Casher promises.

My friend Plowman rather over rates the Beauty of Emily, they are both however very good looking and most excellent girls. I am sorry to say that little Mary has got a very bad cough ; her Mother is of opinion that it is the Hooping Cough. I have been very much occupied at the Admiralty correcting Signals, and I fear we shall not finish before the latter end of this Month, but if I can get away I will pay you a visit early in September. The *Galatea* I believe is still at Portsmouth, I have not seen any of her Officers nor have I heard anything of young Bascomb, I have got an account of the money expended for him, which I will give you when we meet. I hope Cousin Jim shewed you the letter I sent him from Lord Napier [1] when you see him you may say that the *Diamond* will be in England the latter part of September she is now at Lisbon. Of course you have heard of Captn Garth having set off with Lady Astley. I suppose it will annoy the old General very much. The weather continues very warm and the harvest about London is quite finished, the wheat is very good and the Barley very short in straw but on the whole a saving crop. It is very difficult to get a Frank as every body are out of Town. Give my best love to Mrs Hardy, I remain,

My Dear Jos,

Yours affectionately,

T. M. HARDY.

[1] Francis, seventh Baron Napier [1758-1823].

A little later he writes :—

MY DEAR JOS,

I am happy to inform you that my leg is nearly well; the little Doctor put on a long face on Monday morning and said if he had been in Dorsetshire he would not on any account have allowed me to have stirred; however as I was in London he would begin with me in earnest, so he gave me the Black Pill and put on a Swinging Poultice. He now sees the necessity of attending to my stomach, and all is going quite right, and my Nose is not half so troublesome.

My Committee[1] has also indulged me by sitting in my room instead of the Admiralty which has given me the advantage of a comfortable sofa. I am very anxious to hear how Mrs Hardy is; I sincerely hope that she continues to gain her strength; pray give me a line to say how she is, Sir Edward Codrington[2] has been good enough to say he will take young Brown, but the *Asia*, his Flag ship, is not to be commissioned for a month to come.

As we are sitting at 8 Regent Street I fear I shall not be able to get a Frank but I will go out at 4 which is the time we break up and try if I can find my friend Colonel Drinkwater.[3] With best love to Mrs Hardy and hoping that I shall hear favourable accounts of her. I remain,

My Dear Jos,

Yours most affectionately,

T. M. HARDY.

I have written to Augusta this day.

[1] Sir T. M. Hardy was at this time chairman of a committee dealing with the important subject of changes in naval construction.

[2] Admiral Sir Edward Codrington [1770-1851].

[3] Colonel Drinkwater [1762-1844] the historian of the siege of Gibraltar. He subsequently assumed the additional name of Bethune.

Later in this year Rear-Admiral Sir T. M. Hardy was appointed to command the Experimental Squadron organised for the purpose of deciding on the class of ship most suited to the changed conditions of naval warfare. He received his commission on 5th December 1826, and writes to his brother with reference to his new duties :—

PORTSMOUTH, *Decr* 11*th*, 1826.

MY DEAR JOS,

I had the pleasure of receiving your letter of the 9th. I find that young Brown has run from the *Asia ;* it is not worth looking after him so let him remain with his Father. I am very sorry to hear so bad an account of Mrs Hardy, this damp weather is I fear much against her. Little Plowman says that my new command, will do more towards my recovery, than all that he can do for me. I hope he will prove to be right, for I am quite tired of blowing my nose. It certainly is much better than it was, but I am still annoyed by it, in all other respects I never was better in my life. My present command may be honourable but I fear that it will not turn out profitable ; however we must take things as they are, and hope for the best. The squadron which I am to command is built on experiment, and we shall go to sea for the purpose of trying which is the best ship of War. There are four Constructors, all of whom at present are friends of mine. As my opinion (alone) is to be taken at the Admiralty, I much fear that I shall lose three friends out of the four, however I hope and trust my opinion will be impartial ; for the rest I must take my chance. I have not heard anything more about the *Warspite*, when I do I will let you know. I have seen Miss Croan she is looking just the same as she did when you and I paid her Mother and Mrs Pope a visit in, what year shall I say, 1783 or for ought I know some years before that. I am to dine with her tomorrow to meet Mr Thompson, who is also very well. I hope Wm Manfield is getting better, his last letter told me that he had been unwell. With best love to Mrs Hardy. I remain,

My Dear Jos,

Yours affectionately,

T. M. HARDY.

Prior to his start on the "experimental" cruise, affairs in Portugal assumed a critical aspect Dom Pedro had, on the 2nd May previous, abdicated in favour of his daughter, Donna Maria da Gloria. The insurrection of the Marquis de Chaves, in favour of Dom Miguel in October, and the disturbances which followed, caused the Portuguese Government to seek the assistance of Great Britain in maintaining order, and Hardy, on 17th December, with his flag in the *Wellesley*, escorted the expeditionary force to Lisbon.[1] He was soon back again at Portsmouth busy with the Experimental Squadron, his flagship being the *Sibylle*.

Shortly after his return to England he thus writes to his brother :—

PORTSMOUTH, *Febry. 22nd*, 1827.

MY DEAR JOS,

I should have written to you before if I could have given you a favourable answer about Lieutenant Critchell, but I am sorry to say that I have so many of my own followers unemployed, that I cannot hold out to Mr Hawkins the least hope of success for his friend. I am sorry to hear that Mrs Hardy does not gain strength faster ; the cold weather I conclude is the cause. Our Connection Mr Frampton has requested of me to get one of his sons provided for, either in the Marines or otherwise, it is hard that a child should suffer for the sins of the father, but it is

---

[1] A full account of this episode is to be found in the biography of Sir Charles Napier. Our action at that time doubtless laid the foundation of the friendship now existing between Great Britain and Portugal.

quite out of my power to do anything for him. My Squadron are getting in a forward state, and I am in hopes of getting them ready for sea in a fortnight; one of them the *Satellite* has had the misfortune to get on Shore last Sunday in a heavy gale, but fortunately she has not received any damage. My health continues quite good and I do not feel the cold as I used to do. I am sorry to say that my two elder girls are laid up at Paris with severe colds, which I am not much surprised at. Pray offer to Mrs Hardy my best love, I remain,

My Dear Jos,

Yours affectionately,

T. M. HARDY.

Since writing the above, Mr Critchell has introduced himself to me, and as I have given him the same reply as stated in this letter, I hope he is satisfied; if not I am very sorry for it

Of Hardy's opinions as regards the ship of the future at this period, Sir J. H. Briggs says :—

"Sir Thomas Hardy was strongly impressed with the conviction that what the Navy stood most in need of were line-of-battle ships of 120 and 90 guns. He attached as much importance to three-deckers and 90-gun ships as Voltaire did to strong battalions, who is reported to have said with more truth than reverence that he observed that the Almighty generally fought on their side."[1]

In the course of the summer the rear-admiral's flag is transferred to the *Pyramus*, and he thus writes to Mr Joseph Hardy about Portisham business :—

PORTSMOUTH, June 9th, 1827.

MY DEAR JOS,

I had the pleasure of seeing your letter this morning. I shall not at all object to pay the odd £500 for

---

[1] *Naval Administrations*, by Sir J. H. Briggs. London : Sampson Low, 1897, p. 24.

the Rickards[1] Estate as you recommend it, but I will not trouble you to advance the money. My money at present is out on Mortgage; I have called Six Thousand Pounds in, but I fear it will be some months before I can get it; however I have no doubt but Halford will advance the money if I stand in need of it; however I will arrange with William Manfield when I see him. Thank God that I was not returned for Weymouth[2] I have nothing to do with Politics, they are all friends of mine, and I attend to my Orders. I did not intend to have informed you that I had been in correspondence with Mrs Walcott, because I knew it would vex you as my object is to oblige you and not your Nephew in Law. Their folly shall not stand in his way of promotion, I have named him to His Royal Highness[3] who makes no promises, but says he will not forget him. If the young man has patience I think his promotion certain, but pray do not hint it to any of his connections, as it will be deemed by them as a promise from me. It has quite slipped my memory what I said to William Manfield, about young Bascombe, but I should think that I did not speak of his Father, for I consider him as an Orphan and as such I have taken him under my protection. I have seen him and he is looking· very well. Lady Hardy with my girls

---

[1] Sir Andrew Riccard, Kt., was a native of Portisham, of very mean extraction, and who, going to sea young, acquired a great fortune; was an eminent merchant and President of the East India and Turkey Companies. He purchased the manor of Portisham. He was born 1604, and died 6th September 1672. His daughter Christian married John, Lord Berkeley of Stratton. The Hardys had been lessees of part of this estate, and now Sir Thomas Hardy purchased a portion which afterwards came to his nephew, William Manfield.

[2] The Right Hon. Thomas Wallace and Masterton Ure, Esq., this year (1827) became members for Weymouth. If Hardy was a candidate, as it certainly seems to have been the case, this was his third defeat for that constituency (see *ante*, p. 155).

[3] The death of the Duke of York in January 1827 made the Duke of Clarence next heir to the throne. In April of that year he had accepted the office of Lord High Admiral in the Canning administration. He resigned the post in August 1828.

are quite well and staying at Dieppe. I hear that the youngest has grown very much & is much the prettiest of the three. I saw in the papers the melancholy death of poor John Balston, but I have not heard from Augusta since my return. I am sorry to hear that Mrs Plowman is unwell but I hope this fine weather will set her up again. Pray offer to her my best Compliments and with best love to Mrs Hardy, I remain,

My Dear Jos,

Yours affectionately,

T. M. HARDY.

Wm Manfield is not to be alarmed if he sees in the papers of my having sailed. I am only going out for two days to try some new guns.

He next writes on the same subject:—

PORTSMOUTH, Sept 7th, 1827.

MY DEAR JOS,

I am much obliged to you for your letter which I received this morning. I really am very anxious to see you before we sail, which will be very soon after the 15th instant, and if you can make it convenient to come to Portsmouth I shall be delighted to see you. Our Ships are preparing for foreign service, but I do not think that I shall go abroad just now; however I should not like to leave Spithead without seeing you and really I have not time to visit my friends in Dorsetshire. I am not in the least surprised at what you say about our beloved Sister, and I have no doubt but she will keep the little piece of ground which divides your property from that which I have purchased. I can give you a Bed. I am at Meradith's the Tailor 73 High Street opposite the Parade Coffee House. If you will give me a line to say at what time you will arrive I will look out for you. I have told William Manfield that the money to pay the remainder of the purchase is now laying in Cooke & Halford's hands, therefore the sooner it is paid for the better. I wrote to Mr Walcott a few days ago at Doulo [*sic*] but of course the letter will follow him. I fear that I shall find great trouble in getting him promoted for I do not think that he will keep a sufficient time on a foreign station. I have lately heard from my family at Dieppe they are all well and talk of spending the next Winter in England.

Pray offer to Mrs Hardy my best love,

I remain,

My Dear Jos,

Yours most affectionately,

T. M. HARDY.

On Trafalgar Day Hardy struck his flag, and thus writes to his sister at Portisham :—

8 REGENT STREET, *October 26th*, 1827.

MY DEAR AUGUSTA,

I was quite sorry to hear from William Manfield a day or two ago that Martha had met with an accident, pray give me a line and tell me how she is. I have been very much hurried since my return from Sea and I do not quite see when I shall be quiet, for I set off this day for Portsmouth where I purpose to remain until Monday or Tuesday, when I shall again venture to this place. My flag is for the present struck and I do not as yet know if I am soon to hoist it again. I heard a few days ago from my Girls they are all quite well and at Paris. You had better send your letter here as my movements are so very uncertain.

With best love to my Sisters, I remain,

My Dear Augusta,

Your affectionate Brother,

T. M. HARDY.

Rear-Admiral Sir T. M. Hardy was evidently unconscious of the fact that the twenty-second anniversary of the most memorable day in his life was destined to see the end of his active service as an officer in the Royal Navy. It had lasted exactly thirty-five years and three hundred and sixty-four days.

CHAPTER XIX

HARDY RESTS ON HIS LAURELS [1827-1830]. HE
BECOMES FIRST SEA LORD OF THE ADMIRALTY IN
THE GOVERNMENT OF EARL GREY [NOVEMBER
1830—JULY 1834]

A PROLONGED period of almost entire cessation
from active employment followed the Trafalgar
Day of 1827. He was still residing at 8 Regent Street,
where he remained for another two years, removing in
the autumn of 1829 to Addison Villa, Kensington.
Amongst the Hardy papers at Dorchester is a portion
of a letter dated the 4th February 1828, which shows that
he was still negociating for the purchase of the Rickard
(generally written Riccard) property at Portisham.[1] He
refers also to Captain Elliot, who now filled his old post
on board the *Victory*. Hardy's keen interest in Dorset
affairs remained unabated, although he had done for ever
with electioneering at Weymouth.

8 REGENT STREET, *Febry 4th*, 1828.
MY DEAR JOS,

I cannot resist enclosing you a letter which
Captain Elliot of the *Victory* has sent me which he received from Sir Thomas Staines.[2] Should George Feaver
to whom I have written come to you, pray advise him to
take his boy out of the Service. William Manfield when

---

[1] See *ante*, p. 201.
[2] Sir Thomas Staines, Capt. R.N. (born 1776, died 1830).

in Town said that Rickard's Estate would be transferred
to me in 10 days. The Election[1] set him off and I have
heard no more about it.

For nearly a year and three quarters the corre-
spondence leaves no trace, but in the *Life of Admiral Sir
William Parker*[2] may be found the following note, well
worth quotation :—" 18th July 1829—I have," writes Sir W.
Parker, "unexpectedly this day received intimation from
the Admiralty that they have nominated me to meet
Vice-Admiral Sir L. Halsted, Rear-Admiral Sir Thos.
Hardy, Commodore White and Captain E. Brace and
Thos. Hayes in committee for the purpose of revising the
Rigging Warrant and Sea Store Establishment of the
Navy   . I consider the measure very desirable, and
they have wisely included Sir T. Hardy, who is unquestion-
ably the best seaman, and most understanding on the
points to be under consideration, in the service."

A fortnight later, Hardy writes as follows to his old
midshipman of the *Triumph* and *Barfleur* days :—

UNITED SERVICE CLUB HOUSE,
PALL MALL,
August 3rd, 1829.

MY DEAR SIR,

Owing to my being out of Town I did not
receive your letter of the 16th ultimo until my return. I
fear that if it is out of my power to get you employed
either in a packet or in the Transport Service. The
former I think the best employment if you can get an
appointment. Captain Bowles at present is out of Town.
Should you prefer the Preventative Service I will with

---

[1] He evidently alludes to the Weymouth Election of 1828, when
Edward Burtenshaw Sugden became Member in the place of Thomas
Wallace.

[2] *Life of Admiral of the Fleet, Sir William Parker,* by Vice-
Admiral Augustus Phillimore. London : Harrison, 1879, vol. i., p. 494.

great pleasure interest myself with Captn. Bowles on your behalf.

I beg to offer my best compliments to your Brother, and Should Commodore and Mrs Bullen be at Burton will you offer them my best regards.

I remain My dear Sir

Yours very sincerely

T. M. HARDY.

To Lieut. ROBERTS,
Burton Bradstock.

On the 23rd October 1829, he writes a letter to his brother, alluding to his change of residence, and the death of his brother-in-law and Dorset neighbour, John Thresher, of Upway.

PORTSMOUTH, *October 23rd*, 1829.

MY DEAR JOS,

Your letter of the 20th instant gave me the information of the death of our late Brother-in-law Mr Thresher[1] an event which I own I was in some degree prepared for, as I thought him breaking very fast when last I was in the Country. In general occurrences of that nature tend to remove past differences, and I have to regret that the loss of our relation has not brought that consolation. I own from my short but frequent visits into Dorsetshire I never thought that the deceased was the cause of the unpleasant feeling which existed in the family, and I sincerely hope that the few years which may be spared to our Sister, she will employ them in making peace with her brother and Sisters. I have since received a letter from Captain Balston, but it had been detained in London two days. Lady Hardy has given up her intended journey to Paris and all have taken a small house at Kensington situated close to Holland House and she will take possession of it on Monday next. It is called

---

[1] John Thresher, Esq., of Upway, died 18th October 1829, aged 82.

Addison Villa, a finer name than Addison Cottage, which most probably would suit it better. I have been detained here longer than was first expected, but I think we shall finish our labours in ten days when I shall join my family. They are all quite well. Our house is only taken for six months. I see no prospect of employment; unfortunately they do not want any more Admirals, so I must wait patiently. I am rather surprised at Plowmans anxiety to be called father, probably he thinks it would make Mrs P. more obedient, pray remember me to him I am pleased to hear that Mrs Hardy is better and I sincerely hope we shall have a mild winter. Pray offer to her my best love, I remain,

My Dear Jos,

Your affectionate Brother,

T. M. HARDY.

A month later he writes from his new home :—

ADDISON ROAD, KENSINGTON,
Nov. 26th, 1829.

MY DEAR JOS,

You will see by the enclosed note that Bascombe is in the *Donegal* at Sheerness. It is quite possible that he has not as yet written to his Brother to say so. As Sir Jahleel Brenton[1] is an acquaintance of mine I shall take an opportunity of thanking him for taking the youngster but I shall get him into a Sea going ship as soon as any of my friends are employed. I remain,

My Dear Jos,

Yours affectionately,

T. M. HARDY.

[1] Sir Jahleel Brenton, Vice-Admiral (born 1770, died 1844). He commanded *La Minerve* when lost off Cherbourg in 1803 (see *ante*).

The next letter (only a month before he became First
Sea Lord at Whitehall) is as follows :—

SEAFORD,[1] *October 25th,* 1830.

MY DEAR JOS,

We have spent a very pleasant month at this
place, the weather having been delightful.   We return to
Addison Road on Friday next.   Lady Hardy has derived
great benefit from Sea Bathing and is now nearly recovered ;
the young ladies are all quite well they all join me in best
love to you and Mrs Hardy whom I hope is also well.
When you see Cousin James will you thank him from me
for a basket of game which he sent me a short time ago.
The Farmers in this neighbourhood are quite tired of the
dry weather as they cannot commence their wheat sowing ;
however we have had a little [rain] this morning and I have
no doubt but we shall now have enough of it.   I have not
heard of my Sisters since you last wrote to me, but I hope
during this fine weather that they have laid in a sufficient
stock of Health to carry them thro' the Winter.   The
Politics on the Continent continue very unsettled I think
this Country will find great difficulty in keeping out of a
War.[2]   I have applied for the East India Station, in the
event of Sir Edward Owen[3] coming home, which they say
he must do in consequence of ill health, but I cannot get
Lord Melville to give me a promise.   I remain

My Dear Jos,

Your affectionate Brother,

T. M. HARDY.

England was now in the throes of the reform agitation,
which was to have such momentous consequence.   George

---

[1] Seaford in Sussex, 2¾ miles south-east of Newhaven.

[2] The revolution in France was further complicated by the struggle
between the Belgians and the Dutch.   The position of affairs was for
some time very threatening.

[3] Sir Edward Owen, Admiral (born 1771, died 1849).   He did not
return from the East India Station until 1832.

IV. had died four months previously, and Sir Thomas
Hardy's friend and fellow sailor had become King of
England. On the 15th November the Tory Ministry of
the Duke of Wellington was defeated, and William IV. sent
for the leader of the Opposition, Earl Grey. In the Wellington administration Robert, Lord Melville, had filled the
post of First Lord of the Admiralty, an office which he had
held with one brief interval ever since 1812. Lord Grey
proposed Sir James Graham as Lord Melville's successor.
The King at first demurred, and only agreed to the appointment on the understanding that Hardy, with whose views
he was in sympathy, and in whose ability and discretion
he placed entire confidence, should replace Sir George
Cockburn as First Sea Lord: Cockburn, by a strange coincidence, had also been one of Nelson's captains. Sir James
Briggs, in his *Naval Administrations* (p. 14), writes :—

"Sir Thomas Hardy was no politician, had no seat in
Parliament, and was selected solely on account of his
high professional attainments. . . . He did not possess the
gift of eloquence, and could not indite a despatch with the
felicity of Sir George Cockburn though no one knew
better than he what ought to be written, for nothing could
be more true than the remark of Lord Nelson respecting
him that Providence had imbued him with an intuitive
right judgment. . . . Sir Thomas was frequently heard to
say 'that he could not argue against Cockburn, Croker, and
Barrow,[1] for they carried far too heavy a broadside for him.
They would prove him wrong in two minutes though he
knew he was right for all that.'"

In another place (p. 15), Sir James Briggs, who had
himself served under Hardy at Whitehall, says: "The
brilliant services of Hardy as a naval officer are of world-
wide fame, but his administrative abilities as First Sea

---

[1] Sir George Cockburn was First Sea Lord of the Admiralty before
Hardy's appointment. Sir John Barrow held the post of Secretary of
the Admiralty for forty-one years, and John Wilson Croker was for a
long time Political Secretary of the Admiralty.

Lord of the Admiralty have never received a fair meed of honour by the country at large, though thoroughly appreciated in the service. He took a large and comprehensive view of all subjects, and clearly foresaw the many changes which must inevitably take place in the navy. . . . If Sir George Cockburn dreamt of the past, Sir Thomas Hardy lived for the future; he was not only a reformer, but also a most prudent reformer, for he considered how far the leading members of the profession would be likely to go with him, so as not to provoke needless opposition. He was unquestionably thirty years in advance of the opinions held by the admirals of that day; and seemed to behold, in prophetic vision, the mighty changes which science and steam are now effecting in the naval service. He was strongly impressed with the conviction that our naval superiority could only be maintained by large and powerful line-of-battle ships carrying heavy armament, as in action nothing could resist their concentrated fire. He was no less an advocate for numerous and powerfully-armed frigates, as indispensable appendages to a fleet. He considered all large sums of money expended upon small craft as money wasted, as they must necessarily become a prey to vessels of superior force. The policy of Sir Thomas was never to allow any foreign power to gain, even temporarily, an advantage over us. He used to say, 'Happen what will, England's duty is to take and keep the lead.'"

Sir Thomas Hardy lost no time in taking over his new duties. His predecessor (who had always been his senior and formerly his commanding officer in the navy) did his best to make matters smooth; and Sir James Briggs has placed on record an interesting conversation between them, on the occasion of Cockburn "waiting" on his former Lieutenant on board the *Meleager* and *Minerve*, to take his instructions on leaving for the command of the West India Station, which had been given him. Sir James says Hardy always told him he felt in Cockburn's presence just as he did in the old days when their relations were so strikingly different. On the occasion of the above-mentioned interesting meeting, Hardy had requested Sir James (then an Admiralty clerk) to remain in the room. We are gratified, therefore, with the following characteristic account at first hand of what took place [1] :—

"'My dear Hardy,' said Sir George, 'I have come to receive your instructions, as you know I am now under your orders.' Sir Thomas said, 'Pray make any corrections in them you think fit, sir'; when Sir George with a smile replied, 'It is not for me, Hardy, to make corrections, but merely to offer any suggestion that may occur to me for your better consideration.' I then proposed to Sir Thomas Hardy that it might be perhaps agreeable to Sir George Cockburn to take the instructions home with him, so as to peruse them at leisure. Sir George said, 'This seems a good suggestion, Hardy. If you have no objection I will take them with me,' which he accordingly did, and then left, to the great relief of Sir Thomas Hardy. As soon as Sir George had gone, Sir Thomas said, 'I really cannot believe I am First Sea Lord, the tables seem so entirely turned.' Is it not wonderfully strange that a man, the bravest of the brave, who, during the raging of the storm and the fury of the battle, would stand cool and collected and not lose his presence of mind for an instant, should be temporarily disconcerted upon finding himself in authority over one to whom he had for years paid professional obedience? Yet such is the effect of habit and discipline."

The first letter from the Admiralty in the Dorchester correspondence is dated 30th March 1832, but before that its writer was nominated a Grand Cross of the Bath.[2]

---

[1] *Naval Administrations*, p. 19.

[2] Either the officials took their time in sending in their bill of costs, or the new G.C.B. was in no hurry to pay them, for in possession of Mrs J. C. Thynne is the following document :—

"Received, April 19th 1833, of Rear-Admiral Sir Thomas M. Hardy,

This was on the 13th September 1831. This letter is addressed to his nephew, William Manfield, then, like his father before him, a Dorchester solicitor. The First Sea Lord is evidently now in much request as a godfather "down Dorset way":—

ADMIRALTY, *March 30th*, 1832.

MY DEAR WILLIAM,

Doctor Plowman is anxious to Christen his two boys, and as I am to be Sponsor to Thomas Henry, I shall be much obliged if you will get my brother to stand Proxy for me, unless the Doctor will allow you to officiate for me. Lady Hardy and your cousins regret very much that they had not the pleasure of seeing you this morning, but they hope to be more fortunate when next you come to Town.

With best love to your Mother and Sisters. I remain,

My Dear William,

Your affectionate Uncle,

T. M. HARDY.

In August Sir T. M. Hardy goes with Admirals Sir W. Parker and Dundas on a tour of official inspection to Devonport.

Three months later he writes to his brother Joseph as follows:—

ADMIRALTY, *November 9th*, 1832.

MY DEAR JOS,

I am sorry to inform you that our oldest girl Louisa has taken cold, which the Medical men fear will fall on her lungs, if the greatest precaution is not taken.

Bart., G.C.B., the sum of one hundred and sixty-four pounds, seventeen shillings and 2d., the amount of fees due to the several officers of the most Hon. Military Order of the Bath, upon his nomination to be a Knight Grand Cross of the said Order.

"J. PULMAN,

"£164, 17s. 2d. *Receiver of Fees.*"

Lady Hardy, as you may suppose, is very much alarmed about it and has almost made up her mind to go to Malta with her, by the next Packet, leaving the two youngest girls with me. I hope that it is not so serious as the Medical men imagine, but I am sorry to say she has nearly lost her voice.

I have just received a fine turtle and I will send Mrs Hardy some in a few days. It will be ready dressed and all you have to do is to warm it and add a wine glass of Madiera with a little lemon juice ; not more than one small lemon or half a large one. It shall leave London on Tuesday next per mail & it will keep two or three days. I have a good deal to do but my health continues as good as ever. All the rest of the family are quite well & join me in best love to you and Mrs Hardy. I remain,

My Dear Jos,

Your affectionate Brother,

T. M. HARDY.

On the 5th June 1833, Hardy thus writes from the Admiralty to his friend, Sir W. Parker :—

"You see by the papers that there has been a blow up in the House of Lords about the neutrality of Portugal, but you have come off with flying colours. There is to be a trial of strength on the same subject in the House of Commons to-morrow evening. If we are not more successful there I fear that we shall be in a bad way ; but I think the Commons will be on our side, and I do not think the Lords can turn us out."

Five months later, Hardy, still at his desk in Whitehall, writes thus, announcing the approaching marriage of his youngest daughter to Mr John Atholl Bannatyne MacGregor, who, in 1841, succeeded his father as third baronet :—

ADMIRALTY, *Novr 9th*, 1833.

MY DEAR JOS,

It was yesterday settled that Mary is to be married on Thursday next the 14th inst. It is to be as private as possible, and they are to spend the honeymoon at Stoke near Windsor at a Cottage of Lord Sefton's. The ladies are all quite well and join me in best love to you and Mrs Hardy.

I remain, My Dear Jos,

Yours affectionately,

T. M. HARDY.

Sir T. M. Hardy next writes :—

ADMIRALTY, *Decr 4th*, 1833.

MY DEAR JOS,

Perhaps you would like to send the enclosed to Mr Tizard. I have made fifty applications to the Admiral for the promotion of different people but have not been fortunate enough to get one promoted ; the fact is that we are reducing the Naval Establishments in all the different yards, and there is no promotion ; however if you particularly wish it I will write to Admiral Garnett, but I know that nothing can be done for Jos Hawkins.

Lady Hardy and the two girls are at Woburn Abbey with the Duke of Bedford[1] and Mrs MacGregor[2] and her Husband will return to Town in a day or two. I have heard from William Manfield & I will let him know when the boy is to be sent. I remain,

My Dear Jos, Yours affy.,

T. M. HARDY.

[1] John Russell, K.G., sixth Duke of Bedford (born 1766, died 1839). In view of Hardy's birth at Kingston Russell (see *ante*), it is a strange coincidence that Lady Hardy, through the Lennoxes, should be connected with that ancient family. In 1833, John, Duke of Bedford, was the owner of Kingston Russell.

[2] Sir J. A. B. MacGregor, Bart., was the father of Sir Evan MacGregor, K.C.B., now (1905) Permanent Secretary at the Admiralty.

The First Sea Lord was evidently besieged with Dorset aspirants to naval employment. Here are two of his replies :—

ADMIRALTY, *Decr 4th,* 1833.

MY DEAR JOS,

I have nothing whatever to do with the appointment or promotion of the men in the Victualling yards or I should be very glad to attend to the request of Joseph Hawkins. The patronage rests with Rear-Admiral Superintendent Garnett.

I remain, My Dear Jos,
Your Affectionate Brother,
T. M. HARDY.

ADMIRALTY, *April 23rd,* 1834.

MY DEAR WILLIAM,

I have again made application to all my friends, and I hope that your wishes have been crowned with success. Pray let me see you before you go into Dorsetshire.

I remain,
Yours affectly.,
T. M. HARDY.

About this time the First Sea Lord of the Admiralty became a Vice-Patron of the Royal Thames Yacht Club, and so remained till the day of his death. His engraved portrait may still be seen there. He had already been for many years a member of the United Service Club, where his bust now occupies a place of honour. He also belonged to the Royal Naval Club of 1765, and often attended its fortnightly dinners. In 1809, with his friends Berry and Blackwood, he had, in addition, joined the Navy Club of 1785. These clubs since 1888 have been amalgamated under the designation of The Royal Naval Club of 1765 and 1785.

Sir T. M. Hardy's useful presence in the councils of Whitehall was not to last much longer. On the 8th April 1834, he was appointed Governor of Greenwich Hospital, in succession to Sir Richard Keats,[1] but it was distinctly understood (at King William's personal suggestion) that in the event of war Sir Thomas Hardy would again take the command of a fleet and serve his country on the high seas. A few weeks later Lord Grey (on acount of Irish complications) resigned, and was succeeded by Lord Melbourne. Lord Auckland replaced Sir James Graham at the Admiralty, and soon afterwards Sir Thomas Hardy migrated from the Admiralty to the scene of his duties on the banks of the Thames. The following letter shows that before he quitted Whitehall he was already practically in harness at Greenwich :—

ADMIRALTY, *May 12th*, 1834.

MY DEAR LETHBRIDGE,[2]

I sent you last Eveng a lanthorn which was taken in the *Ville de Paris*[3] which I shall be obliged if you will place with other curious things. I now send Commander Fleming's Letter. I also send you a letter from Mr Lene and shall be obliged if you can inform him what vessel his son belongs to. I remain,

Dear Mr Lethbridge,

Yours very truly,

T. M. HARDY.

---

[1] Admiral Sir R. Keats (born 1757, died 1834). Nelson had the highest admiration for Keats, who in 1803 commanded off Toulon the *Superb*, of which ship Hardy became captain fifteen years later. It was in 1803 that Nelson said, " Keats is one of the very best officers in His Majesty's Navy. I esteem his person almost equal to one French 74-, and the *Superb* and her captain equal to two 74- gun ships."

[2] John Arscott Lethbridge, afterward one of Hardy's executors.

[3] A similar lantern still hangs in the hall of Portisham House, the roof of which, tradition says, is supported by oaken beams sent there by T. M. Hardy from "broken-up" battle ships.

His Majesty purposes going to Church at the Hospital on the 1st of June.

Allusion has been made to Sir T. M. Hardy's excusable slips in the matter of orthography, which here and there are observable in his straightforward, downright, matter-of-fact letters. Sir J. H. Briggs (to whom Hardy was a giant amongst First Sea Lords, and little less than a hero), gives the following anecdote on the subject which presumably refers to an occurrence of 1831 : " At this time," he writes (*Naval Administrations*, p. 32), " the officer in command of the Channel Squadron was Vice-Admiral Sir Edward Codrington. He was a Trafalgar captain and the hero of Navarino. Unfortunately he had, about this time, involved himself in some unpleasantness by imprudently preferring certain charges against Captain Dickinson of the *Genoa*, which he failed to substantiate. The squadron being ready for sea, Sir Thomas Hardy asked Sir James Graham, just as the Board was breaking up, what orders he wished him to give to Sir Edward Codrington. He replied, ' I think you had better send the squadron to cruise for three weeks or a month for the purpose of gunnery and exercise. Write a minute to that effect, and give it to Mr Briggs to bring to me.' I went with Sir Thomas Hardy to his private room where he wrote as follows : ' Vice-Admiral Sir Edward Codrington to proceed to sea with the squadron under his command, and to cruise for three weeks for the purpose of exercise, and gunnery off the " Silly " Islands.' I took the minute to Sir James, and handed it to him with a grave face. He smiled upon reading it, and said, ' A very proper place, Mr Briggs, for that admiral to cruise. Nevertheless, we had better insert the " C " before it falls into the hands of the young gentlemen of the office.' "

It is only common justice to the memory of Sir Thomas Hardy to place on record in this volume the following minute made by Sir James Graham before quitting office :—

ADMIRALTY,
4th June 1834.

Understanding that in the new Patent constituting this Board, the name of Sir Thomas Hardy, the Governor of Greenwich Hospital, will not appear, and myself being about to leave an office, in which I have had the honour of serving with Sir Thomas for three years and a half, I cannot omit an earnest recommendation to the Board, that a mark of respect, which was granted to Sir George Cockburn, should be tendered to Sir Thomas Hardy; and that he should be requested to nominate a Commander, a Lieutenant and a Mate for promotion by the Board, before he leaves this Office, as a special mark of gratitude for his services, and of admiration of his Character.

It appears to me conducive to the public good, that this Justice should be rendered to exemplary Merit by Colleagues, who can best appreciate it. The Naval Character of Sir Thomas Hardy will live in the Annals of his Country, while Nelson and Trafalgar are remembered: it is right, that his Civil Services should be recorded at the Admiralty, with some mark of gratitude and respect, which are so justly due.

J. R. G. GRAHAM.

CHAPTER XX

SIR THOMAS HARDY, BART., G.C.B., GOVERNOR OF GREEN-
WICH HOSPITAL (1834-1839). HIS DEATH THERE,
20TH SEPTEMBER 1839

THE last post to which Sir Thomas was ever appointed
must have been one in many ways after his own
heart. Amongst his predecessors at Greenwich Hospital—
the Royal Palace converted into a great naval asylum by
the munificence of King William and Queen Mary in 1694—
were his own ancestral kinsman, Admiral Sir Charles
Hardy (who had died there a little more than half a
century before), as well as such distinguished sailors as Sir
G. B. Rodney, Samuel, Lord Hood (another Dorset "sea-
dog"), and Sir Hugh Palliser. Congratulations came to
him from all sides. Sir William Parker wrote from Lisbon
expressing his hopes that Hardy would "hold the position
long with uninterrupted pleasure."

One of the most prominent characteristics of Hardy's
generous and kindly nature was a solicitude for the comfort
and happiness of those placed under his command. His
anxiety about the young officers and sailors of his various
ships (as constantly shown in his letters to Dorchester) is
often quite touching. Even at that period when the navy
served as a sort of refuge for the very dregs of society he
believed in treating the British sailors as rational human
beings, instead of as animals amenable only to fear of
punishment. In the matter of discipline, Sir Thomas

GREENWICH PENSIONERS IN HARDY'S TIME.

TRAFALGAR DAY.

" Hearts of oak are our ships,
   Jolly tars are our men ;
   They always are ready
   To fight and to conquer again and again."

[To face page 220.

Hardy was far in advance of his times. He was the first who had the courage to trust to the honour of his men and to dispense with the patrol of boats round the ships for the prevention of desertion. He was in the habit of granting shore-leave for forty-eight hours at a time, with no security for their punctual return but their pledged words. The result was the creation of an *esprit de corps*, and on one occasion, when weighing anchor to put to sea, the whole crew was apparently in a ferment of dissatisfaction. It soon became known that the cause of the commotion was the continued absence of two of the sailors on leave, which their comrades regarded as a breach of good faith reflecting on them, one and all. The missing men were seen approaching in a boat, rowing might and main. Three cheers were given, not for them, but for "Cap'n Hardy." At Greenwich Hospital, Sir Thomas Hardy found a new sphere for his geniality and human sympathy. He rapidly became as popular with the pensioners (many of whom had served under him) as he formerly was with the middies and "captain's servants." Many abuses prevailed at Greenwich Hospital when he arrived there, which Hardy at once set himself to remedy. His biographer, in Colbourne's *United Service Journal*,[1] writes as follows:—"With his great kindness of heart, he endeavoured to do away, as much as possible, with the sentence of expulsion from the Hospital—which sentence, as it carried with it the loss of all claim to re-admission as well as forfeiture of pension, he considered highly objectionable, and we believe it was rarely, if ever, resorted to by him. But another sentence, the resistance of which not unfrequently led to expulsion, was felt by him to be of a nature too degrading to be passed upon an old sailor—that of wearing a bright-yellow coat with red sleeves. This punishment was commonly inflicted by the Council when a man had been found drunk upon a Sunday. We are far from advocating drunkenness on any day, and particularly upon the Sabbath; but it must be borne in mind that on that day,

[1] 1839, part iii., p. 385.

more than on any other, the pensioners are visited by their children and friends—an adjournment to the ale-house seems to follow as a matter of course—an extra pint of porter, or a glass of grog too much, is administered, and the old man forgets that it is Sunday. It is surely not such an offence, great though it be in a certain light, as to render it necessary to degrade that man from his station amongst his fellows by putting upon him a badge of infamy. It was in this light that the humane Governor viewed the offence and the punishment, and he never suffered it to be carried into execution. He also requested and obtained his late Majesty's consent to the substitution of trousers for knee-breeches in the dress of the pensioners—an alteration which conferred an incalculable degree of comfort upon the pensioners. But that which most endeared him to every one was his amiable simplicity—a simplicity arising from pureness of heart and intellect, which shed upon all his actions a soft and pleasing light. He was a Christian in profession and practice."

After Hardy's death a Dorset sailor, Mr Edward Thorn, who had served with him as purser on the South America Station (1821-1827),[1] speaking at Dorchester, rendered an eloquent tribute to his large heartedness and consideration for others. Mr Thorn assured those who were assembled to do honour to Hardy's memory, that no Governor of Greenwich Hospital had ever enjoyed anything like so large a measure of popularity with every class of its inmates. Shortly before his death, the visitor had overheard one of the pensioners exclaim: "There goes our good old Governor: God bless him. We honour the very ground he treads on."

At Greenwich, Hardy found his post no sinecure. In addition to his routine duties, he had to arrange the ceremonial for state visits paid there by the King and Queen on the anniversaries of great naval victories, when they happened to fall on Sundays. The "Sailor King"

[1] See *ante*, p. 191.

made these "progresses" one of his rules of life.   An
allusion to the earliest of these royal pilgrimages to
Greenwich occurs in one of the last letters written by Sir
T. Hardy from the Admiralty.   The following communica-
tion relates to the thirty-eighth anniversary of the Battle of
Camperdown :—

GREENWICH HOSPITAL,
Octr. 3rd, 1835.

MY DEAR ELLIOT,

     I have received His Majesty's commands to
inform you that he wishes the Board of Admiralty, now in
London, and also Sir John Barrow to attend Divine Service
in the Chapel at this Institution on Sunday the 11th
instant.   A Guard of Honor of Royal Marines is also to be
provided from Woolwich.   I am also commanded to invite
you to dine at St James' Palace on that Day at 7 o'clock.
Frock Dress.

     I remain, My dear Elliot,

Yours very truly,
T. M. HARDY.

This I hope to deliver in person.

Endorsed—3 *Octr.*—Direct Commandant of Woolwich
to furnish a Guard of Honor consisting of 100 men to
receive His Majesty at Greenwich Hospital at half after ten
o'clock on Sunday the 11th instant.   Orders as on former
occasion, viz., 17 July 1835.—J. H. B.

The following account of the proceedings appeared in
the *Annual Register* for 1835 :—" A large body of the
Metropolitan Police, together with the constabulary force
of Greenwich, attended in the avenues leading to the
Hospital, as well as within the bounds of the Hospital
itself, to preserve order.   A strong detachment of Royal
Marines was stationed in the great quadrangle of the
building, and a guard of honour, selected from the same
Corps, was formed in a line, extending from the great hall

to the chapel.   Exactly at half-past eleven o'clock, His Majesty, accompanied by the Queen and Prince George of Cumberland,[1] and attended by the Royal Suite, in six carriages, each drawn by four horses, and escorted by a detachment of the 8th Hussars, entered the western gates of the Hospital, the band of the Royal Marines performing the National Anthem in a most spirited style, and proceeded to the chapel.   The lower part was chiefly filled by the veteran inmates of the institution; those who had served under Admiral Duncan on the eleventh of October 1797, were conspicuously placed by themselves in a situation opposite to the Royal pew.   The Reverend Dr Cole, Chaplain to the institution, having read the prayers, the Bishop of Hereford[2] ascended the pulpit, and preached a sermon, having selected as his text Ephesians, chapter iv., verse 1.[3]   At a quarter before two o'clock their Majesties and suite left the chapel, and proceeded to Town."

Nearly three weeks later, Hardy thus writes to his daughter, Mrs MacGregor :—

GREENWICH HOSPITAL,
Octr. 20, 1835.

MY DEAR MARY,

Thank you for your little note which I received a few days ago.   We were fortunate in having a fine day on the 11th, and as you will have heard from your sisters that every thing went off quite as well as we could wish.   I dined after at St James', where I had to make a speech, which annoyed me more than fighting the Battle, for which I had to return thanks to His Majesty on the compliments paid to the Officers and Men of the Nile.

I am glad to hear that my Grandson is so well.

In the following year, Sir Thomas Hardy appears to have met the clever but unfortunate Letitia Elizabeth

---

[1] Afterwards King of Hanover.

[2] Edward Grey, D.D., Bishop of Hereford [1832-1837].

[3] " I, therefore, the prisoner of the Lord, beseech you that ye walk worthy of the vocation wherewith ye are called."

Landon at Greenwich. He never could for a moment foresee that this young and enthusiastic woman was pre-destined ten months later to predecease the veteran of 68. She subsequently addressed him the following poem, the original of which, signed " L. E. L."[1] is now amongst the Dorchester correspondence in possession of Mr H. A. Huxtable :—

" Silence is now upon the seas,
    The silent seas of yore ;
The thunder of the cannonade
    Awakes the wave no more.

The battle-flag droops o'er the mast,
    There quiet let it sleep ;
For it hath won in wilder hours
    Its empire o'er the deep.

Now let it wave above their homes,
    Of those who fought afar ;
The victors of the Baltic Sea,
    The brave of Trafalgar.

Upon a terrace by the Thames,
    I saw the Admiral stand ;
He who received the latest clasp
    Of Nelson's dying hand.

Age, toil, and care had somewhat bowed
    His bearing proud and high ;
But yet resolve was on his lip,
    And fire was in his eye.

I felt no wonder England holds
    Dominion o'er the seas :
Still the red cross will face the world
    While she hath men like these.

And gathered there beneath the sun,
    Were loitering veterans old ;
As if of former victories
    And former days they told.

[1] " L. E. L." afterwards Mrs Maclean (born 1802, died 1838).

No prouder trophy hath our Isle,
  Though proud her trophies be,
Than that old Palace where are housed
  The veterans of the sea.

Her other domes—her wealth, her pride,
  Her Science may declare ;
But Greenwich hath the noblest claim—
  Her gratitude is there."

During the latter part of their residence at Whitehall (after Sir Thomas Hardy's nomination to Greenwich), and subsequent to their removal to the hospital, Lady Hardy jotted down in her diary many short memoranda as to the various functions which took place there. As early as May 1834, one finds a note to the effect that "the King sent for Sir Thomas Hardy to tell him he meant to go with the Queen to attend Church at Greenwich Hospital on the 1st June,[1] and desired that Lady Hardy also should be there to receive their Majesties. The King desired that all the survivors of Lord Howe's action should be placed on cross benches, to distinguish them.—The governor's house not being yet ready, the King and Queen could not be entertained, but Sir Thomas and Lady Hardy dined at St James's Palace next evening with the Misses Hardy."

On Saturday, 1st August, in the following year (1835), William IV. and Queen Adelaide came to a breakfast at Greenwich, "His Majesty having desired Sir Thomas and Lady Hardy to invite a suitable party to meet the Queen, the Torys being then in favour." "It was a lovely day," writes Lady Hardy. "The King and Queen and all the Court came down by water in barges, and made a most beautiful procession, about 100 guests. The Queen brought her sister the Duchess of Saxe Weimar, Lady Brownlow, Lady Denbigh, Miss Mitchell, Miss Bagot, Lord Howe (chamberlain to the Queen), Lord and Lady Jersey, Lord

[1] Sunday, June 1st, 1834, the fortieth anniversary of Lord Howe's "Glorious first of June."

Harr.

ROYAL AQUAT C E CURS ON TO GREENWICH HOSPITAL.

[To face page 226.

and Lady Mansfield and their daughters." Sir George
and Lady Seymour and Lady Hardy's three nephews,
Lord Ipswich (afterward Duke of Grafton),[1] Lord Charles
FitzRoy (present Duke of Grafton),[2] and Lord Frederick
FitzRoy, were also present,[3] Sir Thomas took the Queen
down to Luncheon in the large dining room—and the
King took Lady Hardy.   The others went to the other
rooms, where the daughters of the house presided.   Their
Majesties stayed till 6 o'c. and went back by water.   The
Thames was lined with Barges full of people[4] and there
were bands of music all along the river to Whitehall
where they disembarked.   The Band of the Royal Marines
from Woolwich played in the Court before the house."

In the course of 1836 the new railway from Greenwich
to London Bridge was opened.   Lady Hardy made up a
party for a trial trip, and the journey both ways was
effected in twenty minutes.   She adds that "none of the
guests had ever travelled before in the new fashioned
manner."   Sir Thomas Hardy declined to go at any price,
saying it was a needless risk to run, and, until his death
four years later, could never be persuaded to enter a
railway carriage.

The year of Queen Victoria's coronation was a very
busy one for the indefatigable Governor of Greenwich
Hospital, now in his seventieth year.   In May he was
constantly driving up to London to attend the meetings
of the Commission on the "Defences of the Harbours
and Coasts of England," of which he was a member.
He took a very active part in its deliberations.   Doubtless his advice and experience often proved valuable.   In
the late Admiral Colomb's Memoir of the late Admiral
Sir Cooper Key (1898), mention is made of Hardy's in-

[1] The sixth Duke of Grafton (born 1819, died 1882).

[2] The seventh Duke of Grafton (born 1821, and alive at the
centenary of Trafalgar).

[3] Born 1823, and still living.

[4] This fête is evidently the one illustrated in the rare colour-print,
dated 1st August 1838, and now reproduced.

genuity in the matter of a radical change in the mounting of guns afloat. "The great improvement," writes Admiral Colomb, "but only for carronades and lighter guns, had been the invention of Sir Thomas Hardy — Nelson's 'Trafalgar' Hardy—where the gun-carriages, without trucks, slid in and out on iron rails which were fixed to a wooden slide fastened to the ship's side by a pivot, so as to allow of the gun being trained in its port. There was an arrangement called a compressor attached to the carriage, which, dropping through a slot in the centre of the slide, could be set to grip carriage and slide together, and so check the recoil of the gun when fired, reducing the sudden strain on the breeching, and perhaps enabling the space necessary for recoil to be reduced."

On the 10th January 1837, Sir T. M. Hardy by seniority became Vice-Admiral of the Blue. Amongst the few Hardy papers at Greenwich Hospital, is a letter acknowledging the receipt of the notice of this promotion, and less than a month later—viz., 7th February—he was unanimously elected to the honourable and much-sought-after position of an Elder Brother of the Trinity House. He attended the Special Court held on that day, and subscribed the necessary declaration. On the 20th June 1837, Hardy had to mourn the loss of his true friend, King William IV., whom he had known intimately during the later portion of his career, and who was but three years his senior. During Hardy's tenure of office at Greenwich, William IV. had placed a bust there in memory of his predecessor Keats, and had always promised to pay the same honour to Hardy if he survived him. This, however, was not to be, and there is still preserved at Portisham a lock of silvery white hair, sent to the Governor by the widowed Queen, and bearing an inscription in Hardy's handwriting.

Sir Thomas and Lady Hardy were amongst those who attended the Coronation of Queen Victoria, on the 28th June 1838. Lady Hardy notes that they were "in the

Abbey from 5 A.M. to 7 P.M." On the 5th July, Marshal
Soult, the French Ambassador, came to see the hospital,
en route for a review at Woolwich. He was accompanied
by the Prince de Ligne and the Marquis de Miraflore. Sir
Thomas Hardy's almost daily drives to London continued
during the whole of the remainder of the year. In the
early summer of the following year (1839), the last of
Hardy's life, the widowed Queen Adelaide (who shared
her late husband's deep interest in Greenwich), came down
to lunch and see over the hospital. She was accompanied
by the Duchess of Saxe Weimar, Lord Howe, Lady
Georgina Curzon, and Lady Bedingfield.

Once more the old Admiral turns his face Dorsetwards.
This time he does not arrive there in either the "Subscription" or the "Balloon." His visit is announced to his
brother in the following letter :—

GREENWICH HOSPITAL,
August 12th, 1838.

MY DEAR JOS,

As my friend Lord Seaford will pass through
Dorchester in his way to Falmouth, he has been good
enough to give me a place in his carriage, but he is not
yet quite settled the day that we are to quit London, but
it will be either on Sunday Monday or Tuesday next, and
as we sleep at Salisbury I will write to you again before
we leave London. Lady Hardy and the girls start in a
Steamer for Scotland on the 19th inst.

We heard of Mary Manfield & I believe she will dine
with us tomorrow. I am joined by my Family in best love
to you and Mrs Hardy.

I remain, My Dear Jos,
Your affectionate Brother,
T. M. HARDY.

I have written to William Manfield.

As far as can be ascertained, this was the last time Hardy ever saw his beloved " Possum," where his sister still inhabited the old house which had long been their property.   One can imagine " Jos " (now a septuagenarian) coming over from Charminster to show the Governor over the Rickard estate.   It is hoped that partridges were abundant that autumn in the Portisham fields, and that the brothers (now soon to part for ever in this world) had many a pleasant chat of old times in the room adorned with naval relics over " a bottle of the best."

In November 1838 "Tom" Allen, Lord Nelson's old body servant, died in Greenwich Hospital, where, through the instrumentality of the Governor, he had passed the last years of his life in comfort.[1]   Hardy wrote on the 29th November expressing his regret at the " loss of poor Tom Allen," and a little later once more gave proof of his characteristic warmth of heart and his constant regard for his old shipmates, great and small, by causing a memorial to be erected in the Hospital cemetery, bearing the following inscription : " To the memory of Thomas Allen, the faithful servant of Lord Nelson, born at Burnham Thorpe, in the county of Norfolk, 1764, and died at the Royal Hospital, Greenwich, on the 23rd November 1838."

Well before New Year's Day (destined to be the last of Hardy's life) he was, as shown by his action in the matter of Allen, back again at the hospital.   In the letter he now writes to his brother, he shows once more the old desire to give a deserving youngster a helping hand.

GREENWICH HOSPITAL,
17th Janry, 1839.

MY DEAR JOS,

I send you an extract from a letter I have this day received from Captain Napier[2] of the *Powerful*.

---

[1] See *Nelsonian Reminiscences*, by G. S. Parsons, R.N., edited by W. H. Long.   London : Gibbings & Co., 1905.

[2] Afterwards Admiral Sir Charles Napier, G.C.B. [1786-1860].   In 1839 he was sent to the Mediterranean with the rank of Commodore.

"If you will send down your young friend I shall fill up the necessary papers for him."

You had better desire Mr Phelps to proceed as soon as convenient to Sheerness and if he comes by way of London call upon me.

My health continues quite good and I hope my leg is a little better.

I remain, Yours affectionately,

T. M. HARDY.

In March the Rev. Sydney Smith—the witty Canon of St Paul's—sent the Governor of Greenwich Hospital a volume of sermons. Having received an expression of appreciation from Lady Hardy, he wrote her the following letter :—

MY DEAR LADY HARDY,

I would rather have the approbation of Sir Thomas Hardy than that of several Bishops. If Bishops approved, the sermons must be pompous, intolerant and full of useless Theology. If Sir Thomas likes them they are true, honest and useful, and if you add your sanction then at least I am not dull, and I feel that I am helping to pay off the debt we all owe you for looking so well as you do and talking so agreeably.

Ever yours,

SYDNEY SMITH.

March 26, 1839.
33 Charles St., Berkley Square.

As yet there was no sign of a final break in Hardy's health. He is only troubled by his old enemy—rheumatism, and in May he was able to welcome Joseph Hardy and "Cousin Tom" on their return visit to Greenwich. He was apparently as full of activity as ever, and managed to attend certain official meetings in London.

GREENWICH HOSPITAL,
April 29th, 1839.

MY DEAR JOS,

I am enjoined by the ladies to say that we shall be delighted to see you and Cousin Tom on Tuesday the 7 of May I shall be in London on that day to attend the Naval and Military Commission, and if you will tell me where I can pick you up, I will call for you and take you to Greenwich, The Commission assembles at 12 o'clock at No. 10 Downing Street, Whitehall and we generally break up a little before 3, when I will call for you, but probably Cousin Tom will call at 10 Downing Street 5 minutes before 12 when he will find me at the door.

My health is slowly improving but my hands continue very weak.

I am joined by the ladies in best love to you and Mrs Hardy and we all beg to express our regret that Mrs Hardy should continue so unwell.

I remain, My Dear Jos,
Your affectionate Brother,
T. M. HARDY.

This is the last letter of Hardy to be found in the Dorchester correspondence. He became seriously ill during the late summer, but retained his consciousness almost to the last. When all hope was abandoned and Hardy knew his fate, he bade farewell to his wife and children and his beloved brother Joseph, who, with a few intimate friends, surrounded his bed, and faced death with the stoical courage and resignation one would have expected of the captain of the *Victory*. With admirable calmness, he discussed the details of his funeral, and gave certain instructions as to the distribution of a few personal mementos. The certificate of his demise on the 20th September 1839 states that he died from "torpor on paralysis of the intestines."

Eight days later all that was mortal of " Dear Hardy "

was laid to rest in the now abandoned mausoleum of
the old cemetery belonging to the hospital, where, notwithstanding later alterations, his body still remains. The
following description of the funeral appeared in the *Gentleman's Magazine* (1839, Part II., p. 652):—"On Saturday
28th Sept. the remains of this gallant officer were consigned
to their last home." . . . The funeral was in some respects
a public one, but Sir Thomas Hardy himself had strictly
enjoined his executors, Sir John Dean Paul, Bart., John
Arscott Lethbridge, Esq., and Sir George Francis Seymour,
Kt., to avoid any ostentation in the last obsequies. At
11 A.M. the procession set out from the Council Room in
the following order :—

Six boatswains, two and two.

Crew of the Governor's barge.

Colours with crape.   Mace with crape.

Muffled Drum and Fife.

Warder's Gang.

Warders, two and two.

Fifty pensioners, two and two.

The Governor's guard with halberds covered with crape.

Medical Officers, juniors.   Military Officers, juniors.

- Sir J. Brunton, the Lieutenant Governor.

Chaplains in Surplices.

Pallbearers.		*Pallbearers.*
Lieut. Filton.	THE BODY.	Lieut. Tucker.
Lieut. Rivers.		Lieut. Bedford.
Capt. Huskisson.		Capt. Larkan.

Mourners.

Commissioners of the Hospital.

Civil Officers of the Hospital.

Civil Officers of the Schools.

The late Governor's Household.

Pensioners who served with Sir Thomas Hardy in the *Victory*
and other Ships.

Two inspecting boatswains.

Amongst the mourners were :—Lord Euston, Mr Fitz-
hardinge Berkeley, the Hon. Captain Berkeley, Sir John
Paul, Mr Lethbridge (the executors), Sir Richard Dobson,
Chief Medical Officer of the Hospital. Mr Jessep, the long

and faithful friend of the deceased Admiral, and formerly his purser on board the *Ramillies*, and his secretary until appointment to Greenwich Hospital in 1834. Mr W. Manfield of Dorchester and Mr Balston (nephews to Sir Thomas).

Two of the Pallbearers, namely, Lieutenant Rivers and Captain Huskisson, were in the Battle of Trafalgar. The former was Aide-de-camp to Sir Thomas Hardy in the *Victory*, and lost a leg a short time before Lord Nelson was wounded. The latter was a midshipman on board the *Defence*.

With Sir T. M. Hardy was buried a small print of Nelson by which he set some store. This circumstance gave rise to certain rumours at the time which are thus disposed of by the biographers of the *United Service Journal* :—

"The veneration entertained for Nelson by the subject of our memoir was greater than is even generally imagined. A paragraph has gone the round of the newspapers, respecting a small print of the hero, called a miniature, which, it has been stated, was constantly worn round the neck of the subject of this memoir, and that it was his dying request to have it placed in the coffin that inclosed his own remains. That it lies buried with him is true ; in all other respects the paragraph is void of foundation ; but as he was known to have entertained a great value for the picture it was placed by him in death." [1]

The following short obituary notice was penned for the *Gentleman's Magazine* by an official of Greenwich Hospital, subscribing himself R. H. G. :—"On Sept. 20, at Greenwich Hospital, Vice-Admiral Sir Thomas M.

---

[1] In the Memoirs of Sir William Hargood, published two years after Sir T. M. Hardy's death, Mr Joseph Allen writes :—"The late good Sir Thomas Hardy permitted only one of his letters to escape destruction—that one was the first he wrote after leaving his home [see *ante*, p. 21]. It was found in a drawer, after his lamented decease, together with a small portion of Lord Nelson's hair ; which proves that the letter was highly prized by him since it was placed with such a relic."

Hardy, Bart., G.C.B., Governor of that Establishment, eminent for that judgment and self possession without which deeds of honour and arms are seldom achieved, perpetually awake to the various duties of his command, anxious for the improvement of the service to which he had devoted himself, equal to every difficulty which it could present, yet not above its most trivial details, detecting with intuitive facility whatever might require correction, and applying the due remedy, passing readily from the sharpest reproof to the very gentleness of human nature in her best forms; always mindful of those who shared with him the toils and perils of warfare, or were otherwise deserving of encouragement. Sir Thomas Hardy will descend to posterity as one of the truest models in that profession to which the State is so much indebted for its security, its wealth, and its renown.

"R. H. G."

"*21st Sept.* 1839."

As Sir T. M. Hardy left no son, the baronetcy died with him. From Greenwich Hospital his widow and unmarried daughters removed to 3 Chester Square, where they took up their abode; and thence Lady Hardy writes, five months later, the following letter to Mr Joseph Hardy, her brother-in-law :—

3 CHESTER SQUARE,
February 25th, 1840.

DEAR MR HARDY,

I write a few lines not expecting you to give yourself the trouble of answering me, unless your arm has quite recovered its use, but to tell you that Mr Lethbridge will pay you a visit shortly as he is on a visit in Devonshire & will take Dorchester on his way back but it will probably be only for an hour or so.

We are all very well & comfortably settled.

Emily was a little quaking and thin, & so I let her go

by the railroad with the MacGregors to Liverpool about three weeks ago, & she stayed with Lord & Lady Sefton at Croxteth for ten days & they brought her back a week ago in very good care. She had a good deal of riding and the change did her great good. The reports of her marriage to Mr Bruce have been very prévalent, but it is not the case & you never need believe anything that you may hear till you hear it from me, as I shall make it a duty as well as pleasure to let you know the instant anything of the kind could be in question. The MacGregors went on from Croxteth to Edinburgh where he had business for his father to transact, & they are now on a visit near their own home at a Lady Lucy Grant's and will soon get back to Birnam Lodge which is the place they rent near Dunkeld. The children are quite well & were not the least trouble-some on the journey. Little Ally [1] and Emmy [2] grow more & more beautiful & the latter is the most engaging little creature that ever was & walked alone before she left us. I hear great praise of Prince Albert from all sides. I have not seen him as of course I do not go out any where likely to meet him. Sir George Seymour [3] returned the Badge & ribbon of the Bath at the Levee & brought me a very kind message of condolence from the Queen who spoke most handsomely of your poor brother & lamented the loss the Navy had had in him. He was admitted into the Royal Closet for this audience which is not usually done on such occasions, but it was as a mark of respect to the memory of him who had worn that Order.

Colonel & Mrs Dawson Damer were at Cairo & she has been travelling about on a Camel's back all through the Desert, and seems to be as able to bear fatigue as the Colonel, but so can all women if they like what they are

---

[1] Mr Atholl MacGregor (born 1836, living 1905).

[2] Emily Louisa MacGregor, who married Viscount Stormont, and is the mother of the fifth Earl of Mansfeld.

[3] Sir G. F. Seymour, Admiral, G.C.B. (born 1787, died 1870), one of the executors to Sir T. M. Hardy's will.

doing, believe me My Dear Mr Hardy with your Nieces kindest duty & love to you & Mrs Hardy,

Yours affectionately,

L. E. HARDY.

Pray remember me to Augusta when you see her.

Lady Hardy, who afterwards remarried with Lord Seaford, survived her first husband for nearly forty years, dying on the 2nd November 1877, at Hampton Court, where she is buried. Her eldest daughter Miss Louisa Hardy, and her youngest daughter Lady MacGregor (who died in 1896) are buried in the same place.

Hardy's Desk on board the *Victory*, now preserved at Portisham House.

CHAPTER XXI

HARDY MEMORIALS AT GREENWICH HOSPITAL AND IN DORSET : HARDY PORTRAITS

OF the illustrations of the never-to-be-forgotten death scene on board the *Victory*, which began at half-past one and ended at half-past four on the afternoon of the 21st October 1805, the number is almost infinite. They vary from rare and beautiful mezzotints and colour plates down to the roughest and rudest woodcuts and glass-pictures, which at one time were to be found in almost every cottage. In all of these the figure of "Cap'n Hardy" is little less prominent than that of Nelson himself. In the printed descriptions below many of them the name of Hardy is often associated with that of his illustrious chief—"Nelson giving his last commands to Hardy," "Kiss me Hardy," etc. In the majority of these engravings the attempt at any accurate likeness is of the faintest. Most of them were produced and published at high pressure, either in the days which immediately followed the arrival of the news of Trafalgar in England, or in the first fortnight of 1806, when the eyes of all England were directed to the great funeral pageant at St Paul's. This can hardly be said of the beautiful and artistic colour-print of the scene on the deck of the *Victory* just after Nelson had received his death wound,[1] now reproduced. It was engraved by Charles Turner, after a painting

[1] In the collection of A. M. Broadley.

SCENE ON BOARD THE 'VICTORY' JUST AFTER NELSON HAD RECEIVED HIS DEATH WOUND.

by J. Parry. Below it are the words of the familiar Nelson signal. It was published more than a year after the battle, viz., on the 21st November 1806. The publisher was Mr Vittore Zanetti, of 87 Market Street Lane, Manchester. The face and figure of Hardy, as portrayed in this picture, bear a sufficient if not striking resemblance to the hitherto unpublished miniature in possession of Mrs Manfield of Portisham, which forms the frontispiece of this volume, as well as to the recently discovered profile bust in Poole clay, and the large three-quarter-length portrait in oils by Evans, painted at the instance of King William IV. for Greenwich Hospital, while Hardy was Governor. This has been very frequently engraved by H. Robinson and others. There is a good photogravure reproduction of it in Sir J. H. Briggs's *Naval Administrations.* Some replicas of the Greenwich picture also exist, one of them being now in possession of Mrs Thresher of Corfe Hill, Weymouth.

In addition to the Evans portrait in the Painted Chamber, there is a bust of Hardy in the chapel of Greenwich Hospital. This was placed there by public subscription three years after his death. The sculptor was William Behnes, a former student of the Royal Academy, who, in a letter dated 9th August 1842, agreed to provide for the sum of £300, a bust exactly similar to that which Chantrey had executed of Hardy's predecessor, Sir R. G. Keats.[1] To the fund thus organised, of which Sir George Seymour, one of Hardy's executors, was apparently the moving spirit, Queen Adelaide contributed no less than £50; Miss Augusta Hardy of Portisham giving a similar amount. Hardy's old friends and shipmates figure extensively in the list. Amongst them were Sir George Cockburn, Sir R. Hussey, Sir Henry Digby, Sir P. C. H. Durham, Sir Charles Rowley, Sir J. Beresford, Sir J. Whitshed, and Sir G. Martin.

[1] William Behnes, sculptor (died 1864). He was much in vogue as a sculptor of portrait-busts between 1820 and 1845. He died in complete destitution, having quite outlived his fame.

The following inscription was placed below the bust on a tablet surmounted by a medallion of Nelson, and the words: "England expects every man will do his duty."

ERECTED TO THE MEMORY OF

VICE-ADMIRAL SIR THOMAS MASTERMAN HARDY
BARONET AND G.C.B.

GOVERNOR OF GREENWICH HOSPITAL

THE FRIEND AND COMPANION-IN-ARMS OF NELSON

EMINENT FOR JUDGMENT AND SELF-POSSESSION; EVER ANXIOUS
FOR THE IMPROVEMENT OF THE SERVICE TO WHICH HE HAD
DEVOTED HIMSELF; EQUAL TO ALL ITS DIFFICULTIES AND
DUTIES, AND CONVERSANT WITH ITS MINUTEST DETAILS.
THE NAME OF THIS GALLANT AND DISTINGUISHED
OFFICER WILL DESCEND TO POSTERITY AS ONE
OF THE NOBLEST ORNAMENTS OF THE
PROFESSION TO WHICH ENGLAND IS SO
MUCH INDEBTED FOR SECURITY
AND RENOWN

DIED 20TH SEPTEMBER 1839, AGED 70 YEARS

Never probably did any public movement meet with more unanimous approval and general enthusiasm than that for commemorating the "valour and virtues" of Thomas Masterman Hardy in the county of his birth.

On 2nd of March 1844, Lord Ilchester presided at a public meeting in the Town Hall, Dorchester, convened by the Mayor (Mr Charles Criswick), "for the purpose of considering the best mode to be adopted for carrying into effect the wishes of many influential persons in the towns of Dorchester and Weymouth, as well as the general feeling of the county of Dorset that the public services of the late Admiral Sir T. M. Hardy are highly deserving of some public testimonial which would be most appropriately placed on some conspicuous spot in this his native County."

The "Portlanders" offered to provide the whole of the

Thomas Masterman Hardy Bart. G.C.B

Bust of Sir Thomas Hardy
in Dorchester Museum.

stone if the projected column might adorn the " Verne," one of the heights of their peninsula, but the consensus of opinion pronounced itself strongly in favour of the " beacon-mound " on Blagdon Hill, principally because it had once belonged to Hardy, and was in close proximity to Portisham Village and other localities connected with his boyhood, in addition to being the very spot he had selected years before for the erection of a tall rick of furze faggots which should serve as a " sea mark " visible miles away to ships going down Channel.

The projectors of the memorial, now known throughout the length and breadth of Dorset as the " Hardy Monument," were not aware that it also dominated his birthplace at Kingston Russell; but many doubtless remembered that it was there that Joseph Hardy and William Boyt, during the last phases of the Great War (when on the 1st of June 1805, the parole word of the Dorset Yeomanry was " Victory " and the counter - sign was " Howe "), awaited, flint and tinder in hand, the expected signal which would have told all England, in the course of a few hours, that the " Corsican Ogre " had at length effected a landing on the Dorset littoral. Blagdon Hill having been chosen as the site, the design (a massive column with no great claim to artistic merit) sent in by Mr Arthur Dyke Acland was selected. Mr William Manfield, Hardy's nephew, gave the ground, and promised to provide the necessary stone from his quarry at Luckham's Pond. The foundation stone was laid by Mrs Floyer, wife of Mr John Floyer, one of Dorset's representatives in Parliament, and High Sheriff of the County, on the 21st October 1844, the thirty-ninth anniversary of the Battle of Trafalgar. The base of the column is 830 feet above sea-level, and the structure rises 72 feet in height, so that the corona at the top is 905 feet above the waters of Weymouth Bay. Subscriptions poured in from every town and village in Dorset; and four years later (after the satisfactory carrying out of the scheme), the Hardy

Q

Memorial Committee issued, on the 12th June 1848, a final balance-sheet headed by a vignette of the "Monument," showing that they had received and expended £609, 16s.

It soon became a veritable place of pilgrimage. Throughout the "fifties" and the "sixties" of the last century it was the practice of summer visitors to Weymouth, Dorchester, and Bridport to regard the climbing of Blagdon Hill as almost *de rigueur*. And what a treat awaited them after ascending the steep spiral staircase which led to the summit of Mr Acland's massive pillar! Looking seawards, the eye rests on an unbroken panorama of coast-line extending from the Isle of Wight and St Catharine's Point on the east to Start Point and the Tors of Dartmoor on the west. It has even been said that on an exceptionally clear day one can see the Nelson column, far away to the east on the crest of Portsdown Hill in the hinterland of Portsmouth and the Solent. Far down below lie clearly spread out, as if on a map, Weymouth and the Backwater, as well as Portland and the Chesil Beach, while St Aldhelm's Head and the Purbeck Hills to the left, and Thorncombe Beacon with Golden Cap beyond it to the right, stand out, in prominent grandeur. Landwards the view is almost equally magnificent, even if not so extensive. Pillesdon Pen and Lewesdon Hill with Lambert's Castle tower up above peaceful valleys and snug-lying hamlets, the prospect towards the north-east being bounded by the beacon heights of Bulbarrow and Lytchett.

When the novelty wore off, the stranger was content to look at the Hardy column from a distance. It was neglected, if not forgotten—no sustentation fund existing; and a flash of lightning completed the havoc which time had begun. The monument became unsafe, and the internal staircase was closed. Five years ago, however, the structure was completely restored by the instrumentality of Colonel Robert Williams, M.P. of Bridehead, in whose grounds the river Bride takes its rise. There is no fear of the Hardy monument ever again becoming a ruin, for the inscription over the doorway now runs as follows :—

ERECTED BY PUBLIC SUBSCRIPTION, IN THE YEAR 1844,

IN MEMORY OF

VICE-ADMIRAL SIR THOMAS MASTERMAN HARDY

BART., G.C.B.

FLAG-CAPTAIN TO LORD NELSON

ON H.M.S. "VICTORY" AT THE BATTLE OF TRAFALGAR

RESTORED 1900

AND PLACED IN CHARGE OF THE NATIONAL TRUST FOR PLACES

OF HISTORIC INTEREST OR NATURAL BEAUTY BY THE

DESCENDANTS OF SIR THOMAS MASTERMAN HARDY,

ON WHOSE LAND IT STANDS

Hardy, however, needs no visible memorial to keep his memory green in the fair countryside from which he sprang. His name and exploits[1] have become, as it were, part and parcel of Wessex folklore. In out-of-the-way nooks and corners of West Dorset the "Not mortually I hopes, my

---

[1] During the whole of the nineteenth century, the opinions as well as the deeds of Hardy find frequent mention at the hands of nearly all naval historians. In Captain Basil Hall's *Fragments*, i., p. 165, is found Hardy's reply to a query put to him as to the behaviour of the captain of the French privateer *Milan*, captured by the *Endymion* on the 8th November 1810, after a prolonged chase. "This French-man's conduct may teach us the important lesson that an officer should never surrender his ship whatever be the force opposed to him, *while there remains the slightest possible chance of escape*. The privateer you speak of had very nearly slipped through your hands ; and had he knocked away one of your sticks, probably would have done so. It is always useful to have good practical examples of what perseverance and well-directed zeal may accomplish, especially with very small means. I think I have known more than one ship captured, which might, perhaps, have baffled their enemy had they been as stoutly defended as your little privateer. Don't let us forget her example ; for it is no matter whence instruction comes—from friend or from foe—provided it be good."

Lord" is still heard when the mummers enact their Christmas play. It speaks volumes for the enduring fame of Thomas Masterman Hardy amongst successive generations of Dorset men and women, that he is invariably spoken as Hardy *tout court.* It is always Hardy or possibly "Cap'n" Hardy, just as Nelson is Nelson only for Norfolk and the whole world. It has, however, been reserved for the still living Thomas Hardy, to give us in his drama of *The Dynasts* yet another reason for the constant holding in remembrance of his great namesake. Never have the moments of supreme anxiety, which followed the last shot and the last surrender at Trafalgar, been more graphically described than in the lines :—

" ' Pull hard and make the Nothe, or down we go,' one says, say he,
 We pulled ; and bedtime brought the storm ; but snug at home
  slept we.
 Yet all the while our gallants, after fighting through the day,
 Were beating up and down the dark sou' west of Cadiz Bay,
    The dark
    The dark
   Sou' west of Cadiz Bay.

 The victors and the vanquished then the storm it tossed and tore,
 As hard they strove, those worn-out men upon that surly shore.
 Dead Nelson and his half-dead crew, his foes from near and far,
 Were rolled together on the deep that night at Trafalgar,
    The deep
    The deep
   That night at Trafalgar."

CHAPTER XXII

SIR T. M. HARDY IN PROSE, POETRY, AND THE DRAMA.
SOME ADDITIONAL LETTERS AND NOTES

THE references to Hardy in the text of *The Trumpet Major* have already been referred to in the preface, and the description of the captain of the *Victory*, penned by the author of that book from the information given to him by Hardy's daughter, has been transcribed at length. It is thus that Thomas Hardy, the novelist, draws the scene enacted upon the Weymouth Esplanade, on that eventful September day of 1805, when George III. took counsel with the gallant sailor, who was recruiting his shattered health at his Portisham home :—"The town clock struck, and Bob Loveday retraced his steps till he again approached the Esplanade and Gloucester Lodge, where the morning sun blazed in upon the house fronts, and not a spot of shade seemed to be attainable. A huzzaing attracted his attention, and he observed that a number of people had gathered before the King's residence, where a brown curricle had stopped, out of which stept a hale man in the prime of life, wearing a blue uniform, gilt epaulettes, cocked hat, and sword, who crossed the pavement and went in. Bob went up and joined the group. 'What's going on?' he said. 'Captain Hardy,' replied a bystander. 'What of him?' 'Just gone in—waiting to see the King.' 'But he's in the West Indies.' 'No, the fleet is come home; they can't find the French anywhere.' 'Will they go and look for them again?' asked Bob. 'Oh, yes. Nelson is determined to find 'em. As soon as he's refitted, he'll put to sea again. Ah, here's the King coming in.'" In the result, Bob Loveday, as has already been related, took service as a volunteer in the *Victory*, and witnessed the events detailed in the next chapter. In the dramatic version of *The Trumpet Major*, lately presented at Dorchester, no *rôle* was assigned to "Nelson's Hardy," who, however, figures prominently in the first volume of the magnificent poem of *The Dynasts*.

The second scene of the fifth act of the dramatic poem passes on the quarter-deck of the *Victory*. Nelson and Hardy walk up and down, and the following conversation is supposed to take place between them :—

HARDY.[1]—At least let's put you on your old great coat, my lord—
(the air is keen)—
'Twil cover all. So while you still retain your dignities, you baulk
these deadly aims.
NELSON.—Thank'ee, good friend. But no—I haven't time,
I do assure you—not a truce to spare,
As you will see.
                   [*A few minutes later* SCOTT *falls dead.* . . .
                   Immediately after a shot passes between the
                   ADMIRAL *and the* CAPTAIN, *tearing the*
                   instep of HARDY'S *shoe,*[2] *and striking away*
                   the buckle. NELSON *glances round and per-*
                   ceives what has happened to the SECRETARY.]

NELSON.—Poor Scott, too, carried off! Warm work this, Hardy.
Too warm to go on long.
HARDY.—   I think so, too ;
Their lower ports are blocked against our hull,
And our charge now is less. Each shot so near
Sets their old wood on fire.

---

[1] The quotations both from *The Trumpet Major* and *The Dynasts* are made with the sanction and by the kind permission of Mr Thomas Hardy.
[2] See *ante*, p. 142.

NELSON.—   Ay, rotten as peat.
What's that ?   I think she has struck, or pretty nigh !

[A cracking of musketry.]

HARDY.—Not yet.   Those small-arm men there, in her tops,
Thin our crew fearfully.   Now, too, our guns
Have to be dipped full down, or they would rake
The *Téméraire* there on the other side.
     NELSON.—True.—While you deal good measure out to these,
Keep slapping at those giants over here—
The *Trinidad,* I mean, and the *Bucentaure*
To winnard—swelling up so pompously.
     HARDY.—I'll see no slackness shall be shown this way.

[They part, but meet again.]

     NELSON.—Bid still the firemen bring more bucketfuls,
And dash the water into each new hole
Our guns have gonged in the *Redoubtable,*
Or we shall all be set ablaze together.
     HARDY.—Let me once more advise, entreat, my lord,
That you do not expose yourself so clearly.
Those fellows in the mizzen top up there
Are peppering round you quite perceptibly.
     NELSON.—Now, Hardy, don't offend me.   They can't aim ;
They only set their own rent sails on fire—
But if they could, I would not hide a button
To save ten lives like mine.   I have no cause
To prize it, I assure 'ee.—Ah, look there,
One of the women hit—and badly, too.
Poor wench !   Let some one take her quickly down.
     HARDY.—My lord, each humblest sojourner on the seas,
Dock labourer, lame longshoreman, bowed bargee,
Sees it as policy to shield his life
For those dependent on him.   Much more then,
Should one upon whose priceless presence here
Such issues hang, so many strivers lean,
Use average circumspection at an hour
So critical for us all.
     NELSON.—Ay, ay.   Yes, yes ;
I know your meaning, Hardy ; and I know
That you disguise as frigid policy
What really is your honest love of me.
But, faith, I have done my day.   My work's nigh done ;
I serve all interests best by chancing it

Here with the commonest.—Ah, their heavy guns
Are silenced, every one ! Thank God for that.
    HARDY.—'Tis so. They only use their small arms now.

> [*He goes to larboard to see what is progressing on that side of the ship and the* "Santissima Trinidad."]

  .   .   .   .

> [NELSON *is struck and falls.* HARDY *looks round, and sees what has happened.*]

    HARDY (*hastily*).—Ah—what I feared !

> [*He goes towards* NELSON, *who in the meantime has been lifted by* Sergeant-Major SECKER *and two seamen.*]

    NELSON.—Hardy, I think they've done for me at last !
    HARDY.—I hope not !
    NELSON.—Yes. My backbone is shot through.
I have not long to live.

> [*The men proceed to carry him below.*]
>
>   These little ropes

They've shot away, get instantly repaired.

> [*At the sight there is great agitation among the crew.*]

Cover my face. There will no good be done
By drawing their attention off to me.
Bear me along, good fellows ; I am but one
Among the many darkened here to-day !

> [*He is carried on to the cockpit.*]
>
>   *To the* CHAPLAIN.

Doctor, I'm gone. I'm good for none but you.
    HARDY (*remaining behind*).—Hills, go to Collingwood and let him know
That we've no Admiral here.

  .   .   .   .

    The fourth scene of the fifth act is located in the *Victory's* cockpit, where Nelson is lying undressed in a mid-shipman's berth, surrounded by the doctors, chaplain, etc.

    DR MAGRATH (*in a low voice*).—
Poor Ram, and poor Tom Whipple, have just gone.[1]
    DR BEATTY.—There was no hope for them.
    NELSON (*brokenly*).—Who have just died ?

---

[1] See *post*, Chapter XXIII., p. 259.

BEATTY.—Two were badly hit by now, my lord; Lieutenant Ram
and Mr Whipple.

NELSON.— Ah!

So many lives—in such a glorious cause . . .
I join them soon, soon, soon!   O where is Hardy?
Will nobody bring Hardy to me—none?
He must be killed, too.   Surely Hardy's dead?

.   .   .   .

[HARDY *arrives.*]

NELSON.—Hardy, how goes this day with us, and England?

HARDY.—Well; very well, thank God for't, my dear lord.
Villeneuve their Admiral has this moment struck,
And put himself aboard the *Conqueror.*
Some fourteen of their first-rates, or about
Thus far we've yet.

[HARDY *gives details of the prizes, etc.*]

NELSON.—That's well.   I swore for twenty.—But it's well.

HARDY.—We'll have 'em yet!   But without you, my lord,
We have to make slow plodding do the deeds
That spring by inspiration 'ere you fell,
And in this ship the more particularly.

NELSON.—No, Hardy.—Ever 'twas your settled fault
So modestly to whittle down your worth.
But I saw stuff in you which admirals need.
When, taking thought, I chose the *Victory's* keel
To do my business with those Frenchmen in
A business finished now, for me!—Good friend,
Slow shades are creeping on me . . . I scarce see you.

HARDY.—The smoke from ships upon our win'ard side,
And the dust raised by their worm-eaten hulks,
When our balls touch 'em, blind the eyes, in truth.

[HARDY *goes up, but soon re-enters.*]

.   .   .   .

NELSON.—Who's that?   Ah—here you come!   How, Hardy, now!?

HARDY.—The Spanish Admiral's rumoured to be wounded,
We know not with what truth.   But, be as 'twill
He steers away with all he could call round,
And some few frigates, straight to Cadiz Port.

.   .   .   .

NELSON (*arousing*).—Our course will be to anchor.   Let them
know.

HARDY.—But let me ask, my lord, as I needs must,
Seeing your state, and that our work's not done,

Shall I, from you, bid Admiral Collingwood
Take full on him the conduct of affairs.

NELSON (*trying to raise himself*).—
Not while I live, I hope! No, Hardy; no.
Give Collingwood my order. Anchor all.

HARDY (*hesitating*).—You mean the signal's to be made forthwith?

NELSON.—I do! By God, if but our carpenter
Could rig me up a jury backbone now,
To last one hour—until the battle's done,
I'd see to it! But here I am—stove in—
Broken—all logged and done for! Done, ay done!

DR BEATTY.—My Lord, I must implore you to lie calm!
You shorten what at best may not be long.

NELSON (*exhausted*).—I know, I know, good Beatty! Thank you
well.

HARDY.—I was impatient. Now I am still.
Sit here a moment, if you have time to spare.[1]

NELSON.—Come nearer to me, Hardy. One of all,
As you well guess, pervades my memory now;
She, and my daughter—I speak freely to you.

  .   .   .   .   .   . Now she rests
Safe in the nation's honour. . . . Let her have
My hair, and the small treasured things I owned,
And take care of her, as you care for me.

HARDY.—   Now I'll leave,
See if your order's gone, and then return.

NELSON (*symptoms of death beginning to change his face*).—
Yes, Hardy; yes, I know it. You must go.
Here we shall meet no more; since Heaven forfend
That care for me should keep you idle now,
When all the ship demands you. .
My time here is the briefest. If I live
But long enough I'll anchor   But—too late—
My anchoring's elsewhere ordered! . . . Kiss me, Hardy.

             [HARDY *bends over him.*]

I'm satisfied. Thank God, I have done my duty!

             [HARDY *brushes his eyes with his hand, and with-
             draws to go above, pausing to look back before
             he finally disappears.*]

    .   .   .   .

---

[1] For Hardy's reverie on what is passing "down Wessex Way," see
Chapter xv., p. 149.

Since the first issue of the story of " Nelson's Hardy,"
under the title of *The Three Dorset Captains at Trafalgar*,
many additional letters of the most famous of the gallant
trio of naval heroes have come to light.   The one which
follows supplies a link in the correspondence of Hardy
with his brother-in-law.   It would seem to indicate that
the latter availed himself of Hardy's suggestive hint.[1]

"If any of my friends here have a wish to see *San Josef*
they will find her at Torbay all the week after next."

"SAN JOSEF," TORBAY,
Feby 8th, 1801.

DEAR MANFIELD,

We are in Hourly expectation of the *St
George* where the Admiral is to hoist his Flag the moment
she arrives ; myself and all the Officers go with him.   We
shall sail as soon as possible for Portsmouth and from
thence to the North Sea after we have done the *business
there* which we expect to do in about two months.   The
Flag is again to be hoisted in *San Josef*.   The Squadron
under Sir Henry Harvey arrived the day before yesterday
and saild the same even[g] to detach a squadron after the
ships that left Brest about a fortnight ago.

Laurence arrived yesterday with young Roberts ; he is
a fine Lad, and I think will do, but is very young.   The
Adm[l] tells me he saw you when you landed and of course
you made your *Grand Salaam* to him.   I suppose a
number of wonderful stories has been told of *San Josef* in
and about Dorchester.   Our beer is reduced to six Bottles,
and on a moderate calculation that cannot last more than
three days, therefore you will add to the many obligations
I am under to you if you will order our friend Oakley to
send as soon as possible six or eight Doz[n] more directed
for Lord Nelson *St George* Spithead by any vessel that
sails from Weymouth.

With Duty, Love, &c., to all friends

T. M. HARDY.

MR MANFIELD.

[1] See p. 61.

It is not difficult to imagine the Dorchester attorney in his best coat spending a jolly day on board the *San Josef*, and making his "grand salaam" to the famous, but always genial admiral. The next letter is much briefer.

"ST GEORGE," TORBAY,
Feby 20th, 1801.

DEAR MANFIELD,

I have only time to say that we are now getting under weigh for Spithead and shall probably pass Abbotsbury during the Night. Do write to me at Spithead and tell me if the Beer is sent as the Adm[l] *longs* for it every day at Dinner.

T. M. HARDY.

Post mark Brixham, 7d. to pay.

Nelson's appreciation of the merits of Dorchester beer is evident. Songs in its praise date back to the days of the first American War, and the refrain of one of the most popular patriotic songs during the Great Terror ran :—

> " If the Frenchmen a landing should win,
>   In each *County* they'd find we're not slugs ;
> Then with the Land's *End* to begin,
>   In *Cornwall* they'd get *Cornish hugs*,
> In *Devon* they'd dread *Plymouth* fort,
>   Find boxers in *Somersetshire*,
> And in *Dorset* they'd meet pretty sport,
>   From the lads who drink Dorchester beer."[1]

The following letter is in the Nelson collection of Mr F. T. Sabin, by whose kind permission it is published. It discloses the hitherto unknown fact that it was only by a happy accident that Hardy commanded the *Victory* at Trafalgar. On 18th August 1805, he felt so seriously ill that he writes thus to Captain Conn, who some seven weeks later was eventually appointed to the *Dreadnought*.

[1] This song, commended by *The Spectator* to Mr Haldane as a useful aid to military enthusiasm, has been published by Mr Edward Everard of Bristol.

"VICTORY," SPITHEAD,
August 18th, 1805.

MY DEAR CONN,

We are just anchored here and I am sorry to say that the state of my health is so very bad that I have been obliged to apply to the Admiralty for leave of absence. His Lordship has desired me to tell you that he has applied for you to command the *Victory* in my absence. Whether she will go to sea or not is quite uncertain, but I should rather think she will. His Lordship desires me to say to you that all his furniture will be left, therefore you need not trouble yourself to get any. Give my best respects to Mrs Conn and say I hope she will forgive my taking you from her. The Ship is to be considered as Lord Nelson's Flag Ship, and kept in readiness for him. Do answer me by return of post. I think there is no doubt but you will get your Commission, Wednesday or Thursday, as the letter is gone to the Admiral this day. We have had a long round as you have seen by the papers. Keats is arrived here with us, all the remainder are left off Brest. God bless you my dear Conn, and in hopes of seeing you soon   T. M. HARDY.

So magical, however, was the effect of the exhilarating climate of his native Dorset, that in less than three weeks the captain of the *Victory* interviews the King at Weymouth (3rd September), and started the very next day to rejoin his old ship to busy prepare for the voyage which was to gain him the fame so graphically depicted by his namesake in *The Dynasts*.[1]

The relations of Lieut. Roberts and Hardy will be more fully discussed in the next chapter. He thus addressed his former midshipman a quarter of a century after Trafalgar :—

LONDON, *Sept. 18th*, 1830.

I received your letter of the 13th instant yesterday, and I have great pleasure in forwarding to you

[1] See *ante.*, p. 246.

a certificate of my full approbation of your conduct during the time you served under my command and I sincerely hope that your Memorial will procure for you the employment you solicit

T. M. HARDY.

LIEUT. ROBERTS, R.N.

As will be seen when Hardy's services at the Admiralty are dealt with, he was one of the first to recognise the possibilities of steam as regards the futurity of the Navy. In 1834 he thus wrote to the officer who was in later life Vice-Admiral C. E. Binstead [1796-1876] :—

ADMIRALTY, *March 27th*, 1834.

I have this day been favored with your letter of yesterday, and beg to say that I shall have great pleasure in recommending you to Sir James Graham, as a candidate for the Command of a Steam Vessel, but that I think it right to inform you that the first Lord has a large number on his List, and I fear that you will stand a bad Chance of Employment on board a Steam Vessel.

T. M. HARDY.

The following letter to his old shipmate, Captain Young of Exeter, is of later date :—

GREENWICH HOSPITAL,
May 26th, 1836.

I have been favoured with your letter of the 24th instant, and beg to say that I am informed the vacancy caused by the Death of Commander Deacon on the out Pension List of Greenwich Hospital has been already filled up. I shall be very glad to remind the Board of Admiralty of your long services and Claims, but I am sorry to inform you that I have very little interest at the Board. I will make a point of seeing Sir Robert Otway as soon as I possibly can

T. M. HARDY.

CAPTAIN [R. B.] YOUNG.

Amongst Hardy's few intimate friends was Mr Samuel Bagster of Paternoster Row, of whom mention is made in his correspondence. In his autobiography, Mr Bagster says he was, as a boy, sent by his father every Monday morning to Somerset House to find out if Tom Hardy was "made a Lieutenant." After the battle of Trafalgar, Hardy was his guest, and in reply to his host's query as to how the scenes of slaughter affected his mind, the Captain of the *Victory* said :—" I certainly was unmoved, except at one moment when my sympathy overcame my resolution. Good Dr Scott was shot as he stood by my side, and cast into the sea, and in falling his body was caught by the tackle of the ship, and his bowels were torn out! Oh, it excited deep emotion to see that excellent man in that state." Mr Sydney Bagster has kindly forwarded to the writers a letter from Hardy to his ancestor, dated Rio de Janeiro, May 25, 1822. In it Hardy says: "We have just returned from the Pacific, where I have had some trouble, but I have got through it better than I expected. I thank God I enjoy good health, and as my period of service will expire in September or October I shall look for the pleasure of shaking you and all your worthy family by the hand, some time the latter part of this year."

The late Mr Samuel Bagster used also to relate the following anecdote on the authority of his friend Hardy :— "On one occasion Lord Nelson and Hardy were going ashore in the Admiral's barge at Plymouth. One of the Sailors was under the influence of liquor, or some untoward fit of bad temper had seized him, but talk he would and would not keep the stroke of oars. His lordship spoke to him ; he did not desist ; again he was spoken to warmly, but still he was not obedient. His lordship then went to him, and with a light buff glove that he had been swinging in his hand, struck him with it in the face, and said with Nelson Authority, 'Remember for ever you've been struck by your Commander.' It is hardly necessary to say the effect was complete."

CHAPTER XXIII

LIEUTENANT ROBERTS'S LETTERS TO HIS FRIENDS AT BURTON BRADSTOCK, DESCRIBING THE BATTLE OF TRAFALGAR AND THE EVENTS WHICH FOLLOWED IT. THE TRAFALGAR REJOICINGS AT BURTON AND BRIDPORT. THE SONG OF THE BURTON VOLUNTEERS

M ISS M. M. Roberts of Burton Bradstock, whose ready aid has been already acknowledged,[1] has now placed at the disposal of the present writers a bundle of correspondence which throws new and important light on the details of Nelson's "crowning victory" and the part played in it by Hardy. The account of the great battle by Midshipman (and probably acting Captain's Clerk) R. F. Roberts was written almost before the smoke of the contending fleets had cleared away. The replies of the various members of his family afford an interesting picture of the tension of public opinion in a Dorset village towards the end of the Great Terror, and the jubilation caused by the good news brought to England in the manner described. The nation, relieved from the probability of immediate invasion, breathed freely once more. In November 1805, Richard Francis Roberts was the hero of those who then chaunted uproariously "The Song of the Burton Volunteers," discovered by

[1] See Introduction, p. xix.

Miss Roberts amongst the papers of her ancestral kinsman :—

I.

Come my lads of courage true,
　Ripe for martial glory,
See the standard waves for you,
　And leads the way before ye.

Chorus.—To the field of Mars advance,
　Join the bold alliance ;
Tell the blood-stained sons of France,
　We bid them all defiance.

II.

Burton's sons were always brave
　On the land or ocean,
Ready for to kill or save
　When honour's the promotion.
　　Chorus.

III.

Burton long has had a boast,
　And right well deserving ;
For pretty maids a standing toast,
　Of nature's sweet preserving.
　　Chorus.

IV.

Gallia's sons invasion plans [*sic*]
　Threat'ning to destroy us,
Seize our maidens, houses, lands,
　And as slaves employ us.
　　Chorus.

V.

We must fight, or starve, or fly,
　Hope naught else remaining ;
Or wives may faint and children die
　With no hand restraining.
　　Chorus.

Final Chorus—
Lives are lent for Laws and King,
　When that they may need 'em ;
Let us then in chorus sing,
　Give us death or freedom.[1]

---

[1] This song, with the original music, has been published by Mr Edward Everard of Bristol.

Within twenty-four hours or less of the firing of the last shot, Midshipman Roberts wrote as follows:—

"VICTORY," AT SEA,
OFF TRAFALGAR, *22nd Oct.* 1805.

DEAR PARENTS,

I have just time and opportunity to tell you that we had a desperate engagement with the enemy, and, thank God, I have so far escaped unhurt. The Combined Fleet came out of Cadiz on Saturday morning with a determination to engage and blow us up (as the prisoners say) out of the water, but they are much—very much—mistaken. I can't tell you how many we have taken and destroyed, they say fifteen, but it is quite un- certain. *I* don't think it is so many; but none of us know at present, but amongst the taken is a four-decker[1] which struck to the *Neptune*. We engaged her for some time and then she fell astern of us.

I am sorry—very sorry—to tell you that amongst the slain is Lord Nelson, his secretary Mr Scott, and Mr Whipple, Captain Hardy's clerk, whom you know. Out of four marine officers two were wounded and the captain killed. It was as hard an action, as allowed by all on board this ship, as ever was fought. There were but three left alive on the Quarterdeck, the enemy fired so much grape and small shot from the rigging, there was one ship so close to us that we could not run out our guns their proper length. Only conceive how much we must have smashed her, every gun was trebly shotted for her.

We have a great many killed and wounded—danger- ously wounded—21 amputations. I am happy to say Captain Hardy escaped unhurt, but we have one Lieu- tenant killed[2] and two wounded, and one midshipman[3] killed and three wounded. We had no less than ten ships on ours.

I forgot to tell you that we engaged them on Monday,

[1] *Sanctissima Trinidada.* [2] Lieutenant William Ram. [3] Robert Smith.

we began at 12 o'clock and continued till ½ past 4. The enemy consisted of 35 sail of the Line, 4 frigates, 2 brigs; and our fleet of 27 sail of the line, 4 frigates and a schooner and sloop. Unluckily for us Admiral Lewes had been sent a little time before with 5 sail of the line up the Gut.

This morning the enemy are out of sight and we have the prizes in tow, going I believe for Gibraltar. We have several ships fit for the enemy now, and if they should come to attack us we should be able to give them a warm reception, they have most of them had enough of it; there are several lame ducks gone off. The rascals have shot away our mizen mast and we are very much afraid of our main and foremasts. The *Royal Sovereign* has not a stick standing—a total wreck. It was she that began the action in a noble manner, engaging four of them at the same time. Admiral Collingwood had shifted his flag on board of her a few days before. Two of the enemy blew up and one sank. You can have no conception whatsoever what an action between two fleets is; it was a grand but an awful sight indeed; thank God we are all so well over it.

Admiral Nelson was [shot] early in the action by a musket ball from the enemy's top, which struck him a little below the shoulder, touched the rib and lodged near his heart. He lived about 2½ hours after; then died without a groan. Every ship that struck, our fellows ceased firing and gave three cheers like Noble Britons. The Spaniards fought very well indeed, as did the Frenchmen. Scarcely any prizes have a stick standing. One that we had possession of, and struck to us, had 75 killed in her middle deck, and many more in her lower deck. Capt. Duff (I believe he commands the *Colossus*) is killed, but I have not heard of any more captains being killed. I will give you all the particulars in my next, but you must excuse me now as really we are in such confusion that I can't tell how I have written this. I thought you would be uneasy if you did not hear of me by the first ship, so I have as my duty requires written to you.

Remember me to all that ask for me, and believe me

Your dutiful Son

R. F. ROBERTS.

P.S.—We have 40 men wounded, 9 officers, and (I think) as many killed. It was a much harder action than the Nile, several in our ship say so. The carpenter whom you saw at Mr Jacob's was there, and has been in several other actions with Lord Nelson, and he says it is the hardest action he was ever in. There were a thousand shot on each deck, and the middle deck in the action was obliged to be supplied with more. One poor fellow lost both his legs in the action, and is since dead of his wounds.

Lord Nelson's last request was that his body might be taken to England. This ship will not be able to come home with him yet, so I suppose he will be sent by some other. We expect to come to England as soon as we can get a jury mast rigged and a little repaired.

Adieu for the present. Neither Mr Atkinson nor Mr Williams are hurt.

Some time later the following letter was written without date:—

"VICTORY," AT SEA.

DEAR FATHER,

I thank you to shew this plan to Mr Cheney as I promised him he should in my letter to him. I hope Frank has got out of the *Princess of Orange* as she is not a ship for making Prize money. I take this opportunity of writing by the *Belleisle* who is bound to Plymouth with *Pleasure* as we may be 2 or 3 days beating up Channel unless we have a fair breeze. We have had a long and disagreeable passage from Gibraltar, having put in there after the Gale to refit a little. We sailed from thence the 4th Nov.

I have this on the other side by stealth, being a correct account of our ships, how they went into action, and the Enemy's line; likewise an account of the ships which struck to us, &c.; but their number of guns is not correct, the *Sanctissima Trinidada* carrying 140 guns, and the *St Ana* 130, and several that I have marked 74 are 80; but it is correct in every other respect. I wish you not to shew the plan of attack[1] to more than to your friends before it is made public, as I believe it is to be engraved in that way, and no doubt will be given to some particular engraver, and if anyone else were to get hold of it beforehand it would not be quite right in the way I got it. But don't think that their line is at all correct. According to my own observations they were this way

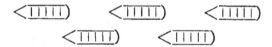

to prevent our ships breaking through their line: but that was impossible. It is beyond description. The way our ships went into action in such an irresistible manner— Words cannot describe it, but the result was glorious.

Lord Nelson was shot by a man in the *Redoubtable's* mizen top, but the rascal was afterwards shot by one of our midshipmen. Poor man; how he wished so much to see England again! But he died about 2 hours after he was shot.

I wrote you shortly after the action, but I have since heard that the letters were put on board the *Euryalus* which had not sailed when we left the Fleet, but we suppose that she will arrive home before us.

Whether this ship will be paid off and the men draughted into other ships will be impossible to say; but I daresay Captain Hardy will put me in another ship if he does not go to sea again; which I do not think

---

[1] The plan of attack mentioned is given at p. 143. The letter shows it was made at the time—a fact which unquestionably gives it additional importance. Midshipman Roberts was evidently a young man of more than ordinary intelligence.

likely as he seems to wish to be on shore for a little time; but I will not answer for it, it will not be for a long time. I have no doubt that the action will make him Sir Thomas, and he well deserves it. Poor Whittle his clerk, whom you saw at Mr Jacob's at Portsmouth, was killed by a splinter.

This ship is very much cut up everywhere; we can count 92 shot that struck her on one side and about 30 on the other. Our mizen mast was shot away, and our fore and main masts very much cut—particularly the foremast. We endured a terrible gale of wind in Cadiz Bay; we expected to go on shore; the captain was afraid of it. Our anchors would have been our last hope which we must have tried in a short time had not the gale abated. We split all to pieces the sails we set and carried away our main yard. The ship laboured very much indeed, but she did not make any water to alarm us, thank God.

I have collected different things previous to the action which I will send you on our arrival at Spithead. I believe the *Victory* must go into dock. If she is fitted out again I hope it will be for the same station as I like it much and the climate agrees with me very well. I feel a great difference now. A hot climate I am certain agrees with me well. I am, thank God, quite free of my complaint, which left me shortly after I was at sea, tho' I took no sort of medicine whatsoever, but I shall again when I arrive in England. I am rated midshipman, so that my Prize money will amount to much more. I was not rated at the time, but Capt. Hardy has been so good as to rate me back, which is equally as well as I shall stand as midshipman in the Prize List. I would thank you to tell me where Frank is that I may write him; likewise Mr Geekie, as I understood before we left England that he had a job somewhere near Portsmouth. Seventeen of our mids are gone into the *Queen* on promotion, where they will be made Lieutenants immediately. Likewise 3 clerks and our 1st Lieutenant is moved into the *Etna* bomb. Mr Williams will no doubt be promoted when we arrive in England.

Amongst the things that I shall send you is an order sent to every captain in the Fleet some time before the action by Lord Nelson, which I would beg you to be careful of and not shew it to any but your friends, as it is not fit for everyone to see—not to be made public.

Give my duty to Mother and love to Sophia, William and Augusta. Remember me to Grandmother, uncle and aunt at Gorwell, Aunt at Brown's Farm. Likewise best respects to Mr Hunter, Mr Travers, Mr Kenway, Mr Margrie and all friends that may enquire for me

Your duteful and affec^{te} Son

R. F. ROBERTS.

P.S.—I dined with Captain Hardy a few days ago, and he asked me if I intended writing a long letter home. I told him yes. He said that I must ask you to go to Portisham and tell his friends that he was well, and that he shouldn't write them, but I believe it was in a joke. However if you have an opportunity of sending I should be much obliged to you as I am greatly indebted to him for his kindness. He was struck two or three times by splinters, but nothing to hurt, thank God![1] I have a small present for Sophia that I bought at Gibraltar and shall send it her when we arrive at Spithead. It is but trifling, but coming from abroad it may be thought the more of, which I must beg her acceptance.

[1] The above postscript throws additional light on Hardy's character. When one considers the variety of emotions he had gone through, and the loss of his dear admiral, and of so many brave shipmates, it would seem as if, beyond the brief epistle he penned to Manfield a week after the battle, he really was unable to indite a lengthy despatch to his own family during those weeks of the homecoming of the Hero's corpse. That his mind was heavily weighted appears from the fact that young Roberts could not make out whether he was joking or not. At any rate, through it all within that middy's heart there shines that enthusiastic love and admiration with which Hardy inspired everyone who served under him.

In another letter (undated) young Roberts replies to a friend's epistle of Saint Nicholas Day concerning Trafalgar :—

Many thanks for your kind and affectionate letter of the 6th Dec., and I sit down as you request with pleasure to answer it.

I was not in much danger of being killed or wounded, though it was not impossible. I was quartered to assist the surgeons, and as you may imagine it was a very disagreeable one, but that was nothing at all after the first. But should it ever be my luck to be in another action I will not if possible be quartered there again. I was happy when I reflected that I had not a relation or dear friend in the Fleet. If I had I am sure I must have felt much more for them than I did for myself, which I assure you was very little, as a person going into action must work up himself to a certain pitch, when all those but cowards are perfectly resigned, when their King and Country need their utmost efforts against the Enemy.

You request me to give you an account of the action, but it would be too tedious to insert in a letter, and I am convinced that you have good accounts in the newspapers; but as you particularly request some account of it I will give you some that lay under my particular observation.

It was a glorious sight to see the *Royal Sovereign* commence the action. The long wished for time for Britons arrived. She fired a most tremendous broadside to begin with, but we did not see her but a very short time, she was soon involved in smoke, and the flash of the guns made it appear awfully grand; and at this time we could see nothing but the Royals above the Clouds. The Van of the Enemy were then firing, when our men were ordered to lay down on the deck and not return their firing; but in a short time the word was passed, "*if you can bring your guns to bear on them fire away*" which was quickly answered with a thundering broadside. We were then steering for the *Bucentaure's* main mast. We continued for about two hours when we had a respite for ten minutes, not choosing to answer their long balls, as there is nothing like close hugs for a Frenchman to make him strike.

About ten minutes after 1 o'clock Lord Nelson was borne down by four of his brave crew wounded in the shoulder mortally. He survived about two hours, when he died in the height of Glory always to be lamented by his country as one of the greatest Admirals that ever existed—perhaps too brave as he exposed himself in his full uniform, and the *Redoubtable* being close alongside of us he couldn't help being observed by them. I have heard it was hinted to him concerning his dress before the action, but he replied, "*I was never afraid of my honour.*"

I was by his side when he expired; he expressed repeatedly a wish to survive to return to his country once more, or even to see the Battle over, which he did knowing we had won the day, but not that *Villeneuve* was taken which was his particular wish before we came into action to conquer him. Every ship that was seen to strike by our men they gave three cheers immediately, which was re-echoed by some of the poor wounded then in the cockpit and it seemed to give new life to Lord Nelson.

[The letter closes with personal matters and the writer's reluctance to be treated as a hero by the enthusiastic Burtonians.]

How the whole populace of Burton Bradstock received the good news of the Trafalgar victory, and especially how the Roberts family took the lead by virtue of having a son in the great admiral's flagship, is shown by the following letters. News travelled fast, and on the very day after the *Victory* anchored once more off the shores of old England, Roberts's father penned the following paternal epistle :—

BURTON, BRIDPORT,
5th Dec. 1805.

MY DEAR RICHARD,

I have just received the happy news of the arrival of the *Victory* at Portsmouth and I sincerely hope you are well. I have only a few days since received your letter written the day after the battle and also Mr Kenway's dated the 27th Oct. from Trafalgar Bay. You cannot conceive the pleasure and happiness it gave your Mother, your brother and your sisters and myself to find you had so happily escaped the fate of the 21st Oct. I will assure you that it was no common feelings that agitated the sensations of the whole family, to which you may add a great many of your friends and acquaintances at Burton, Bridport, and elsewhere as soon as it was known that you were safe. We had the pleasing gratification of congratulations from many friends both by person, letters and messages. This you may be assured was highly gratifying. I have news further to tell you that your Mother, myself and Sophia will very soon be up to see you, Capt. Hardy, and all the brave fellows of the *Victory* whom I have any personal knowledge of; to all of whom I sincerely beg of you to give my most hearty and sincere congratulations for this happy escape. I am told that Captⁿ Hardy is soon to come home as his health is very indifferent. I hope it will not be so before we get up. I have written to Mrs J. Jacobs to try and get me some lodgings with two beds at least and if three the better. I have also written to Captain Rogers to ask for leave for Frank to come to Portsmouth to meet us, which I hope and trust he will do.

I beg you will write to me by return and say how your own health and Captⁿ Hardy's is, also to say what are your proceedings with the corps of Lord Nelson and where the ship is or likely to be, &c.

I leave the other part of the paper for you to receive the congratulations of your Mother, brother and sisters.

I am with the greatest affection

Your father

RICHARD ROBERTS.

In accordance with the father's desire, the children and wife append their letters as follows :—

BURTON, 5*th Dec.* 1805.

OUR DEAR BROTHER,

We beg to offer you our most sincere and earnest congratulations for your late fortunate escape from the dreadful battle you have lately had, and also the lucky escape of Shipwreck, and hope soon to have a pleasing answer from your own hand. We are your loving and affectionate sisters and brother

SOPHIA A. ROBERTS
W. ROBERTS
AG. ROBERTS.

The mother writes the following characteristic note :—

MY DEAR RICHARD,

I sincerely congratulate you on your late preservation from the perilous situation you have lately undergone. It is not in my power to describe the painful anxiety I have felt for your safety, or the joy I felt on hearing you were safe and well, on the receipt of which I returned my thanks to your Almighty Preserver and hope you did not forget to do the same. Hoping to see you in a few days

Your affectionate Mother

M. ROBERTS.

The next day young William Roberts takes pen and paper on the quiet and writes the following boyish account of the high doings in Burton Bradstock in honour of the Great Naval victory, interspersed with details of the home life of the ponies and dogs belonging to the paternal estate.

BURTON, *Dec. 6th*, 1805.

DEAR BROTHER,

Your kind letter on the 22nd of November [*i.e.* October] we were all very happy to receive, and to find you were alive and well. We gave away beer to almost every man in the parish. I was almost drunk myself. Mr T. Fish brought the news and deprived old Jemmy of the pleasure, but we were afraid old Jemmy would not be quick enough. Augusta wishes she could write. Father has bought a little black pony and gave £9, 19s. 6d. for it. It is not broke in yet.

We have raised at Burton and Bridport a subscription for the widows and orphans. They collected at Bridport £14 at the Church door Thanksgiving day, but they got a great deal more than that the day before. We at Burton collected £6, 8s. 1d. Mr Hunter[1] and Father are going all round the parish to those people who were not at Church. Jn° Cheney wants to see you and for that matter so do I too. You will see Father and mother and Sophy. I still remain your affectionate Brother

WM. H. ROBERTS.

P.S.—Please write soon and give me a good account of the battle. We had bell ringing and beer drinking the night that we received the list of the killed and wounded and likewise when we received your letter. The colours were hoisted on the tower. Mother had hard work to keep the beer barrell a running. Our family is increased very much for we have had no less than 13 puppies; Blossom 7 and Clara 6. Ralph, Gipsy, and all are well and hearty. We have been talking about your taking Ralph with you, but I suppose you have enough. I expect you

---

[1] Rector of Burton Bradstock.

home to Burton but none of the rest don't. All the Bridport Volunteers went to Church on Thanksgiving Day. I do not think there is any person in your place. Father will write you soon; he received your letter on the 6th inst. This is all I have at present to say.

Addressed MR RICH^D F. ROBERTS
H.M. Ship *Victory*
Portsmouth
To the care of Mrs J. Jacobs
Ordinance Row
Portsea.

Another Burtonian a day later indites the following epistle to the midshipman. It throws a more refined light on the way in which they relaxed the tension of the mental strain wrought on the dwellers in English seaboard villages by the domination of the Great Terror. At the same time it exhibits the effect of that strain on the educated mind of the country gentleman unversed in nautical terminology, but none the less claiming a share in the national thanksgiving.

BURTON,
Dec. 7th, 1805.

DEAR FRIEND,

'Tis impossible for me to express the happiness that I feel in having to congratulate you on your safe arrival. The many anxious weeks that have elapsed seem for a moment forgotten. I am truly thankful to the Almighty for your preservation. What must have been your feelings in the dreadful conflict you have witnessed! It chills my blood when I think of it, and I am ready to conclude I should not have been able to have endured such a terrible scene.

When I consider your never having been to sea before and the short time that elapsed between your sailing and the battle, together with the distressed condition of your ship since; it seems to me sufficient to determine anyone

to leave it. However, knowing your determination it probably will have the contrary effect, and be the means of your
persevering in the line you are in. If so, I sincerely wish
you every success and that you may become a dignified
character in the British Navy.

We first heard of the engagement on the morning of
the 5th Nov. The account was sent by Mr J. Hounsell
to Burton soon after Lieutenant Lapinoture[1] passed
Bridport. It informed us of the death of Lord Nelson;
and that 19 ships were taken and one blown up. Our
feelings were extremely racked; all deploring the loss of
the Hero; all measureably pleased the victory was so
decisively in our favour. But at the same time our minds
were much distressed on your account. For my own part
I never experienced such incoherent emotions in my life;
one minute hoping you were safe; the next doubting it
from the dreadful carnage that was inevitable in such a
situation. From this dilemma nothing could relieve me
but hearing immediately from you. Every post was
looked for, with indescribable anxiety. Our disappoint-
ment was great in not having the particulars of your ship
in the first Gazette; and the impracticability of it did not
appear till other despatches arrived. During the interval
(which was extremely tedious) every means was used by all
your friends to obtain the earliest information. Captn
Blackwell of the *Euryalus* desired Mrs Fish to present his
compliments to Mr Hardy's Family and your Father saying Captn Hardy was safe and he had no doubt you were
likewise. This was some consolation; but nothing equal
to what we experienced when your name was not to be
found amongst the list of killed and wounded. The news
flew like lightning through the village. The bells rang and
everybody seemed actuated by one general sentiment of
joy. But this however was not the positive intelligence I
wanted; for afterwards a doubt crept in whether your

---

[1] Lieut. J. R. Lapinotière, who brought home the despatches in the
Pickle schooner.

name might not have been omitted, and this was not dis-
pelled till the receipt of your very acceptable letter dated
Oct. 22nd (to your Father) which he received in Bridport
and immediately sent by Mr Fish to Burton. The bells
rang again till several of the ropes broke! They were
repaired next morning. Your Father's colours were
hoisted on the tower and continued flying several days. I
was really astonished to find you were so collected the day
after the action as to be able to write such a letter. It
gave me great pleasure and it does you infinite credit.
Your favour to me of the 27th came at the same time. I
should have written you sooner but did not know where to
direct as we expected the *Victory* home some time past. I
should have thought that you had been so much agitated
by the transactions of the 21st that it would have been
impossible to collect your ideas on paper. It is not to be
wondered at that at the time you did not know the particulars of the action. This has been pretty well supplied by
the public prints, which is astonishing.

What would the English Nation have done with your
gallant Commander had he survived the action and brought
home all the captured ships! Not that it is wanting in
bestowing every encomium on him and on all those under
his command. But surely a new vocabulary must have
been formed, for however verbose our language may be
reckoned it would still have been wanting in epithets.
Great; Magnanimous; Illustrious; would appear too
hackneyed and common. It must have been more than
Invincible Admiral of Admirals and perhaps *Lord of Lords;*
for I think the people would have run into idolatry and
absolutely worshipped him. Pray God may have taken
him to Himself and given him a Crown of Glory.

I have no doubt that the subscriptions now making in
the kingdom to help the widows, orphans, and wounded
will be followed up by others for a remuneration to the
officers and crews of every ship in action. However, I shall
be most happy to hear that you come in for a share of

Prize money; for I am such a novice that I do not know whether clerks have any share.

Decr. 8th.—I left off writing last night thinking there would have been a letter to your Father informing him that you were in harbour, which would have fixed the day of your mother and sisters leaving Burton, but am informed there was no letter. It therefore being uncertain when you will come into port, I thought best to send this and write again by them. I am happy to inform you that your relations and friends in general are well. Mr R. Roberts of Gorwell was here and told me he thought he should go up to see you, but I heard yesterday he has the gravel and is otherwise unwell. I have many times been requested by your friends and acquaintances to present their love and kind remembrances to you when I wrote, which I do unitedly with my own, and remain

Your affectionate Friend

J. Kenway.

"Mr R. F. Roberts, M.D.,
    H.M.S. *Victory*,
      Portsmouth,
        or Elsewhere."

The curtain falls appropriately on the Roberts Trafalgar correspondence, with the joy bells telling out the glorious news of Trafalgar to the dwellers in the lovely Valley of the Bride.[1]

[1] See Chapter III., pp. 12-15.

FACSIMILE OF LIST OF CAPTAIN, OFFICERS, AND COMPANY ON BOARD
THE "VICTORY" who shared in the Government Grant of £300,000 voted
by Parliament for the British Fleet after the Battle of Trafalgar.

[To face page 273.

APPENDIX A

THE MUSTER-ROLL OF THE *VICTORY*
October 21, 1805

Up to the present time it has never been possible to obtain anything like an accurate or complete list of the British sailors who took part in the Battle of Trafalgar. Two very interesting volumes have lately come into the possession of Messrs Maggs of 109 Strand. They consist of two bulky roughly-bound folios of stamped receipts. The earlier, dated August 1806, deals with the division *pro rata* of the £300,000 voted by Parliament for the whole of the British fleet. The later volume, dated April 1807 onwards, shows the distribution of the Trafalgar Prize Money and Bounty Bills.

From these records, by permission of Messrs Maggs, the complete muster-roll of the H.M.S. *Victory* is here presented, containing the names of every one on board the ship who took part in the glorious victory of Trafalgar, October 21, 1805.

The heading of vol. i. is :—

"H.M.S. *Victory*.

"We whose names and marks are hereunto subscribed being the captain, officers, and company of H.M.S. *Victory* under the command of the late Rt. Hon. Lord Nelson at the battle off Cape Trafalgar on the 21st October 1805, do acknowledge to have received by ourselves or our legal representatives through the hands of Messrs C. Cooke and J. Halford for and on account of the Rt. Hon. Lord Howick, John Earl Spencer, and Lord H. G. Petty, trustees for the distribution of £300,000 voted by Parliament, the several sums expressed against our names being the amount of our proportions of the said grant. And we do hereby

273

S

discharge our said trustees as well as the said Messrs Cooke and Halford from all further demand on account thereof :

" * Lord Visct. Nelson   Adml.   £18,517, 13s. 6d.   Pd. exors.
   Lord Collingwood   „   4,629,   8s. 4d.
   Lord Northesk   4,629,   8s. 4d.
   Sir Thos. Louis   4,654,   0s. 0d.
   John Knight, Esq.   „   4,629,   8s. 4d."

The following 18 ships' crews are contained in these volumes H.M.S. *Victory*, Capt. T. M. Hardy.

    „   *Neptune*, Capt. Tho. F. Freemantle.
    „   *Orion*, Capt. Edw. Codrington.
    „   *Polyphemus*, Capt. Richd. Redmill.
    „   *Prince*, Capt. Richd. Grindall.
    „   *Revenge*, Capt. Robt. Moorsom.
        Royal Sovereign, Capt. Edw. Rotheram.
    „   *Spartiate*, Capt. Sir Fras. La Forey, Bart.
    „   *Swiftsure*, Capt. W. G. Rutherfurd.
    „   *Téméraire*, Capt. Eliab Harvey.
    „   *Tonnant*, Capt. Chas. Tyler.
    „   *Thunderer*, Lieut. John Stockham.
    „   *Euryalus*, Capt. the Hon. H. Blackwood.
    „   *Naiad*, Capt. Thos. Dundas.
    „   *Phoebe*, Capt. Hon. T. B. Capel.
    „   *Sirius*, Capt. Wm. Prowse.
        Pickle (schooner), Lieut. J. R. Lapenotière.
    „   *Entreprenante*, Lieut. John Power.
    „   *Enterprise* (cutter), Lieut. R. B. Young.

N.B.—The other 15 ships which fought at Trafalgar were presumably dealt with in the volumes including the earlier letters of the alphabet A to L, which are missing.

Vol. ii., in possession of Messrs Maggs, is headed as follows :

" H.M.S. *Victory*.

" We whose names and marks are hereunto subscribed, being the captain, officers, and company of His Majesty's Ship *Victory* at the Battle of Trafalgar on the 21st October 1805, under the command of the late Rt. Hon. Lord Nelson, do acknowledge to have received of our agents, Messrs Chris. Cooke, and Willm. Rd.

---

* Deceased at time of payment.

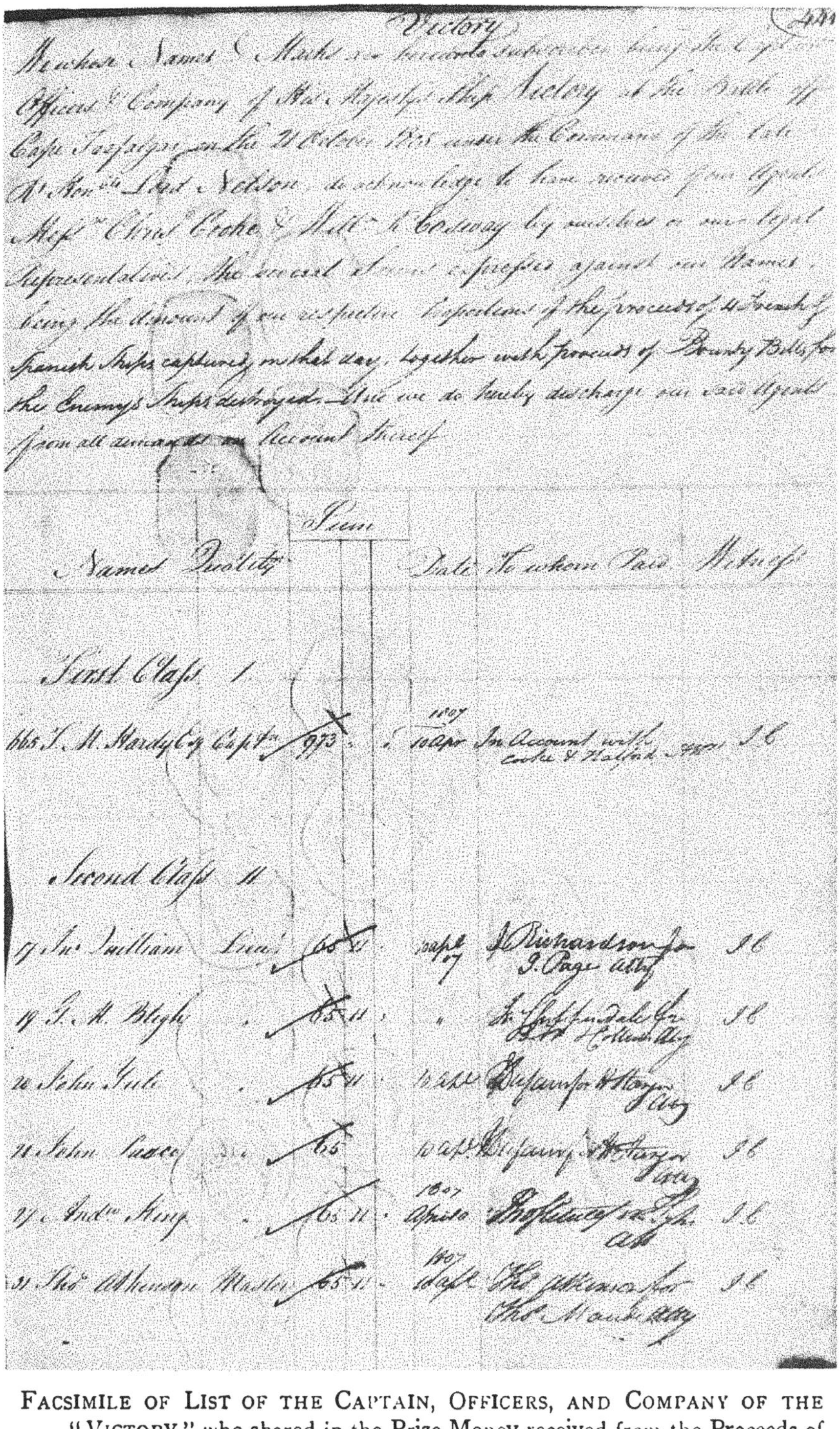

Victory 244

We whose Names & Marks are hereunto subscribed being the Captain Officers & Company of His Majesty's Ship Victory at the Battle of Cape Trafalgar on the 21 October 1805 under the Command of the late Rt Honble Lord Nelson do acknowledge to have received from our Agents Messrs Christr Cooke & Willm A. Conway by ourselves or our Legal Representatives the several Sums expressed against our Names being the Amount of our respective Proportions of the proceeds of 4 French & Spanish Ships captured on that day, together with proceeds of Bounty Bills for the Enemy's Ships destroyed. And we do hereby discharge our said Agents from all demands on Account thereof.

Names	Quality	Sum	Date	To whom Paid	Witness
First Class	1				
665 T. M. Hardy Esq	Captn	973	1807 10 Apr	In Account with Cooke & Halford	J.C.
Second Class	II				
17 Jno Quilliam	Lieut	65 11	10 Apl 07	J. Richardson for J. Page Atty	J.C.
19 G. M. Bligh	"	65 11	"	[illegible] for [illegible] Atty	J.C.
20 John Yule	"	65 11	10 Apl	[illegible] for [illegible] Atty	J.C.
21 John Pasco	"	65	10 Apl	[illegible] Atty	J.C.
27 Andw King	"	65 11	1807 Apl 30	[illegible] Atty	J.C.
31 Thos Atkinson	Master	65 11	1807 10 Apl	Thos Atkinson for Thos Moore Atty	J.C.

FACSIMILE OF LIST OF THE CAPTAIN, OFFICERS, AND COMPANY OF THE "VICTORY" who shared in the Prize Money received from the Proceeds of Four French Ships and Spanish Ships captured on the 21st October 1805.

[To face page 274.

Cosway, by ourselves or our legal representatives, the several sums expressed against our names, being the amount of our respective proportions of the proceeds of 4 French ships and Spanish ships captured on that day, together with Bounty Bills for the enemy's ships destroyed. And we do hereby discharge our said agents from all demands on account thereof."

First Class (1)—6 Aug. 1806, £2389, 7s. 6d. Share Gov. Grant ; 10 Apr. 1807, £973 Prize Money.

T. M. Hardy, Esq., Captn.

Second Class (11)—£161 each of the Gov. Grant ; £65, 11s. each for Prize Money.

Jno. Quilliam, Lieut.
G. M. Bligh, Lieut. (wounded).
John Yule, Lieut.
John Pasco, Lieut. (wounded).
Andw. King, Lieut.
Thos. Atkinson, Master.
Edw. Williams, Lieut.
Geo. Brown, Lieut.
Alex. Hills, Lieut.
*Wm. Ram, Lieut.
*Chas. Wm. Adair, Capt. Marines.

Third Class (16)—£108, 12s. of the Gov. Grant each ; £44, 4s. 6d. each for Prize Money.

Wm. Rivers, Gunner.
Wm. Chaseman, Masr. Mte.
Alex. J. Scott, Chaplain.
Thos. L. Robins, Masr. Mte.
Walter Burke, Purser.
Saml. Spencer, Masr. Mte.
Wm. Beatty, Surgeon.
Wm. Henry Symons, Masr. Mte.
Wm. Willmet, Boatsn.
James Green, Masr. Mte.
Wm. Bunce, Carpr.
Thos. Goble, Masr. Mte.
Jas. G. Peake, Lieut. Marines (wounded).
Lewis B. Reeves, Lieut. Marines (wounded).
Lewis Roatley, Lieut. Marines.
*John Scott, Secretary.

Fourth Class (63)—£26, 6s. each from Gov. Grant ; £10, 14s. each for Prize Money.

Adams, Jas., Qr. Masr. Mte.
Andrew, Geo., Secs Clerk.
Bookless, Robt., Coxswain.
Brown, Lanc., Yeo. P. Room.
Bailey, Thos., Gunr. Mte.
Brown, Jno. (5), Gunr. Mte.
Barton, Rob. C., Mid.
Bulkeley, Rd., Mid. (wounded).
Carslake, Wm. Jno., Mid.
Clements, Michl., Ships Carpu.
Cormach, John, Bos. Mte.
Cary, Hy. Mid.
Dixon, Chrisr., Qur. Mas.
Dowden, Saml., Sergt. Mar.
Elliott, Will., Mastr. of Arms.
Ebbs, John, Gunr. Mte.
Eaves, Fras., Yeo. Shts.
Fenwick, Geo., Gunr. Mte.

* Those marked thus were deceased at time of payment.

Ford, Hy., Qur. Masr.
Felton, John, Mid.
Fearall, Danl., Sergt. Mar.
Grindall, Festing, Mid.
Gillman, John, Sergt. Ms.
Henley, Danl., Ships Carpr.
Hanniford, Josh., Boatn. Mte.
Harrington, Daniel, Mid.
Johnson, Jas., Qur. Mas. Mte.
*Johnson, Thos., Qur. Mas.
King, Thos., Qur. Mas. Mte.
*King, John, Qur. Mas.
Kidd, John, Carpr. Mte.
Lovitt, Peter, Qur. Mas.
Lessimore, Arthr., Qur. Mas.
Leaky, John, Carpr. Mte.
Lyons, John, Mid.
Mannell, Wm., Qur. Mas. Mte.
Maloney, Ml., Qur. Mas. Mte.
Ogilvie, David, Mid.
Poad, Jas., Mid.
Pollard, John, Mid.
*Palmer, Alex., Mid.

Picken, Oliver, Mid.
Rivers, Wm., Mid. (lost a leg).
Robertson, Jas., Mid.
Roberts, Rd. F., Mid.
Spencer, Thos., Yeo. Shts.
Smith, Wm. (1), Sail Mr.
Spencer, Wm. (1), Yeo. P. Room.
Stevenson, Benj., Qur. Mas.
*Smith, Robt.,[1] Mid.
Sach, Andw., Yeo. Shts.
Smith, Neil, Ass. Surg.
Sibbald, Jas., Mid.
Seckar, Jas., Sergt. Mar.
Thorling, Jno., Qur. Mas.
Twiney, Thos., Qur. Mas.
Thovez, Php., Mid.
Thresher, Thos., Mid.
Welstead, Jno., Bos. Mte.
*Whipple, Thos., Clerk.[2]
Westphall, G. A., Mid. (wounded).
Wright, Jas., Bos. Mte.
Westenburgh, Wm., Asst. Surg.

Fifth Class (728)—£4, 12s. 6d. each for Gov. Grant ; £1, 17s. 6d. each for Prize Money.

Astie, Chas., Ab.
Anderson, Thos. (1), Ordy.
Andrews, Isaac, L.M.
Aslett, Anthy., L.M.
Antoine, Antonia, Ordy.
Abrahams, Wm., Ab.
Anderson, John (1), Ab.
Aunger, Geo., Ordy.
Appleby, Jno., Ordy.
Arthur, Jno., L.M.
Atkins, Wm., L.M.
Aldridge, Jas., Ab.
Archibald, Jas., Ordy.
Anderson, Hans, Ab.
Adams, Wm., Ab.
Ansell, Thos., Ab.

Aldcroft, Israel, Ordy.
Abbott, John, Marine.
Altomaro, Gaetano, Marine
Annison, Josh., Supy.
Ashton, Wm., Supy.
Borthwick, Geo., L.M.
Bentole, Jas., L.M.
Bird, Thos., Ordy.
Barry, John, Ordy.
Bryan, Thos., Ordy.
Biggs, Wm., Caulkrs. Mte.
Brown, Josh., Ordy.
Brown, Jno. (1), Ab.
Brashett, Jno., Ab.
Barkas, Saml., L.M.
Butler, Wm., Ab.

* Those marked thus were deceased at time of payment.
[1] Roberts, in his Remark-Book, calls him John Smith.
[2] Captain's Clerk (Roberts).

Beagan, Jas., L.M.
Brown, Josh., Ordy.
Brasby *alias* Brazil, Jas., Qu. Gr.
Bush, John, Ordy.
Barnett, Wm., Gunsmith.
Burton, Geo., Ordy.
Bond, Wm., Ab.
Bell, John, Ordy.
Burgin, Jos., Ordy.
Booth, Wm., L.M.
*Bowler, Jno., L.M. (Pd. to his father John, 9 Apr. 1807).
Butcher, Hy., Ab.
Brown, Jno. (3), Ordy.
Buchan, David, Ab.
*Brown, Wm. (1), Ab. (Pd. to Mary Thomson, administrator, 19 May 1807).
Bird *alias* Boyd, Chas., Ab.
Barrow, Wm., Ab.
Brannon, Timy., Qur. Gr.
Boyle, Bernard, Ordy.
Blake, David, Ab.
Beaumont, Wm., Ab.
Benbow, Saml., Ab.
Buckley, Corns., L.M.
Brown, Wm. (2), L.M.
Browis, Wm., Ordy.
Blumberry, Peter, Ab.
Button, Jos. (2), L.M.
Brady, Will., Ordy.
Boll, Hy., Ordy.
Barrett, Jos., Ab.
Bacon, Richd., Ab.
Beard, Phinias, Trumpeter.
Barrett, Thos., Ab.
Bell, Wm., Ordy.
Bowe, Patk., Ab.
Booth, Thos., L.M.
Boyes, Chas., Ab.
Bush, Fredk., Ordy.
Browne, Jas., Ordy.
Bowen, Robt., Ab.
Benjua, Josh., Ordy.

Baptish, Jno., Ab.
Bomkworth, Jno., Ordy.
Bartlett, Thos., Ab.
Bateman, Jno., Ordy.
Burlingham, Jno., L.M.
Belson, Robt., Ab.
Black, Hugh G. W., Boy.
*Berry, Jas., Drumr. Marines.
Bagley, Richard, Marine.
Brookes, John, Marine.
Blackhorn, Thos., Marine.
Bagley, Wm., Marine.
Bagley, Jas., Marine.
Buckley, Thos., Marine.
Brown, Jacob, Marine.
Brice, John, Marine.
*Brennan, John, Marine (Pd. to John Wolfe of Cork for the widow Johana, 17 Jul. 1807).
Barlow, Wm., Marine.
Buchanan, Jas., Marine.
*Brown, John (1), Marine.
Brown, John (2), Marine.
Bradford, John, Marine.
Browning, W. D., Marine.
Bennett, Richd., Marine.
Baker, Saml., Marine.
Bullock, John, Marine.
Beeton, Wm., Marine.
Burgess, Jas., Marine.
Bower, Vale., Marine.
Borrow, Patk., Supy.
Borrow, Philp., Supy.
Carroll, Chas., Cook.
Conn, David, L.M.
Caharty, Patk., Ab.
Cope, John, Ab.
Chapman, Jas., L.M.
Campbell, John (1), L.M.
Connell, Josh., Ordy.
Corten, Geo., L.M.
Cary, Hy. (1), Ordy.
Cooper, John, L.M.
Connor, Jas., Ordy.

* Those marked thus were deceased at time of payment.

Collins, Rd., Ab.
Colliver, Rd., L.M.
Cornwall, Thos., Ordy.
Caton, Jas., L.M.
Chant, Isaac, Ab.
*Cramwell, Hy., L.M. (Pd. to mother Jane, 17 Apr. 1807).
Cruize, Thos., Ordy.
Callaghan, John, Ordy.
Curry, Jas., Ab.
Coates, Josh., L.M.
Clarke, Hy. (1), Ab.
*Cale, Wm.,¦L.M. (Pd. to Ann Cale, 11 Sep. 1807).
Connolly, Thos., Ordy.
Cole, Nathl., Ab.
*Cornwarder, John, Ordy. (Pd. to Eliz. Harris for the mother, 21 Apr. 1807).
Clarke, Jas., Ab.
Collard, Thos., Ab.
Clarke, Wm., Ab.
Clarke, Hy. (3), L.M.
Cooper, Saml., Ab.
Campbell, John (3), Ab.
Coleman, Benjn., Ordy.
Curran, John, Ordy.
Crawley, Timy., Ordy.
Casey, Dennis, Ab.
Clarke, Saml., Ordy.
Casewell, John, Ordy.
Collins, John (2), Carpr. Crew.
Cepell, Jas., Armr.
Cosgrove, Jas., Purs. Std.
Camelaire, Eml., Ordy.
Clarke, Geo., Ordy.
Christopher, Jas., Ab.
Caldwell, Wm., Ab.
Chapman, Jas., Ordy.
Crooke alias Crookes, Math., Ab.
Castle, Wm., Ab.
Clay, John, Boy.
Carroll, Corns., Boy.
Cogswell, Wm., Corpl. Marines.

Coulston, Geo., Marine.
Crofton, Thos., Marine.
Chappell, Chas., Marine.
Cownley, Thos., Marine.
Cowling, Wm., Marine.
Coburne, Wm., Marine.
Carrick, Wm., Marine.
Crofts, Rd., Marine.
*Cockran, Geo., Corporal.
Cooke, Benj., Marine.
Church, John, Marine.
Cooke, Wm. (1), Marine.
Cummins, Wm., Marine.
Chambers, Tho., Marine.
Cappell, Jacob, Marine.
Cooke, Wm. (2), Marine.
Chivers, John, Marine.
Cloughton, Robt., Marine.
Chevalier, Hy. Lewis, Retinue (Lord Nelson's Steward).
Carr, Wm., Supy.
Collingwood, Fras., Supy
Chappell, Chas., Supy.
Catling, John, Supy.
Cavanaugh, Arr., Supy.
Dinton, Jas., Ordy.
Dixon, Thos., L.M.
Donnelly, Chas., Ab.
*Daniels, Thos., L.M.
Darby, Geo., Ordy.
Davis, John (1), Ordy.
Drake, Saml., Ordy.
Duffy, Siam., Ordy.
*Davis, Chas. (1), Ordy.
Davis, Chas. (2), Ab.
Darby, Robt., Ab.
Darnold, Wm., Ordy.
Dixon, John, L.M.
Downes, Wm., Ordy.
Dowding, Thos., Qur. Gr.
*Davidson, Robt., Ab. (Pd. to his father Thomas, 2 June 1807).
Dubine, Domk., Ordy.
Dunkin, John, Ordy.

* Those marked thus were deceased at time of payment.

Dennison, Thos., Ab.
Davidson, Jas., Ordy.
Dobbin, Peter, Ab.
Dupuis, John, Ordy.
Dobson, Isaac, Carpr. Crw.
Dizmont, Danl., Ordy.
Double, Rob., Carpr. Crw.
Druce, Edw., Ordy.
Doak, Wm., Boy.
Downes, Wm., Marine.
Dutton, John, Marine.
Dean, Nichs., Marine.
Dunn, John, Marine.
Drummond, Rob., Retinue.
Dear, Thos., Retinue.
Edmund *alias* Henman, John, Ordy.
Evans, Jas., Ordy.
Evison, Thos., Ab.
*Edsworth, John, Marine.
Flynn, Matth., L.M.
Ford, Wm., Ordy.
Flemming, Wm., Ab.
French, Geo., Ordy.
French, Jas., Ab.
Fennell, Jas., Ab.
Forbes, Wm., Ab.
Flynn, Bernd., Ordy.
Fitzgerald, John, Ordy.
French, Fras., Ab.
Francois, John, Ordy.
Fall, Wm., Ab.
Fairman, John, Ordy.
Foley, Thos., Ordy.
Fisser, John, Ab.
Ferrins, Wm., Ab.
Foley, Stepn., Ordy.
Finlay, Rob., Ab.
Flight, Hy., Carpr. Crew.
Farecloth, Rob., Ab.
Ferris, Wm., Boy.
Feagan, Jas., Marine.
Ford, Wm., Marine.
Flinn, Edw., Marine.

Garrick, Jas., Ab.
Gibson, Rob., Ab.
Gray, John, Ab.
Graham, Thos., L.M.
Griffen, Wm., Ordy.
Gillett, Wm., Ordy.
Goodchild, Thos., Ordy.
Gasby, Saml., L.M.
Grey, Edw., Ordy.
Gibbons, Wm., L.M.
Gallachan, Edw., Ordy.
Gill, Jas., Ab.
Green, Tho. (1), Ab.
Green, Jas., Qur. Gr.
Green, Tho. (2), Ordy.
Graham, John, Ab.
Gantlett, John, Ab.
Griffith, Griffith, Ab.
Griffiths, Michael, Ab.
Gutlipster, John, Ordy.
Godby, Philip, Ab.
Gentile, Domque, Marine.
Ging, Michael, Ordy.
Graham, Tho., Ab.
*Gordon, Josh., Ab.
Giddice, Josh., Ab.
Greenfield, Geo., Ab.
Griffiths, Wm., Boy.
Gregory, John, Marine.
*Green, Jas., Marine.
Graves, Geo., Marine.
Green, Saml., Marine.
Guinti, Giovanni, Marine.
Geoghegan, John, Supy.
Hall, Peter, L.M.
Honnor, Wm., Qur. Gr.
Highland, John, L.M.
Hoffman, Peter, Ordy.
Hulbert, Jas., L.M.
Hawkins, Benjn., Ab.
Hayes, James, Ordy.
Harris, George, Ab.
Hodgkins, Josh., Ordy.
Hartnell, James, Rope Mr.

* Those marked thus were deceased at time of payment.

Haggerty, John, Ab.
Heath, John, Carpr. Crew.
Hampton, Saml., Ordy.
Hallet, Wm., Ordy.
Hall, John, Ordy.
Hunter, John, Ab.
Hall, Wm., Ab.
Hughson, Lawe., Ordy.
Hartley, Matth., Ab.
Howard, John, Ordy.
Harrison, Wm., Ordy.
Humphries, Wm., L.M.
Hannam, Wm., Ordy.
Harvey, Wm., Ab.
*Herwin, Arthur, Ordy. (Pd. to mother Elizth.).
Heaver, Richd., Ordy.
Hardy, Jonn., Ordy.
Hubert, Aaron, Boy.
Huns, John, Boy.
Huchinson, Wm., Boy.
Haile, John, Marine.
Hodges, Geo., Marine.
Henrix, Thos., Marine.
Harding, Henry, Marine.
Harding, Robt., Marine.
Hanbury, Wm., Marine.
*Hillier, Danl., Marine.
Harris, Isaac, Marine.
Hines, James, Marine.
Hawkins, Thos., Marine.
Heath, Isaac, Marine.
Hammond, Chas., Supt.
Inwood, Wm., Ab.
Jackson, Wm., Ordy.
Johnson, John, Ordy.
Jacobs, John, Ordy.
Jefferson, John, Ordy.
Jago, Thos., L.M.
*Jewell, Richd., Ordy. (Pd. to Martha Jewell).
Johns, Thos., Ab.
Jones, Wm. (1), Ordy.
Jameson, Saml., Ordy.

Jarvis, Thos., Ab.
Jones, James, Ab.
Johnson, Wm., Ordy.
Jewer, Andw., Ab.
Jones, Morgan, Ab.
Jones, Wm. (2), Ab.
Jones, Wm. (3), L.M.
Johnson, Saml., Ab.
Jones, Peter, Ab.
Jackson, John, Ab.
Johnson, Ezechiel, Ordy.
Johnston, Wm. (2), Ab.
Ireland, Geo., Ab.
Johnson, Thos., Boy.
Jackson, John, Marine.
Jennings, Hy., Marine.
Joey, Wm., Marine.
*Jones, Wm., Marine.
Johnson, Wm., Supy.
Kendall, John, Ordy.
King, Wm., Ordy.
Kenney, Stephn., Ab.
Kennedy, John (2), Ordy.
Kennensaw, Steph., Ordy.
Killy, Peter, Ordy.
Killen, Peter, Ab.
Kennedy, Archd., Ab.
*Kennedy, Geo., Marine.
Knight, Wm., Marine.
Lambkin, Wm., L.M.
Leeds, Thos., Ordy.
Leek, Wm., Ab.
Laundry, Thos., Ab.
Legg, Chas., L.M.
Lawrie, Thos., Ordy.
Lavenny, Jas., Ordy.
Lewis, John (1), Ordy.
Loft, William, Ordy.
Leary, Danl., Ab.
Lay, Jas., L.M.
Lewis, John (2), Ab.
Lemon, John, Ab.
Lovitt, Saml., Ab.
Lenham, Jas., Qur. Gr.

* Those marked thus were deceased at time of payment.

Leary, Jas., Ordy.
Lowrane, Chas., Ab.
Lever, John, Ab.
Lewis, Edw., Ab.
Legg, Peter, Ordy.
Levericks, Thos., Ordy.
Longshaw, John, Ordy.
Le Dam, Hans, Ordy.
*Laing, Geo., Carpr. Crew (Pd. to Harry Laing, father).
Lancaster, Hy., Boy.
Ludford, Jas., Boy.
Leech, Wm., Marine.
*Lewis, Jer. G., Marine.
Long, Jas., Drummer.
Le Couteur, Nich., Supy.
Lerosa, Degara, Supy.
M'Pherson, Jos., L.M.
Mansell, Jas., Ab.
Munro, Danl., Ab.
M'Kenzie, Lewis, Ordy.
M'Beth, Alex., L.M.
M'Pherson, Danl., L.M.
M'Kennan, Langn., Ordy.
M'Donald, Jas., Ab.
Mann, John, Ab.
Matthews, Tho. (1), L.M.
Maloney, Tho., L.M.
Mitchell, Pat., Ab.
Magee, Peter, Ab.
M'Laughlin, Jas., L.M.
M'Guire, Edd., Ab.
M'Donald, Mich., Ordy.
Marsh, Hy., Ordy.
Moon, Simeon, Ab.
Manning, John, Ordy.
Martin, Sam., Ordy.
Murray, Robt., Ordy.
Martin, Geo., Ab.
M'Manners, Owen, Ab.
Minute, John, Ab.
Mason, John, Ab.
Morris, Wm., Ab.
Marshall, John (1), Ab.

Milebury *alias* Munbury, John, Arms. Mate.
Morris, John, Ordy.
*Muck, Wm., Ab.
Miffen, David, Ab.
Marshall, Wm. (1), Ordy.
Marshall, John (2), Ab.
Monday, John, Ordy.
Mainland, Wm., Ab.
M'Williams, Andrew, Ab.
M'Connell, John, Ordy.
Moss, John, L.M.
M'Dowell, Alex., Ordy.
Murray, Josh., Ab.
Morton, Wm., Ab.
Mooney, Edw., Ordy.
Marr, Edw., Ab.
M'Donald, —, Ab.
Merrygan, Pat., Ordy.
M'Donald, John, Ordy.
M'Donald, Angus, Ab.
Murray, Alex., Ab.
Murphy, John, Ab.
Morley, Geo., Ordy.
M'Connerky, Alex., Carpr. Crew.
M'Clements, Gilbt., Ab.
Mullen, Jas. S., Ab.
M'Indoe, Archd., Ordy.
Matthews, John, Ab.
Mitchell, Wm., Boy.
Moss, John, Boy.
M'Donald, Archd., Ordy.
Matthews, Wm., Ab.
*M'Pherson, Jas., Boy.
Mitchell, Wm., Ab.
Moss, Josiah, Ab.
Magee, John, Marine.
Morgan, John, Marine.
Melvin, Jas., Marine.
Matthews, Rob., Marine.
Moore, John, Marine.
M'Elroy, Thos., Marine.
Mead, David, Marine.
Marston, Thos., Marine.

* Those marked thus were deceased at time of payment.

Molloy, Philip, Marine.
Matthews, Benjn., Marine.
Magolina, Anto., Marine.
*Myers, Lamt., Marine.
*M'Manus, Bernd., Marine.
Mason, Geo., Supy.
Morgan, Michl., Supy.
Marat, Thos., Supy.
Mason, John, Supy.
*North, James, Ordy.
Nutting, Rob., Ab.
Norville, Rob., Ordy.
Nicholls, Hy., Ordy.
Nipper, Jas., Ab.
Northwood, John, Marine
Nicholls, Chas., Marine.
*Norgrove, Jas., Marine.
Nash, John, Marine.
Nicholls, Hy., Retinue.
Nevill, Hon. R., Supy.[1]
Neale, Pat., Supy.
Ogilvie, Geo., Ordy.
*Onions, Wm., Ordy. (Pd. to sister
   Sarah Stephens).
Owen, John, Ab.
Osborne, Wm., Ordy.
Peters, Valier, L.M.
Phillips, Robt., L.M.
Peters, John, Ab.
Powell, Richd., Ordy.
*Park, Jas., Ordy.
Penny, Alex., Ab.
Palmer, Thos., Ordy.
⌠Packett, John, Ab.
⌡alias Fernie, Peter, Ab.
Patterson, Wm., Ab.
Prescott, Geo., Ordy.
Prout, Tho., Ordy.
Pain, John, L.M.
Padaro alias Panaro, Fras., Qur.
   Gr.
Pelcone, John, Ordy.
Pille, John, Ab.

Page, Jas., Ab.
Pickering, Thos., Ordy.
Pooley, Isaac, Ordy.
Pillique, Stromblo, Ordy.
Painter, Josh., Ab.
Piercey, Tho., Ab.
Pritchard, Robt., Ab.
Pritchard, Wm., Ab.
Pirch alias Nicholas, Nathl.
   Ordy.
Pennell, Michl., Ab.
Parker, Jas., Ordy.
Price, Thos., Ab.
Pitt, Geo., Ordy.
Pope, Wm., Boy.
Peppett, Jas., Boy.
Portfield, Hugh, Boy.
Perrion, Wm., Boy.
Parry, John, Marine.
Pritchard, Saml., Marine.
*Perry, Wm., Marine.
Pearson, Geo., Marine.
Powell, David, Marine.
*Palmer, John, Marine.
Parnell, John, Marine.
Pitney, Fras., Marine.
Powell, Thos., Marine.
Padden, Edw., Marine.
Porter, Abrm., Supy.
Penning, Rob., Supy.
Quinton, Geo., Qur. Gr.
Recain, John, L.M.
Ryan, Stephn., L.M.
Ross, John (1), Ab.
Ritchie, Peter, Ordy.
Roberts, David, Ab.
Reynolds, Peter, Ab.
Ryan, Geo., Ordy.
Read, Danl., Ordy.
Richards, John, Ab.
Ross, John (2), Qur. Gr.
Randall, Thos., Ab.
Richards, Saml., Ab.

---

* Those marked thus were deceased at time of payment.
[1] Afterwards Viscount Nevill, Captain, R.N.

Ross, Robt., L.M.
Rawlins, John, L.M.
Remmington, Stephn., L.M.
Rome, John, L.M.
Rowe, Michl., Ab.
Russell, Wm., Ab.
Rowe, Jas., Ab.
Richards, Wm., Ordy.
Rylett, Hy., Ordy.
Robinson, John, Ab.
Rey, John, Ordy.
Rey, John, Ordy.
Randall, Wm., Boy.
Rawlinson, Jas., Boy.
Robbins, Saml., Boy.
Rayner, Saml., Marine.
Rawlinson, Tho., Marine.
Reece, Saml., Marine.
Rogers, Jas., Marine.
Rowland, Lewis, Marine.
Reece, Wm., Marine.
Richards, Nathl., Marine.
Raymont, John, Marine.
Rackhams, John, Marine.
Riggan, John, Supy.
Riceri, Simini, Supy.
Swain, Wm., L.M.
Shadd, Robt., L.M.
Stiles, Hy., L.M.
Smith, John (2), Ordy.
Stevens, Saml., L.M.
Stevenson, John, Ab.
Saunders, Wm., Ab.
Summers, John, Ordy.
Stanford, Wm., Ordy.
Stevens, Hugh, Armr. Mte.
*Shaw, Wm., L.M.
Stevenson, Anty., Ordy.
Stake *alias* Hake, Geo., Ab.
Shimmel, Josh., Ab.
Straker, Wm., Ab.
Selby, Wm., Ordy.
Smith, Tho. (1), Ab.
Simms, Wm., Ab.

Stapleton, Geo., L.M.
Sutherland, Jas., Ordy.
Syms, John, Ab.
*Smith, Geo. (1), L.M.
Stevenson, Geo., Ab.
Searle, Richd., Ab.
Simpson, Tho., Ab.
Stayham *alias* Strawn, Tho., L.M.
Smith, Jas., Ab.
*Smith, Wm. (2), Ordy.
Smith, David, Ordy.
Sedgwick, Thos., Qur. Gr.
Smith, Geo. (2), Ab.
Shinner, Wm., Ordy.
Sarson, Wm., L.M.
Sexton, Thos., L.M.
Smithson, Jas., Ab.
Sayking, Chas., Ordy
Starr, John, Qur. Gr.
Stewart, Chas., Ab.
Sheppard, Wm., L.M.
Stacey, Jas., Ordy.
Searchwell, Hy., Ab.
Smith, Chas., Carpr. Crew.
Stallet, Andrew., Ab.
Scott, Andrew, Sailmaker's Mate.
Sullivan, Jerie., Ab.
Smith, Wm. (4), Ab.
Spencer, Wm. (2), Ab.
Stewart, David, Ab.
Stair, John, Ab.
Studdy, Fras., Ordy.
Sherman, Jas., Ordy.
Smith, Jno. (3), Ab.
Saunders, Isaac, Ab.
Stead, John, Sailmaker's Crew.
Sweat, Wm., Ordy.
*Skinner, Wm., Ordy.
*Skinner, Jas., Ordy.
Scott, John, Boy.
Smith, Geo., Boy.
Sabine, Stephn., Boy.
Saunders, John, Boy.
Smith, Wm., Marine.

* Those marked thus were deceased at time of payment.

Smith, John, Marine.
Sutton, Geo., Marine.
Sullivan, Corns., Marine.
Smith, John, Marine.
Sheppard, Wm., Marine.
Scattergood, Wm., Marine.
Salluzzd, Crescenzo, Marine.
Staples, Richd., Marine.
Spedillo, Gaetano, Retinue.
Sarr, Jas., Supy.
Sloane, Andrew, Supy.
Thompson, Stephn., L.M.
Thomas, Chas., Ordy.
Tomlinson, Tho., Carp. Crew.
Thomas, Tho. (1), Ab.
Thompson, Wm. (1), Ordy.
Taylor, Alfred, Ab. (Pd. to Mother Isabella).
Thomas, Jeree., Ab.
Thomas, John (1), Ordy.
Terrant, Wm., Qur. Gr.
Terry, John, Ab.
Tobin, Richd., Ordy.
Temple, John, L.M.
Thomas, John (2), Ordy.
{ Thomas, Thos. (2), alias Thomas, John (3), } L.M.
Turner, Fras., L.M.
Taylor, Wm., Ordy.
*Thompson, Wm. (3), Ab.
Thompson, Wm. (4), Ordy.
Thompson, Robt., Ordy.
Taylor, Geo. A., L.M.
Tart, John, Ordy.
Toole, Chrisn., Ab.
Tater, Mark, Ordy.
Twitchett, Robt., Boy.
*Turner, Colin, Boy (Pd. to Mother Jane).
Twitchett, Tho., Boy.
Taft, Wm., Corpl. Mar.
Turner, Wm., Marine.
Thompson, John, Marine.
Tuck, John, Marine.

Tadd, Wm., Supy.
Upton, Robt., Ab.
Vincent, John, Qur. Gr.
Vent, Jas., Ordy.
Vava, Filippo, Marine.
West, Jas. (1), L.M.
West, Richd. (1), Ab.
Wilkins, Hy., Ordy.
Walton, John, L.M.
Waddle, Wm., L.M.
Wood, Wm. (1), Ordy.
Wilkinson, Benj., Ordy.
Walton, Wm., L.M.
Willoughby, Tho., L.M.
Warden, Alex., Ab.
White, Richd., L.M.
Wilson, Wm., L.M.
Waters, Chas., Ab.
Wood, Thos., Ordy.
Welch, Wm., L.M.
Welch, John, L.M.
Walker, John, Ab.
White, Wm., Ab.
Willan, John, Ab.
Watson, Thos., Ab.
Waters, Wm., Ordy.
Wood, Wm. (3), L.M.
*Wharton, John, Ordy. (Pd. W. C. English for father John).
Winnigle, Wm., Ab.
*Waters, Edw., Ab.
Whitton alias Bitton, John, L.M.
Wood, Thos. (2), Ab.
Wilkins, Geo., Ab.
Williams, Jas., Ab.
Warrandall, John, Ab.
Which alias Ulrick, Peter, Ordy.
Williams, John (3), Ab.
*Walker, John, Ab.
Whitton alias Bitton, Thos., Carp. Cw.
Williams, Richd., Ordy.
Welsh, John (2), Ab.

* Those marked thus were deceased at time of payment.

Walker, Geo., Ordy.
Williams, John, Ordy.
*Ward, Josh., Ordy.
Wise, Edw., Ab.
*Wilson, Geo., Boy.
Worson, Thos., Boy.
Wright, Wm., Marine.
Wilton, Tho., Marine.
*Wilkes, Saml., Marine.
Warner, Jas., Marine.
Walker, Saml., Marine.

*Wilmot, Geo., Marine (Pd. to mother Elizth.).
Wells, Wm., Marine.
Witchall, Chrisr., Marine.
Ward, Edw., Marine.
Wizzen, Geo., Marine.
Webster, Wm., Supy.
White, Wm., Supy.
Ward, Geo., Supy.
Yaul, Hans, L.M.

* Those marked thus were deceased at time of payment.

TOTALS.

CLASS I. 1
  „   II. 11
  „ III. 16
  „   IV. 63
  „   V. 728
                                 ———
Total of the *Victory* 819

Total of those deceased 56

N.B.—Hardy's letter says 54 killed on the *Victory*. So does Roberts' Remark-Book, adding that 57 were wounded. The official returns say 57 killed on the *Victory*. No other English ship had so many killed. It should be remembered that Nelson, writing to Sir T. Troubridge, 21st December 1803, said : "We are not stoutly nor in any manner well manned in the *Victory*, but she is in very excellent order, thanks to Hardy, and I think woe be to the Frenchman she gets along side of."

APPENDIX B

R. F. Roberts, midshipman in the *Victory*, enters the following notes in his "Remark-Book" :—

"Defects to H.M.S. *Victory*, 5th December 1805. Thos. M. Hardy, Esq., Captain.

"The hull is much damaged by shot in a number of different places, particularly in the wales, strings, and spurketing, and some between wind and water. Several beams, knees, and riders, shot through and broke ; the starboard cathead shot away ; the rails and timbers of the head and stem cut by shot ; several of the ports damaged, and port timbers cut off ; the channels and chainplates damaged by shot, and the falling of the mizen mast ; the principal part of the bulkheads, halfports, and portsashes thrown overboard in clearing ship for action.

"The mizen mast shot away about 9 feet above the deck ; the main mast shot through and sprung ; the main yard gone ; the main topmast and cap shot in different places and reefed ; the main topsail yard shot away ; the foremast shot through in a number of different places, and is at present supported by a topmast, and a part of the topsail and crossjack yards ; the fore yard shot away ; the bowsprit jibboom and cap shot, and the spritsail and spritsail topsail yards, and flying jibboom gone ; the fore and main tops damaged ; the whole of the spare topmast yards, handmast, and fishes shot in different places, and converted into jury geer.

"The ship makes in bad weather 12 inches water an hour."

APPENDIX C

GRANT OF ARMS TO THOMAS MASTERMAN HARDY,
Esq., dated 18th January 1806

To all and Singular to whom these Presents shall come, Sir Isaac Heard, Knight, Garter Principal King of Arms, and George Harrison, Esquire, Clarenceux King of Armes of the south-east and west parts of England, from the river Trent southwards, send Greeting.

Whereas Thomas Masterman Hardy, Esquire, Captain of His Majesty's Ship the *Victory*, under the command of the ever-to-be lamented Hero, Vice-Admiral Lord Viscount Nelson, in the late memorable and glorious Engagement with the Combined Fleets of France and Spain off Cape Trafalgar, second son of the late Joseph Hardy of Portisham, in the County of Dorset, Esquire, deceased, hath represented unto the most noble Charles, Duke of Norfolk, Earl Marshal and Hereditary Marshal of England, that His Majesty having been graciously pleased to signify his intention of conferring upon him the Dignity of a Baronet of the United Kingdom of Great Britain and Ireland, and being informed that the arms used by his family have not been duly registered in the College of Arms, and that such registry is necessary on the present occasion. He, therefore, requested the favour of his Grace's warrant to the Kings of Arms concerned, for their granting, confirming, and exemplifying the same, with such variations or distinctions as may be necessary to be borne by him and his descendants, and by those of his said late father, Joseph Hardy, deceased, viz., Joseph Hardy of Portisham, aforesaid, Esquire, John Hardy, Esquire, Elizabeth, wife of John Thresher, Gent., Anne Hardy, Mary, wife of James Balston, Gent., Catherine, wife of John Callard Manfield, Gent., Martha Hardy and Augusta Hardy, with

due and proper differences according to the Laws of Arms.   And
for as much as the said Earl Marshal did, by warrant under his
hand and seal, bearing date the seventeenth day of January instant,
authorise and direct us to grant, confirm, and exemplify to the
said Thomas Masterman Hardy the Armorial Ensigns used by his
family accordingly.

KNOW YE, THEREFORE, that we, the said Garter and Clarenceux,
in pursuance of His Grace's warrant and by virtue of the Letters
Patent of our several offices to each of us respectively granted, do
by these Presents grant and exemplify to the said Thomas
Masterman Hardy the arms following, that is to say :

PEAN ON A CHEVRON OR, BETWEEN THREE ESCALLOPS ARGENT,
THREE DRAGONS' HEADS ERASED OF THE FIELD,

and for a Crest,

OUT OF A NAVAL CROWN OR, A DRAGON'S HEAD PEAN,

as the same are in the margin hereof more plainly depicted, to be
borne and used for ever hereafter by him the said Thomas
Masterman Hardy and his descendants, and by those of his said
late father, Joseph Hardy, deceased, viz., Joseph Hardy of Portisham aforesaid, Esquire, John Hardy, Esquire, Elizabeth, wife of
John Thresher, Gent., Anne Hardy, Mary, wife of James Balston,
Gent., Catherine, wife of John Callard Manfield, Gent., Martha
Hardy and Augusta Hardy, with due and proper differences
according to the Laws of Arms.

IN WITNESS whereof, we, the said Garter and Clarenceux
Kings of Arms, have to these presents subscribed our names, and
affixed the seals of our several offices this eighteenth day of
January, in the forty-sixth year of the reign of our Sovereign
Lord, George the Third, by the grace of God of the United
Kingdom of Great Britain and Ireland, King, Defender of the
Faith, etc., and in the year of our LORD One thousand eight
hundred and six.

Seals and signatures of Sir Isaac Heard, Garter Principal King
Arms, and George Harrison, Clarenceux King of Arms.

From the original in the possession of W. Hardy Manfield,
Esq., of Portisham House, Dorset.

HARDY'S BUST AND MONUMENT IN THE CHAPEL OF GREENWICH HOSPITAL.
(See page 239.)

[To face page 288.

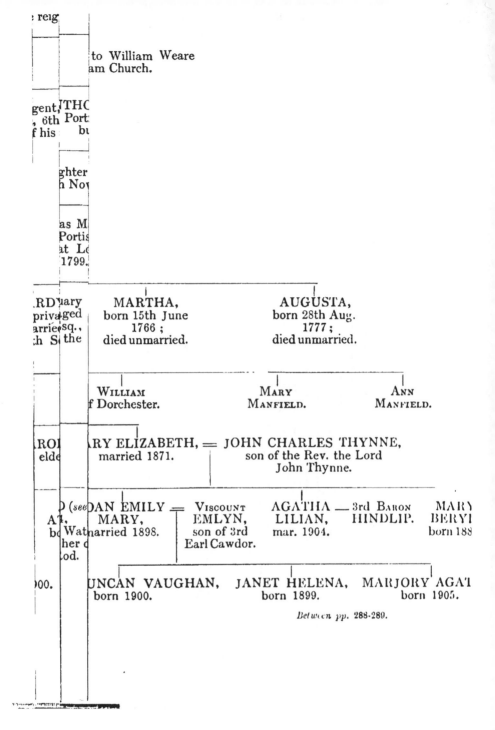

: reig

to William Weare
am Church.

gent, THC
, 6th Port
f his   bu

ghter
n No\

as M
Portis
at L
1799.

RD ary
priva ged
arrie sq.,
h S the

MARTHA,
born 15th June
1766 ;
died unmarried.

AUGUSTA,
born 28th Aug.
1777 ;
died unmarried.

WILLIAM
f Dorchester.

MARY
MANFIELD.

ANN
MANFIELD.

RO
elde

RY ELIZABETH, = JOHN CHARLES THYNNE,
married 1871.   son of the Rev. the Lord
                       John Thynne.

D (see AN EMILY = VISCOUNT   AGATHA — 3rd BARON   MAR\
A1,   MARY,   EMLYN,   LILIAN,   HINDLIP.   BERY1
b Wat married 1898. son of 3rd mar. 1904.   born 188
her d   Earl Cawdor.
od.

00.

UNCAN VAUGHAN,   JANET HELENA,   MARJORY AGA1
born 1900.   born 1899.   born 1905.

Between pp. **288-289.**

APPENDIX D—PEDIGREE OF THE HARDYS OF PORTISHAM, CO. DORSET.

CLEMENT LE HARDY, Bailly of Jersey, 1488, Lieutenant-Governor, 1486 =

From whom Sir THOMAS HARDY, Vice-Admiral, who died 10th August 1732, and his buried in Westminster Abbey.

APPENDIX E

WILLS OF THE HARDYS

THE will of John Hardy, senior, of Portisham, co. Dorset, gentleman, is dated the 8th May 1704. He desires that his body may be buried in the Parish Church of Portisham. To his son, John Hardy, he bequeaths household goods and furniture. To his son, Joseph Hardy, his large chests and other furniture. Residue to his daughter, Anne Hardy, whom he appoints to be executrix of his will.—Witnesses, Richard Baily, Edward Fooks, and Katharine Michell. Sealed with the Hardy Arms.

The will was proved by the executrix at the Court of the Archdeacon of Dorset, the 6th March 1705, and is endorsed "Mr John Hardy Senr's Will."

The will of Thomas Masterman of Kingston Russell, co. Dorset, gentleman, is dated the 12th February 1763. He bequeaths legacies to several servants. To his son-in-law, Joseph Hardy, the younger, of Portisham, bequeaths the remainder of his estate for term of years in Carrents Farm, in Winterborne St Martin, Dorset, which he holds on a lease from William Pitt, Esq. All the rest of his lands are bequeathed to his loving brother-in-law, Thomas Rawlins of Druce, in Puddletown, gentleman, Charles Masterman of Friar Waddon, gentleman, and to the testator's nephew, William Masterman of Abbotsbury, gentleman, executors in trust for the testator's daughters, Mary Masterman and Nanny, wife of Joseph Hardy aforesaid, equally. Sealed with these arms —*A cross coupé between four pears.*

The will was proved by the executors in the Court of the Archdeacon of Dorset, the 20th January 1764.

Will of John Hardy of Portisham, Dorset, gentleman, dated the 4th February 1809. He bequeaths all his personality, the stock on his farms, etc., to his sisters, Anne Hardy, Martha Hardy, and Augusta Hardy, to be equally divided, and he appoints them to be executrices of his will. Witnesses, John Templeman and Francis Oakley, junr.

The testator died the 25th of April 1822. The will was proved at Blandford, in the Court of the Archdeacon of Dorset, the 29th April 1823. Sworn under £2000.

The will of Vice-Admiral Sir Thomas Masterman Hardy, Bart., G.C.B., Governor of Greenwich Hospital, is dated the 10th June 1839.

He appoints Sir John Dean Paul, Bart., Sir Francis Seymour, K.C.H., and John Arscott Lethbridge, Esq., to be his executors in trust for the equal division of his estate between his three children, viz., Louisa Georgina Hardy, Emily Georgina Hardy, and Mary Charlotte MacGregor, wife of John Atholl Bannatyne MacGregor, Esq. His wife, Lady Anne Emily Louisa Hardy, is provided for under her marriage settlements. He bequeaths an annuity to his sister, Miss Augusta Sarah Master man Hardy of Portisham, Dorset. Power is reserved to his executors to dispose as they shall think fit of all household effects which Lady Hardy might not choose to retain.

Testator died at Greenwich Hospital, the 20th September 1839. The will was proved in the Prerogative Court of Canter bury by the executors, the 7th November 1839. Sworn under £25,000.

[Reference, P.C.C. 690, Vaughan.]

The will of Joseph Hardy, Esq., of Charminster, in the county of Dorset, is dated the 7th March 1840. He bequeaths to his three nieces, the daughters of his late brother, Sir Thomas Masterman Hardy, Bart., the sum of £5000. To his nieces, Mary Manfield and Anne Manfield, £1000 each. To his nephew, Thomas Balston, gentleman, of Broadway, Dorset, £1000. An annuity of £100 to his sister, Miss Augusta Sarah Masterman Hardy of Portisham, Dorset. Legacies to his servants. Life interest in his estate to his wife, Mrs Mary Hardy. Residue to his nephew, William Manfield of Dorchester, attorney-at-law, whom he appoints to be executor.

The testator died at Charminster on the 6th May 1841. The will was proved by the executor in the Prerogative Court of Canterbury, on the 22nd July 1841.

[Reference, P.C.C. 1841, No. 500.]

APPENDIX F

OFFICIAL LIST OF THE NAVAL SERVICES OF REAR-ADMIRAL SIR THOMAS MASTERMAN HARDY, BART.

Ships.	Entry.	Quality.	Discharge.	Yrs.	M.	Ms.	Days.
Helena	30th Nov. 1781	Capt. Servant*	9th April 1782	...	4	2	5
Seaford	30th April 1782		26th April 1783	...	12	3	5
Carnatic	24th Jan. 1784		16th Oct. 1784	1	9	2	0
Hebe	5th Feb. 1790	Midshipman	7th ... 1790	...	10	3	5
Hebe	8th Dec. 1790	Master Mate	5th ... 1792	1	3	0	4
Tisiphone	6th ... 1792	Able	16th Oc 1792	...	8	0	1
Tisiphone	17th Oc 1792	Midshipman	23rd ... 1793	...	7	3	2
Amphitrite	24th ... 1793	„	26th Nov. 1793	...	6	2	5
Meleager	27th Nov. 1793	Lieutenant	17th Aug. 1796	2	9	2	0
La Minerve	20th ... 1796	„	15th June 1797	...	10	2	6
Mine	16th June 1797	...er	3rd Aug. 1798	1	1	3	0
Vanguard	4th Aug. 1798	...in	7th June 1799	...	11	0	0
Foudroyante	8th June 1799		12th ... 1799	...	4	2	1

Ship	Date	Capacity	Date				
Princess Charlotte	14th Oct. 1799	Captain	10th Nov. 1799	...	1	0	0
Namur	21st Nov. 1800	"	27th do. 1800	...	1	1	2
San Josef	28th do. 1800	"	10th Feb. 1801	...	1	2	3
St George	11th Feb. 1801	"	17th Aug. 1801	...	6	2	6
Isis	31st Aug. 1801	"	21st June 1802	1	10	2	1
Amphion	11th July 1802	"	30th July 1803	2	0	2	6
Victory	31st July 1803	"	15th Jan. 1806	2	6	0	1
Sampson	27th March 1806	"	14th May 1806	3	1	3	0
Triumph	15th May 1806	"	15th May 1809	3	0	0	1
Barfleur	17th May 1809	"	15th Sept. 1812	3	4	1	3
Ramillies	8th Oct. 1812	"	13th June 1815	2	8	3	4
Princess Augusta (yacht)	23rd June 1815	"	5th May 1818	2	11	1	2
Superb	30th Nov. 1818	Commodore	11th Aug. 1819 Struck his Flag	...	9	0	3
Superb, Creole, et c.	12th Aug. 1819	Rear-Admiral	23rd April 1824	4	5	3	4
Experimental Squadron	5th Dec. 1826	Co mander-in-Chief	21st Oct. 1827	...	11	1	6
			Total	35	12	3	6

NAVY OFFICE, 7th May 1830.   (Signed)   JMES LAINE.

* This ... has ... gen rise to the most absurd misconceptions—one biographer asserting that Hardy served in the cook's galley. As a ... of ... it was a ... good form of entering the Navy, the reg ... was prescribing that "No ... on the sh ips ... who is under 13 years of age, ... he be the son of an officer, and is not to be under 11." The ... ... is fully ... in ... after C. N. Robinson's The ... ..., pp. 18, etc.

APPENDIX G

STATEMENT OF ACCOUNT BETWEEN HARDY
22ND MAY 1794

Dr.

1794.

May 22. To paid Fees on his confirmed Commission -		£1	1	6
1795.				
Feb. 17. „ paid his Draft, 11th Oct. 1794, to G. Cockburn		40	0	0
18. „ pd. do., Decr., to do.		20	0	0
Dec. 31. „ interest, £2, 13s. 9d., and postage, 7s. -		3	0	9
		£64	2	3

1796.

Jan. 1. To balance of last year - - - - - -		£64	2	3
10. „ pd. Draft, 4th Novr., to D. H. Garrott -		30	0	0
Apl. 12. „ pd. do., 15th Feby., to Thos. Pollard		40	0	0
Oct. 17. „ pd. do., 1st Augst., to J. R. Wilson		31	10	0
Dec. 31. „ difference of int., £5, 5s. 2d., and postage, 5s. 6d.		5	10	8
		£171	2	11

1797.

Jan. 1. To bal. of last year - - - - - -		£137	18	5
Mar. 9. „ pd. Draft, 20th Augt. 1796, to J. R. Wilson		33	0	0
Apl. 9. „ pd. do., 31st Decr. 1796, to J. Culverhouse -		40	0	0
June 4. „ pd. do., 13th April 1797, to G. Cockburne		25	0	0
Dec. 12. „ pd. do., 13th Octr. 1797, to J. Lampiere -		30	0	0
31. „ difference of int., £10, 10s. 0d., and postage, 5s. 1d.		10	15	1
		£276	13	6

1798.

Jan. 1. To balance of last year - - - - -		£276		6
Mar. 10. „ pd. his Draft, 3rd Janry., to J. Lampiere -		35		0
„ pd. do. 13th Janry., to Jn. Robin, Esq. -		30		0
Nov. 28. „ pd. do. 1st Aug., to do.		10	9	0
14. „ pd. Fees on your Commissions as Comr., *Falcon* and Post-Captain *Alligator* - - - -		6		
30. „ his Order, 5th Augst., to Capt. Berry - -		14	1	
Dec. 31. „ difference of int., £13, 6s. 7d., and postage, 3s. 6d.		13	16	8

Carry forward -		£386	4	7

AND HIS AGENT, GEORGE HARTWELL, TO 16TH JULY 1799.

1795.
Dec. 31. Balance due G. H. - - - - - - - £64 1

£64 :

1796.
Apl. 16. By Prize Money of Poulain & Keys, *Tisiphone* for
          L'Ontardo - - - - £34 1 6
       „ Commission - - - - 0 17 0
                                              £33 4 6
       „ Balance due G. H. - - - - - - 137 18 5
                                              £171 2 11

1797.
Mar. 29. By Prize Money, *Amphitrite* for *Prince Royal of
          Sweden*, captured 5th Augst. 1793, and an
          oil boat - - - - - - - - - £0 4 0
Dec. 31. „ Balance due G. H. - - - - - - 276 9 6

£276 13 6

1798.
June 2. By Messrs Cook & Halford, P.M., 14th Feb.
          (*Minerve*) - - - - - £113 12 6
       „ Commission - - - - 2 17 0
                                              £110 15 6
Dec. 19. „ Wages, *Tisiphone*, 1st May '92 to
          23rd May '93 - - - - £17 18 6
       „ Wages, *Amphitrite*, 24th May '93
          to 26th Nov. - 9 1 0
                                              £26 19 6
       „ Commission - - - - 0 13 6
                                              26 6 0
                         Carry forward - £137 1 6

Dr.
1798.

Brought forward   £386   4   7

$$£386 \quad 4$$

1799.

			£	s	d
Jany.	1.	To balance of last year -	£32	13	3
	12.	„ paid his Draft, 11th Octr. 1798, to Jos. Littledale	70	0	0
May	25.	„ paid do. (no date), to Messrs Littledale & Brodrick	70	0	0
July	16.	„ interest - - - - - - - -	3	3	4
			£175	16	7

ACCOUNT—*continued.*

1798.

Brought forward $£$137 1 6

Dec. 31. By Pay, *Meleager*, 27th Nov. '93 to
31st July '96 - - - - $£$192 5 6
„ Compensation - - - - 26 8 6

Paid— $£$218 14 0
Carr Journals $£$0 1 6
Passing do.
and dispens-
ing Order - 0 17 6
——————
$£$0 19 0
Commn. - - - - 5 9 6
——————
6 8 6
——————
212 5 6
Dec. 31. By do. do., 1st to 19th August '96 - - 4 4 4
„ Balance due to G. H. - - 32 13 3
——————
$£$386 4 7
══════

1799.
July 16. By cash of Messrs Cooke & Halford $£$175 16 7

$£$175 16 7
══════

Errors Excepted,

G. HARTWELL,

LONDON, 16th July 1799.

Hardy's Monument, Blagdon Hill, Dorset.

INDEX

The figures in square brackets refer to the notes only.

299

PRINTED BY
OLIVER AND BOYD
EDINBURGH

Lightning Source UK Ltd.
Milton Keynes UK
UKOW06f1856180815

257149UK00016B/534/P